'LIBRO DE BUEN AMOR' STUDIES

'LIBRO DE BUEN AMOR' STUDIES

EDITED BY

G. B. GYBBON-MONYPENNY

TAMESIS BOOKS LIMITED
LONDON

Colección Támesis

SERIE A - MONOGRAFIAS, XII

SBN: 900411   04   X

Depósito legal: M. 841 - 1970

Printed in Spain by Talleres Gráficos de EDICIONES CASTILLA, S. A.
Maestro Alonso, 23 - Madrid

for

TAMESIS BOOKS LIMITED
LONDON

TABLE OF CONTENTS

EDITOR'S FOREWORD

The eleven studies presented in this volume are not the product of a master plan nor of any kind of editorial direction as to scope or content. They are individual essays by Hispanists who have something they wish to say about the Libro de buen amor *and who have been attracted by the idea of doing so in a volume entirely devoted to that work. Even the choice of contributors was not the editor's nor was he required to canvass the project: as soon as word of it got about the offers of contributions rapidly produced a total higher than that originally envisaged by the editorial board of* Tamesis. *The enthusiasm of the contributors is thus one of the happiest features of the volume. A less happy result has been that the need to limit the size of the volume made it impossible to invite contributions from other scholars, both British and foreign, who are known to have a keen interest in the* Libro de buen amor *and who might well have proved willing and able to respond to such an invitation.*

The fact that each contributor chose his own topic and the manner of dealing with it means that it would be a mistake to look for agreement or consistency between these eleven essays in theme, approach or point of view. It is interesting to observe, however, that there is much common ground in what might be called the basic preoccupation of these essays: they all illustrate in different ways the richness and the variety of Juan Ruiz's literary background. The studies of Janet Chapman, Rita Hamilton, Kemlin Laurence and Roger Walker bring home to us the dominance of the Church over men's minds in the Middle Ages; the Libro *is shown to reflect this, not only in the author's attitudes and preoccupations but also in the very techniques of literary expression. The importance of the secular Latin tradition, not only literary but scientific, is underlined in the studies of Peter Dunn and the editor, while Brian Dutton and Brian Tate illustrate different aspects of Juan Ruiz's familiarity with and use of vernacular literary conventions. Alan Deyermond and Ian Michael concern themselves with different aspects of Juan Ruiz's methods of literary expression, while Kenneth Adams studies the technical problem posed by the rhyme scheme of the* cuaderna vía *form and his skill in coping with it. One might almost suggest as a subtitle for the volume «Juan Ruiz the Writer: His Sources and Resources».*

There are, inevitably, instances of the same passage of the Libro *being discussed by more than one contributor and views are stated that conflict. Contributors have been given an opportunity to take each other's views into account in such cases, but no attempt has been made editorially to reconcile such differences as have remained. Where appropriate, the reader's attention is drawn to the fact that the same matter is discussed elsewhere in the volume.*

The proliferation in recent years of publications concerned with the Libro de buen amor *is fitting testimony to the fascination of one of the most perplexing and challenging works to survive from the Middle Ages. At the same time this very proliferation is in danger of provoking a reaction, if not of hostility, at least of weariness and indifference among scholars — appalled as they must be by the ever-mounting tide of bibliographical items that they are called upon to take note of. It is with some trepidation, therefore, that this collection of essays is offered to the public. To know that it will be duly card-indexed by scholars and deposited on the shelves of libraries will hardly be sufficient reward for its contributors. Their hope must be that the unusual nature of the concept of this book will provide an initial* captatio benevolentiae *among scholars and that on examination it will be found to make a genuine if modest contribution to the corpus of useful scholarship.*

The customary expressions of the author's gratitude to those who have helped him cannot in the nature of things have a place in this foreword. Contributors read and commented upon each others' work in typescript and all will surely agree that that the benefits have been mutual. But a special word of thanks is due to the General Editor of Tamesis Books, Professor John Varey, for his initiative in launching this volume and, subsequently, for his patience and helpfulness in seeing the project through to its completion.

Manchester

G. B. Gybbon-Monypenny

NOTE

It is clearly desirable that quotations from the text of the Libro de buen amor *should be standardized throughout the volume. When it was planned, however, there was still no reliable critical edition that could be chosen as the basis, though it was rumoured that no less than three were in preparation. In the circustances it seemed best to ask all contributors to base their quotations on the palaeographic edition of Jean Ducamin (Toulouse, 1901) which has been the stand-by of serious students of the* Libro *ever since its appearance. The three new editions —the palaeographic edition of M. Criado de Val and Eric W. Naylor (Madrid, C.S.I.C., 1965) and the critical editions of G. Chiarini (Milano-Napoli, 1964) and Joan Corominas (Madrid, Gredos, 1967)— have now all appeared in print, but none has yet established itself as an accepted version of the text of the* Libro. *Ducamin's edition has therefore remained the source for all quotations, though contributors have taken the new editions into account. The orthography has been brought into line with modern typography and the editor assumes responsibility for over-all standardization. Thus the text used by contributors is principally as represented by the Salamanca manuscript, though where manuscript variations are sufficient to affect the sense of a passage, this is indicated. «Editing» of this text has been confined to using modern forms of letters, supplying accents (except, for typographical reasons, on stressed vocalic y) and punctuation, and regularizing word spacing and certain features such as the sibilants and vocalic and consonantal u and v. Obvious errors by the copyists (usually indicated by Ducamin with a sic) are corrected.*

* * *

Bibliographical references are normally given in footnotes as the occasion arises, but no separate bibliography has been included. A general bibliography which was merely the sum of all works referred to by contributors (which include items not directly concerned with the Libro) *would be a miscellaneous list serving no particular purpose, while a bibliography on Juan Ruiz, containing as many items as have come to our notice, is scarcely called for in a volume of this character and would duplicate lists to be found elsewhere. It may be helpful, however, to draw attention to several recent bibliographies on Juan Ruiz. The most nearly complete is that given in J. Simón Díaz, Bi-*

bliografía de las literaturas hispánicas, *2nd edn. (Madrid, 1963) III.i., pp. 222-236; there are also bibliographies in María Brey Mariño's modernized version of the* Libro de buen amor, *4th edn. (Valencia, «Odres Nuevos», 1965), in Chiarini's edition (mentioned above), in Carmelo Gariano,* El mundo poético de Juan Ruiz *(Madrid, 1968) and in the editor of this volume's «Estado actual de los estudios sobre el* Libro de buen amor», *AEM III (1966), 575-609. All bibliographies are, alas, out of date, sometimes even before publication, and the periodical bibliographies of such journals as* PMLA, RFE *and* NRFH *must be consulted regularly.*

ABBREVIATIONS

AEM	*Anuario de Estudios Medievales.*
BAE	Biblioteca de Autores Españoles.
BdeF	*Boletim de Filologia.*
BFC	*Boletín del Instituto de Filología de la Universidad de Chile.*
BH	*Bulletin Hispanique.*
BHS	*Bulletin of Hispanic Studies.*
BRAE	*Boletín de la Real Academia Española.*
CHE	*Cuadernos de Historia de España.*
CMC	*Cantar de Mio Cid.*
DCELC	*Diccionario crítico-etimológico de la lengua castellana,* by Joan Corominas (Madrid, 1954-7).
EETS	Early English Texts Society.
ELu	*Estudios Lulianos.*
HR	*Hispanic Review.*
LBG	London, Brussels and Göttingen mss. of the Latin *Romulus* (see Karl Warncke, *Die Fabeln der Marie de France,* Halle, 1898).
MHRA	Modern Humanities Research Association.
MP	*Modern Philology.*
NRFH	*Nueva Revista de Filología Hispánica.*
PAPS	*Proceedings of the American Philosophical Society.*
PLPLS	*Proceedings of the Leeds Philosophical and Literary Society.*
PMLA	*Publications of the Modern Language Association of America.*
PQ	*Philological Quarterly.*
RABM	*Revista de Archivos, Bibliotecas y Museos.*
RET	*Revista Española de Teología.*
RF	*Romanische Forschungen.*
RFE	*Revista de Filología Española.*
RFH	*Revista de Filología Hispánica.*
RHi	*Revue Hispanique.*
RO	*Revista de Occidente.*
RomN	*Romance Notes.*
RPh	*Romance Philology.*
SATF	Société des Anciens Textes Français.
VR	*Vox Romanica.*
ZRP	*Zeitschrift für romanische Philologie.*

KENNETH W. J. ADAMS

Juan Ruiz's Manipulation of Rhyme: Some Linguistic and Stylistic Consequences

Introductory remarks

In the *Libro de buen amor* it is quite apparent that Juan Ruiz regards the mastery of rhyme as an essential ingredient of verse making. So much so, in fact, that it is my contention in this article that rhyme constitutes an element of considerable importance in the composition of the work. I hope to show that the implications of rhyme in the *Libro de buen amor* have a bearing on several aspects of the book.

Mention has naturally been made in previous studies of the phenomenon of rhyme in the *Libro de buen amor*. Adequate lists of endings appear in Lecoy, pp. 56-62, and Chiarini, pp. LIV-LXIX. [1] Rhyme has been taken into account by the major editors of the work, though not always in a thoroughly consistent fashion. [2] Aguado, *DCELC*, Morreale and Richardson have had occasion to mention rhyme, but almost exclusively to establish the mere existence of a particular form. [3] Most serious critics have referred to Juan Ruiz's awareness of the art of versifying and to his comments on the subject, yet very little has been said about the effect the choice of rhyme has on the composition of the individual line or strophe and eventually of the whole work. [4]

[1] F. Lecoy, *Recherches sur le 'Libro de buen amor'* (Paris, 1938); Juan Ruiz, *Libro de buen amor*, ed. G. Chiarini (Milano-Napoli, 1964).
[2] I have compared the variant readings of the *Libro* in the light of Juan Ruiz's rhyming techniques; in nearly every case ms. *G* is most reliable. This concurs with the view of Corominas in his edition of the *Libro* (Madrid, 1967): see especially pp. 28-29, though Corominas does not refer specifically to rhyme, but to general linguistic authenticity and reliability.
[3] See J. Aguado, *Glosario sobre Juan Ruiz, poeta castellano del siglo XIV* (Madrid, 1929); *DCELC*; Margherita Morreale, «Apuntes para un comentario literal del *Libro de buen amor*», *BRAE* XLIII (1963), 249-371; H. B. Richardson, *An Etymological Vocabulary to the 'Libro de buen amor'* (Yale U. P. 1930).
[4] See, for example, A. N. Zahareas, *The Art of Juan Ruiz, Archpriest of Hita* (Madrid, 1965), pp. 62-69.

1

Variety of rhymes

The sheer variety of rhyme terminants in the *Libro de buen amor* is impressive. While it is perhaps surprising to discover that the *Libro de Alexandre* and Berceo employ as many as 130 and 115 rhyme endings respectively, Juan Ruiz's achievement is quite exceptional, since he surpasses these totals by at least one hundred in his *cuaderna vía* poetry alone.[5] Some of the many examples in the *Libro de buen amor* which do not appear in other *cuaderna vía* poets are: —*aco*/—*aca*, —*adan*, —*agre*, —*allen*, —*amo*/—*ama*, —*ançe*, —*anga*, —*apa*, —*arta*, —*eça*, —*ema*, —*epa*, —*erro*, —*ezno*, —*icha*, —*iervo*, —*ijo*/—*ija*, —*ima*, —*obra*, —*olo*, —*oma*, —*onda*, —*onja*, —*orra*, —*ueda*, —*uerda*, —*urra*, —*uxo*. A further contrast can be made with the excessive poverty of rhymes in works such as the *Poema de Fernán González* and the *Libro de Apolonio*.[6] Furthermore, Juan Ruiz experiments with even more types in his poetic pieces not written in the *cuaderna vía* form, where we find the following additional endings: —*abras*, —*ercia*, —*iéredes*, —*iestra*, —*uegras*, —*uerça*.

The motive behind this independence of rhyme must be a desire to break the monotony of the commonest endings employed by the previous *cuaderna vía* poets.[7] Juan Ruiz clearly saw that these conventional, facile rhymes would not permit him to display his brilliance as a *trobador*. The figures again support the point. He rhymes some 136 stanzas in —*ado*/—*ada*, or approximately 8 % of his total output of *cuaderna vía* poetry. Berceo has 600 such stanzas, i. e. 18 % of his verse, *Alexandre* 23 %, *PFG* 20 %, *Apolonio* 24 %. A similar differential exists with regard to —*ar*, the next most prolific rhyme ending after —*ado*/—*ada*. The consequence, therefore, is that Juan Ruiz reduces the number of purely morphological rhymes, which helps to

[5] *Alexandre: Libro de Alexandre*, ed. R. S. Willis (Princeton-Paris, 1934). I give Willis's own composite stanza numbers, but indicate by *O* or *P* if one ms. reading is preferable. As for Berceo, there are some differences between individual works, but they do not change my conclusions significantly with respect to Juan Ruiz. Specific editions of Berceo will be referred to as I have cause to mention them separately. Lastly, the figures and percentages given here and subsequently are based on my own reckonings and make no claim to absolute mathematical accuracy.

[6] *PFG: Poema de Fernán González*, ed. R. Menéndez Pidal in *Reliquias de la poesía épica española* (Madrid, 1951), 34-153; *Apolonio: Libro de Apolonio*, ed. C. Carroll Marden, Elliott Monographs Nos. 6, 11, 12 (Baltimore, 1917-22).

[7] The extent of this monotony is referred to in two articles: G. Cirot, «Sur le *mester de clerecía*», *BH* XLIV (1942), 5-16; H. H. Arnold, «Irregular Hemistichs in the *Milagros* of Gonzalo de Berceo», *PMLA* L (1935), 335-351.

break the repetitious structure found in these poems. A similar awareness is seen in Juan Ruiz's use of imperative forms in — *at* and plural nouns in — *amos;* this varies the monotonous effect of consecutive
abstract nouns in — *at* or plural verb forms in — *amos.*

While scarcely any other terminants can match — *ado/ — ada* and
— *ar* in quantity, there are several others such as — *al/ — ales,* — *ano/*
— *ana,* — *ava,* — *emos,* — *ir,* — *ura,* which appear rather less frequently
in the *Libro de buen amor* than in the other works. At the same time,
a number of those rhymes which appear only in the *Libro de buen amor*
are not restricted to single appearances; this is true, for example, of
— *aca,* 616, 919, 1201; — *amo/ — ama,* 101, 197, 812, 830, 857, 936, 1181,
1355; — *ardo/ — arda,* 455, 749, 1566; — *ega,* 1176, 1250, 1374; — *ico,*
247, 869, 1013; — *id,* 52, 258, 1079, 1450, 1496, 1605; — *orre/ — orres,*
512, 1007, 1465; — *os,* 661, 1193, 1290, 1705; — *oya,* 699, 937; — *uerte,*
166, 584, 1118, 1217, 1580. Besides, many of those rhymes which appear very rarely in the other works are employed by Juan Ruiz rather
more often, e. g. — *abo/ — aba,* 398, 560, 1453, 1624, cf. *Alexandre* 683;
— *ago/ — aga,* 3, 204, 400, 467, 1436, cf. *Alexandre* 74, 925, *Santo Domingo* 64; — *esa,* 298, 1078, 1166, 1221, 1274, 1470, 1702, cf. *Alexandre* 336, *Apolonio* 483; — *ete,* 406, 1232, 1257, 1400, cf. *Alexandre*
436, *Apolonio* 502; — *il,* 65, 463, 486, 600, 1096, 1690, cf. *Alexandre*
857; — *ora,* 78, 111, 397, 462, 738, 799, cf. *PFG* 689, *Milagros* 304,
Apolonio 272, 580, *Oria* 123; — *ud,* 582, 911, 1511, cf. *Apolonio* 20;
— *uego,* 262, 423, 690, 734, 1608, cf. *Alexandre* 352, *Apolonio* 151;
— *uso/ — usa,* 363, 364, 412, 472, 519, cf. *Santo Domingo* 662, *Loores* 37. [8]

Needless to say, several of the above examples contain imperfect
rhymes. However, this is an intrinsic difficulty which the language is
inadequate to solve and we shall see later that Juan Ruiz himself is obliged to resort to a type of assonance to complete some of his more
troublesome stanzas. The important point is that, even with the enor-
mously increased range of endings in the *Libro de buen amor,* this happens much more frequently in the other poets. Lastly, it must be
stressed that Juan Ruiz chose the difficult task of finding new rhymes,
where simpler ones would have satisfied the remaining poets. If we

[8] I use the following abbreviations for Berceo's works: *Loores, Loores de
Nuestra Señora,* ed. F. Janer, BAE vol. LVII (Madrid, 1864), 93-103; *Milagros,
Milagros de Nuestra Señora,* ed. A. García Solalinde (Madrid, Clásicos Caste-
llanos, 1922; *Oria, Vida de Santa Oria,* ed. C. Carroll Marden in *Cuatro poemas
de Berceo* (Madrid, *RFE* anejo IX, 1928), 73-94; *Santo Domingo, Vida de Santo
Domingo de Silos,* ed. J. D. Fitz-Gerald (Paris, 1904); *San Millán, Estoria de San
Millán,* ed. G. Koberstein (Münster, 1964).

are to accept recent findings on the stylistic qualities of some of the other poems, it may be that the more difficult rhymes were deliberately avoided before Juan Ruiz. [9]

Consecutive rhymes

Concomitant with the excessive use of the same rhymes, such as *— ado* and *— ar,* in *cuaderna vía* poetry, is the tendency to repeat the same rhyme in consecutive stanzas. While there could be a stylistic reason for this device in some instances, which may be compared to the *laisse* structure of the epic, it is probable that the majority of cases is due to careless composition. As in the case of frequently repeated rhymes, Juan Ruiz does not go so far as to eradicate the phenomenon entirely, but once again severely limits its use. I have found up to six consecutive stanzas in the same rhyme in e. g. *Alexandre* 1942-47 (I include here as identical from a stylistic viewpoint such series as contain merely morphological variants of the same rhyme, i. e. *—ado/ —ada/—ados/—adas*); examples of five stanzas of this type (*Alexandre* 2510-14) and four (*Alexandre* 2576-79) also occur. Juan Ruiz allows himself three stanzas to a rhyme on only three occasions (131-133, 369-371, 1412-14); contrast this with eighteen and sixteen such instances in *Alexandre* and Berceo respectively. As for two consecutive stanzas in the same rhyme, the difference between the poets is equally marked. Juan Ruiz has as many as thirty-one instances, but *Alexandre* has 110 or so and Berceo reaches 130. There is evidence too that Juan Ruiz is being clever in some of his instances; for example, he repeats the comparatively rare and difficult ending *—ote* (1477-78) and changes from masculine to feminine in 363-364, where *— uso* is followed by *— usa.*

Influence of rhymes upon each other

Although Juan Ruiz seems to have limited drastically the use of repeated consecutive rhymes, he does allow his rhyme to be suggested to him by its predecessor. This is fairly common in the *Libro de buen amor* and may be due in part to aural association of a spontaneous

---

[9] See, for example, J. Artiles, *Los recursos literarios de Berceo* (Madrid, 1964), and C. Gariano, *Análisis estilístico de los Milagros de Nuestra Señora de Berceo* (Madrid, 1965).

4

nature, but could also illustrate Juan Ruiz's desire to be clever at-
versifying. After all, such a feature is not easy to spot if the reader
does not deliberately look for it, taking the rhymes in isolation.

In all I have found some fifty groups of rhymes of this type. A few
of the more outstanding examples will suffice, e. g. 275-276 — ata/ — anta;
382-384 — ona/ — ana/ — anga; 391-392 — ina/iñas; 470-471 — ero/ — edo;
473-474 — ana/ — aña; 523-524 — asa/ — anssa; 757-758 — illa/ — ía; 925-
926 — or/ — orra; 1011-12 — ista/ — isa; 1274-75 — esa/ — erça; 1606-07
— oco/ — uego. Virtually all of the possible examples I have found
elsewhere concern very easy and common rhymes, so that the likelihood
of pure coincidence is high; compare for example, Alexandre 2116-17,
2229-30, 2270-71 (all — ado/ — ano combinations) or Milagros 477-78
— ades/ — adas or San Millán 49-50 — ares/ — ales.

Assonance and consonance

The poet is confronted with a simple choice when he is unable to find
enough rhyming words to complete his stanza: either he re-writes in
a simpler rhyme or he contents himself with incomplete rhymes. Juan
Ruiz clearly refused to reject many opening lines once they had been
written, even though they ended in extravagant rhymes. It was also
undoubtedly part of his purpose to stretch his own ingenuity in this fashion. [10] We shall see, however, that his solution to the difficult rhyme
problems is much more accomplished than mere assonance.

In the majority of cases, he is able to maintain a degree of consonance; in most of these instances too the near adequate rhyme of line *b*
becomes the rhyme for lines *c* and *d*. Over fifty cases arise, but since
several of them are set out by Lecoy (Recherches..., pp. 53-54), I will refer
here to only a handful of examples, e. g. 940 — ardan/ — adan; 1601 allen/
— alen; 1239 — armen/ — amen; 159 — obre/ — onbre; 1392 — oça/
— orça; 972 — ovia/ — oya. Similar associations uncharacteristic of
other *cuaderna vía* writers (see also Lecoy, Recherches..., p. 54) are
the rhyming of *ie* with *e* and *ue* with *ie* or *e*, e. g. 301, 1458, 1524, 1593.

A simpler solution is assonance. Although Juan Ruiz has only a half
dozen or so examples in his whole work, even these rarely concern more
than one of the four rhyming words, e. g. 1603 — uno/ — deyuso. By

---

[10] Aguado, Glosario..., p. 97, regards these cases as mere «infidelidades rí-
micas» and is surely wrong, too, in attributing their existence to the «cambio de
la rima consonante por el asonante que entonces comenzaba».

contrast, the near consonance of imperfectly rhyming stanzas is not so much practised by the other poets, who have no qualms about using assonance. Compare, for example, *San Millán* 208, *—ençio/—erio* or *San Millán* 470, *—inio/—ilio/—içio.*

Elaborate rhyme

A significant feature of Juan Ruiz's verse is the elaboration of the basic requirements for rhyme.[11] The phenomenon certainly exists in other *cuaderna vía* poets, though neither to the same extent nor with such success. Internal evidence definitely suggests that, apart from the occasional unintentional alliteration or other syllabic association, the elaboration is deliberate, either as a trick of style, or at its worst, as a hackneyed, facile means of finding a rhyme word.

The elaboration generally consists in creating an association between the rhyme words of a given stanza in addition to the consonance of the stressed syllable and any following syllable. This may take the form of a simple initial alliteration or the more subtle shape of an association between or repetition of a syllable or syllables preceding the stress. To refute in statistical terms the notion that such associations may be entirely fortuitous, we can compare the number of times they do occur with the number of times they might have occurred, where the necessary conditions are present. While I see no need to quote figures where three and even all four of a stanza's rhyme words are specially interrelated, it is clear that coincidence could be more likely when only two lines are involved. Thus, referring to each of the the four lines as *a, b, c, d,* we can see that a deliberate association of rhyme words would be more conceivable in the combinations *ab, bc, cd,* than elsewhere. Only

---

[11] Each of the devices with which I shall deal has its respective technical term, set out principally in the *Leys d'amors:* see M. Gatien-Arnoult, *Monuments de la Littérature Romane,* Tome I (Toulouse, 1841), 1-363. Although this work was not composed until 1356, it assembles what had been common practice amongst Provençal poets for centuries previously. See also E. Faral, *Les Arts Poétiques au XIIe et au XIIIe Siècles* (Paris, 1924), especially pp. 55-98. For a discussion of the appearance of some of these devices and terms in Spain, see P. Le Gentil, *La Poésie Lyrique Espagnole et Portugaise à la Fin du Moyen-Age,* Tome II (Rennes, 1952), pp. 111-158, and M. de Riquer, *La lírica de los trovadores* (Barcelona, 1948). Also relevant, although it deals principally with particular usage at the end of the fifteenth century, is the article by K. Whinnom, «Diego de San Pedro's Stylistic Reform», *BHS* XXXVII (1960), 1-15. However, there is very little to suggest that Juan Ruiz was not writing more or less spontaneously, or at most drawing only indirectly upon a cultural background influenced by such techniques.

in the event of complete four-line symmetry could we conceive of the associations *ac, ad, bd,* when we would expect the patterns *ad/bc* or *ac/bd.* The fact that the series *ab, bc, cd,* outnumbers the second, *ac, ad, bd,* by 6 : 1 in Juan Ruiz, 9 : 1 in *Alexandre* and 8 : 1 throughout Berceo, makes it most likely that there is a degree of intention present or in any case a subconscious aural attraction. [12]

Taken as proportions of the whole output of these poets, the respective totals show c. 17 % of strophes with such lines in Juan Ruiz (i. e. 254 pairs of rhyme words), 12 % in *Alexandre* (317 pairs) and 9 % in Berceo (299 pairs). Before giving a selection of examples of this device, where only two lines are involved, I will deal with the rather smaller, but not insignificant, number of four- and three-line associations. To begin with, nearly 5 % of Juan Ruiz's *cuaderna vía* stanzas show complete four-line relationships beyond the mere essential rhyme. There are some eighty stanzas involved. I find no more than twenty-seven such possibilities in *Alexandre* (i.e a mere 1 % of the poem). As for Berceo, there are eighty-six or so instances, which would amount to 2½ % of his poetry; however, some sixty-four of these concern the rhyme *—ón* and are facile *—ción, —zón,* or *—sión* endings. How little conscious Berceo was of this type of symmetry is illustrated by the fact that he only achieves the feat with six rhyme types, all of which are very common endings, e. g. *—ar* (once only), *—ia* (twice), *—iento* (five times, all nouns in *—miento). Alexandre* is more varied, with fourteen different rhymes in the twenty-seven cases mentioned. Juan Ruiz, however, has recourse to twenty-four different rhyme endings here.

The rhyme ending with which Juan Ruiz achieves most sucess in this technique is *—ar;* there are several instances, e. g. *—allar* (1010), *—brar* (289, 1585), *—char* (1433), *—dar* (401), *—gar* (55, 278, 442, 629, 867, 1018), *—mar* (12), *—xar* (387). Another successful elaboration is *—í,* e. g. *—dí* (1339), *—ntí* (1368), *—ví* (107), and *—ía* appears more than once in this way, e. g. *—sía*(319), *—zía* (1182 *—* although the example is still valid, Corominas has *—zié* here). Several other examples cannot go unmentioned, e. g. *—mó* (196), *—tura* (263), *—sada* (1330), *—ender* (1523). The device known as *annominatio* (see E. Faral, *Les Arts Poétiques...,* pp. 93-96, 169, 323) is also very like the above cases and itself appears a few times, e. g. 215 *—dicha* or 80 *—puesta.* In such examples, successive compounds of the same verb are employed and

---

[12] The combinations *ad/bc* and *ac/bd* do occur occasionally in the *Libro,* e. g. stanzas 60, 225, 524, 778, 958, 1442, 1479, 1492. For examples of *ab/cd* see 198, 254, 345, 859, 885, 1540, 1597.

whatever the rhetorical origins of the device considerations of rhyme are clearly uppermost here. One further example, 95, is rejected by Corominas who prefers *sotenten* in line *d;* he may be right in implying that this is only a case of partial *annominatio* (i. e. lines *a-c*), but comparison with some of the above examples could mean that Ducamin's *someten* was correct after all.

While Juan Ruiz greatly surpasses his predecessors in the success of this type of composition, he is not a complete perfectionist. Frequently he produces the same effect in only three of his four lines. Obviously, the fourth word may be very difficult to find or even non-existent, but he does not re-write these stanzas. In fact, he is probably proud of these too. Again in terms of proportions, this three-line association is more frequent in Juan Ruiz (122 stanzas, or c. 8 % of his total) than in Berceo (124 stanzas or c. 3 %) or in *Alexandre* (99 stanzas, c. 3 %). The bald totals are not too dissimilar, but these are obviously less meaningful than the proportions. In any case, Juan Ruiz is again superior in variety and quality. In fact, he is able to find such associations for some sixty different rhyme endings. This applies both to rhymes already used in the four-line series above, such as *— ado, — ar, — i, — ia* and to a host of others. Furthermore, he is able in several instances to avoid having recourse to the same words as he used in the four-line combinations. Outstanding examples of three-line associations are:
180 *seo/asseo/deseo;* 244 *silla/rrenzilla/manzilla;* 277 *locura/rrencura/cura;* 632 *rreferteras/rregateras/arteras;* 745 *Endrina/golondryna/madrina;* 942 *falcón/ryncón/tocón;* 982 *almozar/solazar/amenazar;* 1021 *talla/pyntalla/trotalla;* 1088 *javaly/don aly/valy;* 1199 *leydas/caydas/oydas;* 1266 *contar/yantar/cantar;* 1296 *carrales/parrales/corrales;* 1304 *Ssevilla/villa/maravilla;* 1319 *ya qué/pequé/saqué;* 1325 *verssos* (clearly pronounced *viessos;* Corominas in fact has this reading)*/aviesos/traviesos;* 1392 *Garoça/orça/roça;* 1576 *sepultura/soltura/altura* (if we accept Corominas' reading for line *c, boltura,* we have in fact another four-line combination; the *— ltura* throughout would seem to provide a justification for his reading which he does not refer to).

The examples so far mentioned all concern associations within the body of the words involved. At the same time, Juan Ruiz is not averse to using the rather easier device of alliteration in these three-line groups, e. g. 780 *dañoso/deseoso/desdeñoso;* 1174 *corvillo/canistillo/cantarillo;* 1393 *camarones/caçones/capones;* 1417 *melezina/madrina/mesquina.* Further well contrived instances are 126 *almas/armas/anbas* (where the consonance would be much better if we pronounced the last word **amas)*

8

and 976 *conbidas/comidas/midas*. Finally, it is important to note that Juan Ruiz is often able to find a fourth rhyme which is phonetically not too distant from the other three, even if it is not completely consonant, e. g. 160 *—tura/ —tura/ —tura/ —dura,* 526 *—dura/—dura/ —tura/—dura.* Compare, too, unvoiced *t* and *c* in 1021 *talla/ —talla/ —talla/ —calla* and voiced *d* and *g* in 199 *—gavan/ —davan/—gavan/ —gavan.* Likewise, the assonance is preserved in 1088, *—aly/ —a'i/ —aly/—aly* and a close approximation to consonance appears in 244 *—silla/—zilla/ —zilla/—stilla.*

While I have stressed the argument that Juan Ruiz is supreme in range and quality, it would be unfair to some of the other *cuaderna vía* poets to suggest that they knew nothing of such tricks of style. However, since fairly easy associations are generally made by them and with respect to rather simple rhyme endings, it might not be hazardous to say that the search for such words was not often made by them for reasons of style, but much more for the elementary purpose of composing the next line. Compare for example *Santo Domingo* 398, (*—t'ral?*) *natural/mortal/otra tal*; *Alexandre* 470, *lidiar/livrar/levar*; *Oria* 163, *logar/rogar/folgar*. Examples of more satisfying associations are *Alexandre* 124, *prestar/preçiar/pechar; Santo Domingo* 276, *reglares/logares/pulgares; Alexandre* 532 (ms *O*), *logal/lo al/çervigal/igual.*

Nevertheless, such combinations are quite infrequent in these poets and can often be attributed to coincidence or at best to a not very powerful aural impulse. On the other hand, it would seem that the impulse is a very potent one in Juan Ruiz's case.

I will move next to sound associations which concern only two of the four rhyming words of a stanza. Here clearly the chances of purely accidental juxtaposition are quite high. However, some judgements can be made which are in keeping with what has already been said and which once again show that Juan Ruiz is the superior craftsman. Firstly, the simple alliterative type is extremely common in all the major *cuaderna vía* poems except the *Libro de buen amor;* in these cases the successive rhyme words merely begin with the same sound (see examples on p. 7). The comparative figures are quite interesting; *PFG* has 54 % of its two-line associations in this category, *Apolonio* 50 %, Berceo 48 % and *Alexandre* 30 %. Only 10 % of Juan Ruiz's two-line series are of this type. Next, a further important group of associated rhyme words is formed by homonyms or near homonyms. We should naturally not expect Juan Ruiz to depart from this tradition, which is also present in other poets, since he is able to find several clever exam-

9

ples of his own, as well as having recourse occasionally to the homonyms used by others. Examples peculiar to Juan Ruiz's particular mentality are 201 *sobyr/servir*; 313 *denteras/delanteras*; 330 *veynte/vente*; 338 *ovejas/arvejas;* 410 *enojo/ynojo;* 752 *plaça/pelaça*; 979 *yradas/aradas*; 1093 *çeçina/ coçina*. A few further examples outside of the *Libro de buen amor,* which are quite original, may be compared, e. g. *Milagros* 523, 865, *mediçina/mezquina*; *Oria* 74, *paredes/perdredes*; *Santo Domingo* 448, *avredes/abredes*; *San Millán* 428, *generaçion/guarniçion*; *Alexandre* 1171, (ms 0), *lana/llana*; *Alexandre* 141, *rancado/regnado*. However, the humorous punning, which is apparent in some of Juan Ruiz's examples, is not a feature of the other poems. In fact, virtually all of the examples from the *Libro de buen amor* just quoted would seem to serve this purpose.

In considering the remaining subdivisions of two-line combinations, all of which are within the body of the words concerned, we can observe a further divergence between Juan Ruiz and his predecessors. I refer to the frequent use of combinations in which part or all of the first word of the pair is repeated, in sound though not always in spelling, in the second word, [13] e. g.:

94 *çaraça/rraça;* 337 *descomulgado/legado* (I prefer Corominas's reading here); 178 *mazillero/çillero;* 750 *villana/llana;* 1253 *dineros/tardineros;* 1305 *Toledo/ledo:* 1468 *vegadas/cavalgadas;* 1548 *fermosura/mesura.*

There are in fact nearly fifty such instances in the *Libro de buen amor,* or nearly 25 % of the whole series of two-line associations. While the process for the poet himself may well be without complexity — its sole purpose being to associate syllables as they occur to him — it is important to note that other *cuaderna vía* poets do not think of it very often. It should be remembered too that this type of trick had been held in repute by sophisticated poets from Provence and those influenced by them. Yet it can certainly be argued that these combinations could well occur to the poet aurally, not visually. In this way, the similarity between the over-contrived tricks of the *troubadours* and some of Juan Ruiz's devices might just be accidental, since the syllabification of speech is not that of writing. Nonetheless these conflicting points have to be considered in the light of Juan Ruiz's obvious knowledge of «metrificar e rrimar e de trobar» (*Libro de buen amor,* prose prologue, Ducamin, p. 7).

---

[13] See also Le Gentil, *La Poésie Lyrique...*, II, p. 154, «Rimes contrefaites», and the *Leys d'amors,* p. 158, «rim consonan leyal».

A related series of examples is that where the extended rhyme is divided between different words. This also would seem more probable in speech than in writing. The device is not abundantly employed and is certainly not the easiest to achieve of those dealt with so far. Here once more very few instances are to be found outside the *Libro de buen amor* amongst the *cuaderna vía* poets. [14] Some of Juan Ruiz's more successful examples are:

4 *Susaña/tu saña* (cf. *conpaña/tan maña* in the same stanza); 5 *la ballena/la mar llena;* 84 *comiese/que omne viese* (Corominas' reading); 104 *mal va/malva;* [15] 267 *sobida/su vida;* 567 *por ty/departy;* 917 *dia ver/aver/horaña ser/nasçer;* 699 *viejas Troyas* (or *croyas* in Corominas' edition)/*orejas oyas;* 957 *con quexa/coneja;* 1097 *viernes yd/desid;* 1227 *con flores/colores;* 1298 *verdat son/rraçón;* 1333 *dies años/sosaños;* 1368 *arrepenty/en ty;* 1510 *alvalá/tal ha* (ms. *G*); 1690 *don Gil/non vil;* 1375 *vyanda/y anda;* 911 *ver pud'/virtud* (probably pronounced *vertud* as in Cejador's edition (Clásicos Castellanos, Madrid, 1955, 7.ª ed.).

Poems not written in cuaderna vía

These pieces of poetry are those for which Juan Ruiz has become famous as a poet. I have concentrated most of my own analysis on the *cuaderna vía* sections and am concerned here only with making a few technical comparisons. The poems in question have attracted considerable attention for their metrical variety, versatility, fine quality and not the least for their apparent originality and their appearance in Spanish literature at such an early date. It is quite clear that they are the work of the same man as the author of the *cuaderna vía* portion. I have observed many of the same tricks and resources of composition in all types of verse in the *Libro de buen amor*.

The same variety of rhyme terminants is present as before, the same freedom is exercised, e. g. the rhyming of *—ueno/ —eno* (28) and of *—uerto/—ierto* (1066), or the approximation of similar sounds in 1027, *—oça/—osa* and 1042 *—aje/—aze*. The same solutions to dif-

---

[14] Le Gentil, *La Poésie Lyrique...*, II, p. 155, is, then, only partly right in affirming that «On ne recontre point, au Sud des Pyrénées, de ces longues rimes à la fois *équivo,ues* et *léonines* qu' appréciait déjà Gautier de Coincy». Compare also Faral, *Les Arts Poétiques...*, p. 93, and the *Leys d'Amors*, p. 162, on «simple leonisme contrafag».

[15] Within the group of examples I quote, a distinction must clearly be drawn between genuinely contrived instances and those which supply an obligatory rhyme.

ficult rhymes are adopted, e. g. 991 _—ada/—arda,_ (cf. 749), 1719 _—amas/—almas_ (cf. 936). Again, 1039 _—ura_ is probably prompted by _—ora_ in the same stanza, while 1719 _—amos/—amas_ is also typical of Juan Ruiz.

Homonyms and near homonyms again appear, e. g. 965 _vino/vino;_ 1005 _comides/conbides_ (cf. 976); 1642 _cuanta/canta._ Identical or very similar sound associations occur again, e. g. 120 rhyming in _—jero_ or 1710 in _—dar;_ 35 _oviste/rresçebiste/oíste/conçebiste;_ 1726 _galardón/perdón._ We can observe, too, the same special types of which Juan Ruiz is so fond, e. g. 968 _asadas/amassadas;_ 1637 _naçiste/rremaneçiste;_ 969 _hadeduro/duro._ The rhyme which extends over more than one word is again present here, e. g. 959 _como andas/demandas_ (ms _G.;_ Corominas rejects this reading, but the presence of the sound association would seem to justify it); 1025 _bien corres/engorres;_ 1026 _fermosura/por mesura;_ 1040 _merchandía/buen día;_ 1638 _por o/tesoro_ (Cejador's reading). Such special similarities are clear evidence of the singleness of authorship of the whole of the _Libro de buen amor._

Breadth of vocabulary

It is a well known fact that Juan Ruiz has recourse to a superabundant vocabulary. However, no systematic attempt has yet been made to relate this wealth of words to the practical problems of poetic composition. It has become quite clear in the course of my own investigations that the vocabulary of the _Libro de buen amor_ is in no small way dependent on the choice of rhymes. [16]

Thus, more than seven hundred words only appear in rhyme in the _Libro de buen amor;_ in fact, some five hundred of these appear once only in the work. At the same time, Juan Ruiz's obvious delight in parading his lexicon before us cannot be minimised in view of the fact that a further five hundred words appear once only and not in rhyme. Similarly, more precise orientation is provided by the knowledge that nearly half of the seven hundred words mentioned above do not seem to appear in rhyme for any obvious technical reason. That is to say, the rhyme could have been supplied by a number of other words. It can, nevertheless, be shown that the remaining three hundred and fifty words do seem to owe their presence to the choice of rhyme.

[16] On the lengths to which rhymesters can go, compare Tirso's humorous _glosa_ «por ser el bastón de enebro...»; see E. Díez-Echarri, _Teorías métricas del siglo de oro_ (Madrid, _RFE_ anejo XLVII, 1949).

As for the rather large number of words which appear in rhyme for no obligatory reason, where the choice of words available is reasonably wide, it is still possible to suggest two or three feasible causes. Firstly, there is an obvious desire on Juan Ruiz's part to break away from the monotony of some previous poets. Where more was this monotony to be felt than in the trite, repetitious rhyme words of the *cuaderna vía* stanza? Juan Ruiz probably felt that the rhyme word was, or could be used as, the key word in the line, since it occupies a position of emphasis. [17] This word could make or mar the whole line, especially if we imagine the book being read aloud. Secondly, Juan Ruiz seems to be reasonably aware of the words he has already used in a particular rhyme terminant and seems to be striving to avoid, where possible, undue repetition. A third and perhaps less contributory reason is that Juan Ruiz may have had a natural tendency to think of the unusual word, especially if he found himself in difficulty.

Although the above group of words and the additional large number within the line are sufficient to guarantee that Juan Ruiz did not just use strange vocabulary for rhyme, it cannot be denied that such is the reason for the appearance of a considerable variety of words in the *Libro de buen amor*. Such words clearly owe their presence to the paucity of items available in the particular rhyme required. [18] For example, the following words appear only once in Juan Ruiz and in addition the rhyme is employed only in the one stanza: [19]

246c *aguaducho,* 1306a *almagra,* 1228d *apriscarse,* 1488a *baço,* 1466d *bayle,* 947a *coxixo,* 1490d *debuxar,* 712c *desmoler,* 1718a *diestro,* 420c *encobo,* 968a *enhoto,* 966d *escarcha,* 1544c *escuerço* (ms. T), 926b *handorra* (Cejador), 1017d *hueco,* 1311a *lastro,* 219c *lepra,* 1544d *mestuerço,* 390d *mijo,* 712b *moler,* 1001a *muedo,* 517c *palanca,* 1015d *parva,* 926a *porra,* 384c *rremangarse,* 779a *rrodezno,* 773c *sojorno,* 968b *ssoto,* 779c *torrezno.* Many other words occurring once only end in rhymes used by Juan Ruiz on more than one occasion, but there is still a pauc-

---

[17] The significance of the rhyme and other positions is also mentioned by Artiles, *Los recursos literarios...,* p. 65: «En realidad, lo que importaba aquí a Berceo era colocar las palabras más importantes al final de los hemistiquios.» He does not, however, mention the possibility that they might be important for technical reasons, such as rhyme, number of syllables, stress, etc.

[18] The *Leys d'Amors,* p. 150, advised strongly against the use of too extravagant rhymes, «Quar poucas dictios ni sillabas poyria hom trobar semblans ad aquelas per far leyal acordansa».

[19] I have taken most of my evidence for the number of appearances from Aguado, *Glosario...,* and Richardson, *An Etymological Vocabulary...* Although they are not always absolutely reliable, I do not believe this interferes to any great extent with the principles involved, nor with the conclusions drawn.

ity of new words available to him if he is to avoid repeating the same four in each stanza concerned, e. g. 302c *adyvas*, 1007c *alhorre*, 1076a *almofalla*, 241a *çermeña*, 173d *enviso*, 815b *estricote*, 400c *fadraga*, 1477b *galeote*, 266c *goma*, 569b *haça*, 1293 *heliçes*, 119b *marfuz*, 1453d *menoscabo*, 171c *mita*, 1232a *panderete*, 439a *paviota*, 242c *prizes*, 1350d *rraso*, 1176a *rrepegar*, 542b *rrevertir*, 1207d *sofraja*, 1031d, *som⁊*. 1598c *tableta*, 812a *trama*, 1436d *trasfago*, 1607d *troco*, 499c *tyña*.

The special features of Juan Ruiz's rhyme schemes, with which I dealt earlier (pp. 2-11), play a large part in the choice of vocabulary. Indeed they contribute to its further specialisation. Thus, another body of words appears once only, or very rarely, because of the fullness of rhyme Juan Ruiz desires to achieve, e. g. 114b *aburrir*, 153d *acabesçer*, 1290b *alfoz*, 1001a *altybaxo*, 1510b *alvalá*, 710a *conosçienta*, 107c *deservir*, 1539b *desferrar*, 1276c *enbudo*, 633b *enfaronearse*, 271b *enpendolado*, 80b *enpuesto*, 179b *ensillar*, 1430b *entropeçar*, 1018c *espulgar*, 795d *haçerio*, 1277c *pajar*, 1296c *parral*, 752d *pelaça*, 632c *rregatero*, 1430c *retaçar*, 361b *rretachar*, 982b *solasar*, 95a *someter*, 523c *traspassar*. Compare also the following examples which appear more than once but are once again limited to the rhyme position:

700d (ms *G*), 938d *atahona*; 263d, 1364b, *aturar*; 874a, 1188c, *beçerro*; 17d, 1213c *cañavera*; 247b, 869b, *çatico*; 242a, 1293d, *çerviz*; 1235c, 1709b *clerizón*; 285d, 1001d *denodarse*; 780c, 1671c *desdeñoso*; 442b, 467d *despagarse*; 131b, 137c *despeñar*; 376d, 1492c *engraçiarse*; 392a, 918a *enveleñar*; 463d, 600c, *gentil*; 1110b, 1516b *marco*; 618d, 1482d *perjuro*; 356d, 379c *posponer*; 311c *sañoso*; 1036a, 1457d, *sarta*; 514d, 1607c *trocar*.

From the lexicographer's point of view it is significant that many of the words used by used Juan Ruiz only in rhyme appear to be the first evidence of their existence in Spanish. In a general way, we can accept *DCELC*'s authority for the first appearance in Spanish of numerous words in the *Libro de buen amor;* if there are errors of detail, these can only be rectified by exhaustive searches beyond the scope of this study.[20] The following words are found by *DCELC* for the first time in the *Libro de buen amor;* further, they appear once only in the work and then in rhyme:

1010d *aballar*, 420d *ajobo*, 1157a *arapar*, 1228b *arisco*, 406a *brete*,

---

[20] While I have consulted principally *DCELC*, I have taken into consideration the modifications to that work suggested since its publication, for example in Corominas's own *Breve diccionario etimológico de la lengua castellana* (Madrid, 1961).

14

288c *carrizo,* 1008d *çeñiglo,* 241a *çermeña,* 1276c *enbudo,* 1507a *ende-cha,* 1498c *esgrima,* 815b *estricote,* 266c *goma,* 1308d *lobuno,* 957a *ma-dexa,* 119d *marfuz,* 1014b *moxmordo,* 17b *peñavera,* 293b *postema,* 1699a *prebenda,* 1230d *prisco,* 1219b *rrabygalgo,* 499c *tyña,* 1443d *to-ronja,* 1021c *trotalla,* 507a *tuero,* 183b *vira.*

Other words which appear more than once are again found only in rhyme and are again discovered by *DCELC* for the first time in the *Libro de buen amor,* e. g. 874d, 1188b *çençerro;* 207a, 299d *contrallo;* 1025d, 1465d *engorrarse;* 288d, 992d *erizo;* 749c, 1566d *escardar;* 1120b, 1713b *estrena;* 845c, 977b *pepita;* 222c, 341c, 1493c *picaña.*

The words so far discussed illustrate the wealth of Juan Ruiz's vocabulary and its independence of previous poets. There are, lastly, several words used by Juan Ruiz in rhyme only which had already been virtually limited to this function by previous writers. These 'traditional' words were again largely forced upon the poets by the choice of rhyme made, e. g. *almofalla* 1076a, cf. *Alexandre* 888b; *belmez* 1521a, cf. *Alexandre* 694b, *Apolonio* 107a; *aturar* 263d, 1364b, cf. *Apolonio* 52b; *çerviz* 242a, 1293d, cf. *Alexandre* 1854b, 2342c, *Apolonio* 17b; *confuerto* 301a, 651c, cf. *Alexandre* 253c (ms. *O*), *PFG* 244c, *Santo Domingo* 404b, *Milagros* 243c, *Apolonio* 458d; *enviso* 173d, cf. *Milagros* 14c (*anviso*); *pelmazo* 744a, cf. *Alexandre* 1033c, *Santo Domingo* 687b; *rrebata* 952a, cf. *PFG* 652b; *sañoso* 311c, 1685d, cf. *Alexandre* 1824d, *Milagros* 391b, 775b; *sobejo* 251b, 604d, 688d, 839b, 1117c, 1332d, 1479b, cf. *Alexandre* 1479b, *PFG* 762d, *San Millán* 28b, *Santo Domingo* 209b, *Milagros* 544b; *vedeganbre* 414b, cf. *Alexandre* 792a, 2343b.

In the above section I have been discussing Juan Ruiz's vocabulary in accordance with frequency of appearance within the *Libro de buen amor* and the position of the words in his rhyme schemes. A few reservations should be made. Firstly, it is not certain in what order the lines were composed, but it is reasonable to assume that line *a* came first; this is evident in several cases where the odd rhyme words do not appear until lines *c* or *d,* i. e. when the poet has exhausted his supply of normal words. Yet it is also possible that other methods of composition were employed, or that line *a* was sometimes corrected in the light of the remainder of the stanza. In this way, though my general argument is unchanged, some of the above examples which occur in line *a* might have to be reconsidered. Secondly, I must state here that there is no reason why many of the words appearing within the line should not also be artistically or technically poetic. I limit my discussion here, however, to the rhyme words, which do offer us a special yardstick not easily available in other parts of the line.

Further, it is obvious that not all of the words dealt with above are of particular linguistic interest, since they existed long before Juan Ruiz and still exist to-day. The interest that these words arouse, in such instances, is not linguistic but rather stylistic. I will proceed now to subdivide the rhyming vocabulary of the *Libro de buen amor* according to both philological and stylistic criteria.

Abstract Nouns

It would clearly be tedious to give more than a brief summary. However, it is quite evident that many nouns in *– ança, – at, – ençia, –eza, – ía, – ión, – miento,* and *—ura* owe their presence in the *Libro de buen amor* to the exigencies of rhyme. The opportunities for facile rhyming with such endings are obvious and although Juan Ruiz does not use them to the same excess as earlier poets, he is often unable to avoid having recourse to them. Very few such nouns occur exclusively out of rhyme. In addition many of the ideas expressed in rhyme would be expressed differently in other genres. The contrast is further underlined by comparing the frequency of appearance of certain synonyms in and out of rhyme. In the following cases, the first mentioned word is either unique or considerably more frequent in rhyme than elsewhere:

mançebez 157*a/mançebía* 245*a,* 626*a,* 643*c,* 673*b,* 726*a,* 1363*d; dubdança* 141*c,* 1665*f,* 1669*c/dubda* 534*a,* 594*d,* 616*b,* 690*a; rresponssión* 371*a/rrespuesta* 48*d,* 80*d,* 338*c,* 349*c,* 423*a,* 604*c; ardura* 605*b/ardor* 379*c,* 639*b,* 1703*c; calentura* 1006*b/calor* 1270*c,* 1289*b; quexura* 365*a,* 594*a,* 605*d,* 652*a,* 659*d,* 675*d/quexa* 211*d,* 639*d,* 662*a,* 703*a, quexo* 792*b; salvamiento* 1674*d/salvaçión* 9*b,* 35*c* and prose prologue; *orgullía* 214*c,* 245*b/orgullo* 304*b,* 1223*c.* Likewise, *tristura* (four appearances) and *tristençia* (one appearance) are found only in rhyme by contrast with *tristesa* and *friura* is also restricted to rhyme.

Adjectives

The distribution of adjective endings in the *Libro de buen amor* is very similar to that of abstract nouns. Several adjectives in *—ero, – iente, – or* and *– oso* are found only in rhyme. Again, examples like

16

paresçiente or *estorvador,* etc., would be expressed differently out of rhyme. The comparison of different endings for the same adjectival stem again produces interesting results. The first adjective in each of the following pairs is more or less restricted to rhyme and generally less frequent than the second:

çertero 324*b,* 480*d,* 1034*c,* 1569*c/çierto* (passim); *coytoso* 819*d,* 1172*a,* 1427*b/coytado* 1*d,* 543*c,* 587*b,* 590*b,* 602*c,* 651*a; dolioso* 1172*c/ doliente* 82*a,* 237*d,* 251*d,* 373*b,* 649*a,* 893*a; engañador* 220*b,* 1716*d/en- gañoso* 627*c,* 665*b,* 1257*c,* 1600*b* and prose prologue; *sañoso* 311*c,* 1685*d/sañudo* 85*d,* 94*c,* 181*b,* 314*b,* 423*b,* 563*c; segurado* 609*c,* 646*d,* 1435*b/seguro* 209*d,* 365*d,* 595*c,* 656*d,* 822*d; sobervioso* 1665*i/sobervio* 236*a,* 238*b,* 241*d,* 243*d,* 245*b,* 1209*b; tardinero* 477*c,* 1068*c,* 1253*d/tar- dío* 1017*d.*

A few other adjectives appear only in rhyme, e. g. *profundo* 1552*a* (cf. *fondo* passim), or nearly always in rhyme, e. g. *tamaño* 4*c,* 474*b,* 621*d,* 1333*c,* 1425*d,* 1644*b,* 1686*f* (this is a little surprising since the adjective is still quite common in the works of Don Juan Manuel). Further, the use of the ending —*illo* is not entirely restricted to rhyme for adjectives, but would be severely limited without the many rhym- ing examples, e. g. *agudillo* 434*c, apartadillo* 434*b, angostillo* 434*d, cor- tillo* 1240*c.* A few more adjectives, not uncommon in other positions, have less common synonyms in rhyme, e. g. *amargo* (cf. *agro, azedo*) *alegre* (cf. *ledo*), *egual* (cf. *parejo*).

Verbs

A large number of verbs in the *Libro de buen amor* appear once only and then in rhyme; they are clearly not indispensable as far as mean- ing is concerned, e. g. *ajobar* 402*c, arapar* 1157*a, devallar* 1601*a, enbo- tar* 1518*b, enrizar* 75*d, rretachar* 361*b.* Synonyms for these and for many other verbs, readily used elsewhere in the line, give a more ac- curate picture of the normal language of the time. Compare, for example, within the *Libro de buen amor* the use and distribution of the following, where the first form appears only in rhyme:

aforrar 512*c,* 1125*b (lýbrar, soltar); aturar* 263*d,* 1364*b (durar)*— on this occasion both verbs have the same rhyme ending, i. e. —*ura(r)* but the examples of *aturar* (i. e. *atura*) both follow lines ending in *na- tura* —*avenir* passim (*pasar, acaesçer, contesçer*); *comedir* passim (*coy- dar, creer, pensar*); *condesar* 635*c,* 1206*c (asconder, çelar); departir*

691d (apartar); departir 567b, 655b, 789b, 842a, 850a, 1128b (dezir, fa-blar, parlar); desconortar 1519b (doler, penar, coytar, desagradesçer); devallar 1601a (derribar, destruir); enartar 182c, 403a, 1195c, 1457c (engañar); engorrar 1025d, 1465d (detener, tardar, parar); erzer 319c, 1441a (erguir, levantar, alçar); pechar 256b, 1433c 1507c, 1517d — this last example out of rhyme— (pagar); punir 358c (castigar); rrefertar 68d, 295c (rretraer, quexar, denostar, despreçiar); rremaneçer 1637f (quedar, fincar); trançar 904d, 1587c (destruir, roer).

Despite the occasional additional shade of meaning to be found in some of the above examples, there is little to suggest that this was the real reason for their appearance. In fact the merely apparent special meaning and even the misuse of words in rhyme could be the reason for the difficulty of some of Juan Ruiz's lines. That is to say that the possibility that a word might be forced into a line because of its phono-logical make-up is one which can in no way be ruled out.

Variant forms

Rhyme is once more a significant contributory factor to the existence in the Libro de buen amor of alternative forms of the same word. Beginning with nouns, we find a number of forms both in — e and — o. I give the form found in rhyme only first:

> rribalde 1461b/rribaldo 46c, 51b, 55d (NB also rribal in ms.
> G, 46c); alardo 455d/alarde 1082d, 1090a; unguento 1050b/
> unguente 1057b; talento 735d/talente passim; alanes 1220a/
> alano(s) 175b, 226a, 227b, 1014a; instrumente (estrumente) 355a,
> 1263b/instrumento passim.

The above division still seems to me to be valid, although I would mention here the fact that Corominas, in his recent edition, makes a few modifications to these forms. He does not accept the form rri-baldo, substituting for it on each occasion ribald, nor does he allow alarde, preferring alardo on every occasion; he also reads ungento 1057b, again removing the duality of form. To proceed with my own observations, it is further interesting that escantamente and falimente only occur in rhyme, though the evidence is not complete since their counterparts in — o do not appear at all in the book. Both confuerte and confuerto are restricted to the rhyme position, a fact which sug-gests the archaic nature of this word (see also p. 15). Other interesting pairs are *mercadero* (rhyme only) and *mercador, pastrija* (rhyme only) and *pastraña, pesa* (rhyme only) and *peso, consseja* (rhyme only) and *conssejo.* The words *pelleja* and *pellejo* are both found in and out of rhyme, though the former is more common, while of the three forms *val/valle/vallejo,* the last appears in rhyme four times out of five. Another case is *vergüenza/vergüeña/vergoña;* while the first of these is well nigh impossible in rhyme, it appears several times elsewhere, the other forms being both rare and restricted to rhyme. A few further examples are interesting; *dona* scarcely ever appears out of rhyme, *don* being preferred on those occasions; the same can be said of *laçerio* (mostly rhyme) and *laçeria, rama* (rhyme) and *ramo.* Lastly, Juan Ruiz resorts very occasionally to feminine endings unnecessary to his meaning but essential to his rhyme, e. g. *coneja* 957d, *galga* 1219d; the reverse process is used once to splendid effect (see 909a, *endrino*).

Diminutive, augmentative and other suffixes do not play as large a part in Juan Ruiz's technique as might be imagined, especially when rhyme is considered. It has already been seen that a number of adjectives in *—illo* appear in rhyme and very little elsewhere (see p. 17). Some points can also be made with regard to nouns. There is for example not a single animal in *—illo* restricted to rhyme alone. This clearly indicates that such forms are deliberately used for other than purely technical reasons. On the other hand, Juan Ruiz is not much attached to using *—illo* with other nouns. Amongst the few nouns denoting miscellaneous objects which have the *—illo* ending, only *casilla* 973d and *odreçillo* 1233c, 1516c, appear outside of rhyme. From this we can suggest that words such as *canestillo* 1174b, 1343d, *cantarillo* 1174c, *çestilla* 870c, *soguilla* 870b, and even those denoting time, distance or quantity such as *ratillo, poquillo* passim, *pasillo* 718c are to Juan Ruiz nothing more than rhyme fillers, since they all appear exclusively in that position. It is of course impossible to ascertain the origin of these forms from this evidence alone and there is no need to assume that Juan Ruiz just attached *—illo* at will; many of these forms may have existed somewhere at some time in their own right, but it is important to note that Juan Ruiz is probably forcing them in for technical motives. As for the other suffixes, some of which admittedly do not supply particularly difficult rhyme series, it might well be that forms such as *albogón,* 1233a, *clerizón* 1235c, 1709b, *tendejón* 1107d, *vyllanchón* 1115a and *panderete* 1232a owe their existence to rhyme.

Several positive conclusions emerge from an investigation of the

3

verb in the *Libro de buen amor* with respect to variant forms in and out of rhyme. The apocopated forms *faz, fiz, diz, yaz,* appear in any position, but *pon, tien, detien, mantien, vien, avien, pid* and *pud* are limited to the rhyme position. Of the infinitives *fer* and *far*, the latter is found only in rhyme. Also in rhyme only are the imperative forms *crey* 309d, *vey* 1021d, *pid* 52c, and *yz* 881c. The last of these may be invented to fit the rhyme but compare *catat* 482c. This form too should be pronounced *cataz* to fit the rhyme and since it is in the midst of the *Pitas Payas* story, such a 'foreign' form could be allowed. We might compare here Amado Alonso's discussion (in *De la pronunciación medieval a la moderna en español*, Madrid, 1955, p. 7, note 3) where «catad que no comaz» is evidence of «vaga caracterización leonesa». A further form, *vedes,* which Richardson (*An Etymological Vocabulary...*, p. 233) supposes to be an imperative is surely used interrogatively in the present indicative (see 873b — this time, however, rhyme is not involved).

As for individual tenses, the situation is fairly straightforward. One example of *seye* 1279b, appears out of rhyme, and indeed Corominas rejects this form in favour of *reyé*. Four cases of *seya* are found in rhyme; the form *era* is found frequently in all positions. In the preterite, *priso* is only found in rhyme (214b). Some fluctuation seems still to exist between *estude* and *stove*, etc. but *estido* appears twice, in rhyme both times, 481c, 608c — here I agree with Corominas in rejecting the form *estudo.* Lastly, one example of *veno* appears, again in rhyme.

Similar data are available for the past participle. I find *rrepiso* 77b, 935c only in rhyme — here again Corominas is probably right to read *repeso,* but the fact is that the strong participle is restricted to rhyme. Likewise, *aducho* 342c and *quisto* (usually as an adjective and fairly common) appear only in rhyme. The form *nado* appears twice, both times in rhyme, 798b, 1506c, but *nasçido* is not restricted thus. Again, *aperçebudo, atrevudo, arrepentudo* and *perdudo* are limited to the end of the line; examples of *aperçebido, arrepentido* and *perdido* appear elsewhere. The strong form *preso* continues in all positions though *apreso,* in the forms *bien apreso* and *mal apreso* is found only in rhyme (see 935a, 1373d, 1470c, 571c, 1078c).

Before proceeding to the next section, I should like to stress the fact that the distribution of words in the above study is presented as an illustration of Juan Ruiz's particular usage. Considering the many forms the language can take and the partial nature of the evidence, it would be somewhat presumptuous to pronounce categorically on the appearance, disappearance and reappearance of this or that word or to attempt to fix firm limits to such a fleeting subject. Yet, while I do not believe that the division between 'rhyme only' words and the remainder is necessarily evidence of general practice at the particular time, it must surely correspond to some preference on Juan Ruiz's part at least and not be a mere accident. Further, on comparing Juan Ruiz's vocabulary with that of certain prose authors, although there is the occasional appearance there of words which I have tried to show are principally poetic, the pattern is remarkably similar. Thus, the majority of Juan Ruiz's 'rhyme only' words have no great currency in these authors. [21]

Rhymes and structure

My conclusions here are rather negative. The distribution of Juan Ruiz's special rhyming techniques throughout the *Libro de buen amor* is extremely uneven. Further, this irregularity does not really correspond to the many *volte-faces* of the work and does not provide us with a simple guide to the identification of serious and not so serious portions. The section on the Seven Deadly Sins, however, does contain very little elaborate rhyme and likewise nearly all of the *enxienplos* contained in it. Yet consistency is hardly Juan Ruiz's strong point, so at the same time there is not much clever rhyme in some of the later *enxienplos* (e. g. 1348-1411) and in other sections, such as 1485-1490 *(De las figuras del arçipreste)* or 1606-17 *(De las propiedades que las dueñas chicas han)*, which might have been exploited, are similarly impoverished. Contrast the comparative abundance of rhyme elaborations in stanzas 199-216, 1225-1314 or 1425-36. It would appear, then, that with few exceptions the distribution of these devices is quite random.

Thus, the only way to account for yet another apparent inconsistency in Juan Ruiz's work is to assume that his rhyming mood had little

[21] See particularly, F. Huerta y Tejadas, «Vocabulario de las obras de don Juan Manuel», *BRAE* XXXIV (1954), cuad. 41; A. García Solalinde, *Antología de Alfonso X el Sabio* (Madrid, 1960); V. Fernández Llera, *Gramática y vocabulario del Fuero Juzgo* (Madrid, 1929); *Los Fueros de Sepúlveda*, Publicaciones históricas de la Excma. Diputación Provincial de Segovia (Segovia, 1953). I am also grateful to Miss L. E. Ingamells for allowing me to consult her London M. A. Thesis (1962), *A Linguistic Analysis of Book Two of «El Especulo» of Alfonso el Sabio.*

to do with his thematic purpose, or better perhaps, that the same rhyming techniques had to serve a variety of purposes. We must finally remember that rhyme is only one aspect of Juan Ruiz's poetic composition, even if it is a highly significant one.

Some stylistic considerations

The choice of difficult rhymes by a poet means that he is often obliged to use words for their phonological make-up. In so far as these words condition the content of their respective lines and even stanzas, it can be said that the poem to some extent composes itself. Hence the intrusion into the *Libro de buen amor* of a large number of lines which are totally dependent on the rhyme word; hence the introduction of several items, often of a too specialised nature, in which it is likely Juan Ruiz had no particular interest.

Once we accept this intrinsic difficulty and the inevitable appearance of often highly unpoetic objects, it is still possible to distinguish good lines from bad. For example, I consider the following lines quite adequately contrived, some excellently:

1252 *açafrán*, 1099c *alas*, 126b *armas*, 1120c *ballena*, 1250d *bodega*, 1350b *brasa* (ms. G), 778c *cabçe*, 151b *cabestro*, 1359c *conejo*, 1114d *correa*, 219b *estepa*, 219c *lepra*, 1457d *sarta*, 1400c *tapete*, 415d *tenaças*, 1164b *trucha*, 1323c *vara*, 950c *vyanda*. On the other hand, the dangers of being a rhymester are emphasised by many other lines, which I consider somewhat weak, e. g.

700d, 938d *atahonas*, 835d *ballena*, 954d *barvecho*, 875d *clavo*, 773d *forno*, 1109d, 1472d *gato*, 1492d *palaçio*, 753c *palas*, 1220c *panes*, 410d, 953d *rastrojo*, etc.

A further tendency, which varies in its effect from neatly epigrammatic to far-fetched and virtually incomprehensible, is the recourse to elliptical and loosely connected expressions. This I feel also is due in no small way to the problems of fitting in the rhyme word. Hence a phrase or *refrán* may occur to the poet because of its rhyme word; there is often a missing link between such lines and their predecessors. For example, adequate continuity is provided in 219b-c *estepa/lepra*, 390c-d *aguijo/mijo* or 1490c-d *aduxo/debuxo*. The link is however more tenuous in 246b-c *ducho/aguaducho*, 712b-c *muele/desmuele*, 517b-c *manca/palanca* (perhaps redeemed poetically at least by the alliterative *peña... pesada... palanca* of the line), 384c-d *arremanga/remanga*,

1544*c-d escuerço* (ms. G)/*mestuerço,* 1007*a-c corre/torre/alhorre,* etc.

There is, then, an abundance of such lines in the *Libro de buen amor,* some splendid, some mediocre, some totally inadequate, which give the work an uneven quality. It is quite possible that further investigation into the methods and difficulties of composition could lead to the elucidation of difficult passages. Certainly several of the lines discussed by Morreale (see the entry under the relevant stanza number in her article referred to in note 4) concern the rhyme word, though this is hardly mentioned, e. g. 616*a achaca,* 857*c derrama,* 712*c desmuele,* 733*c despecho,* 752*d pelaça,* 653*a plaça,* 504*c rraças,* 735*d talento,* 550*d traspaso,* 302*d yvas* and even 1660*d tos.*

I will discuss next the extent to which Juan Ruiz has recourse to the trite phrase or stop-gap expression to complete his line. In the context of the purest poetry, the device is inexcusable, but of course Juan Ruiz is by no means alone in this. The point of departure is again the rhyme word or the terminant required. The first series of examples I wish to discuss is the expression of lack of worth of the type *non val un figo* (e. g. 359*c*). Such expressions are clearly fill-ins at all times, but can vary in cleverness of contrivance. Juan Ruiz does not limit their use drastically, as we might have expected from other developments noted so far. However, he uses them in an apparently much more vivid fashion, adapting some of those used previously by other poets. It would be attractive to attribute this to a positive desire on Juan Ruiz's part for graphic, lively expression; it would also be nice to suggest that he was poking fun at some of his predecessors by such alterations. It is nevertheless a fact, however sad, that the variety is a direct consequence of the abundance of rhyme endings in the *Libro de buen amor.* Hence even if Juan Ruiz's original motive in employing so many terminants was the revivification of a hackneyed form, the widening of the range of such expressions is an automatic outcome of that choice. Thus, of some sixty examples in the *Libro de buen amor,* more than forty appear in line *d,* only two in line *a.* Further, the number of items for comparison in such phrases is only marginally higher this time than in the *Alexandre,* though rather more extensive than in the works of Berceo. While it seems certain that the motivation is a technical one, some of Juan Ruiz's examples are quite original, e. g. 241*a non valya una çermeña,* 270*d preçiávala más que saya* (I include this example here because of the use of *saya* in the rhyme position, while realising fully that its meaning is the very opposite of «lack of worth»; however, the point made is still valid); 390*d,* *non me val tu vanagloria un vil grano de mijo* (notice the fine alliteration here and compare *Alexandre 656d quanto valié un grano,* or *Santo Domingo 478d non pareçió... un grano); 392d pyñones en pyñas; 599b dos viles sarmientos; 820d la seca sardina; 1230d non vale un prisco; 1443d es podrida toronja* (ms. *G*).

Another element of Juan Ruiz's composition which is largely attributable to rhyme is the linking of the rhyme word to the preceding word or phrase by *e* or *nin*. By so doing, he not only achieves several «adecuaciones» and «repeticiones sinonímicas» (see Morreale, «Apuntes...», p. 268 and p. 303), but allows himself a less restricted development for the remainder of the line, i. e. the part which precedes the rhyme, since it is no longer entirely dependent on the rhyme for its composition. Obviously, the rhyme cannot be entirely isolated and will usually prompt the synonym, but the scope for the composition of a more normal line is widened. The device can be described rhetorically as *interpretatio* (see Faral, *Les Arts Poétiques...,* pp. 63, 277, 355), but Juan Ruiz's motivation again seems to be principally technical. He is not so much vaunting his knowledge of rhetorical devices as employing them, knowingly or not, to extricate himself from difficult situations once more provoked by the choice of rhyme. Though there are some four hundred lines affected in this way, I will give here a mere handful of examples: *14d se usa e se faz; 58c con paz e con sosiego; 61d con saña, con ira e con cordojo; 85b buena e sana* (or according to Corominas *más ligera e más sana); 124d su fado e su don; 171b non paños e non cintas; 191c con una e con más non; 231c mugeres cassadas e esposas; 255d rroçio e feno; 294a gula e tragonía* (presumably *gula* would prove impossible as a rhyme); *391a de rey nin de reyna; 452b nunca muere nin pereçe; 504d tordos nin picaças.* In nearly every case the rhyme word is the less current and more specialised of the pair; very often the rhyme word does not naturally form a happy connection with the main verb or is less idiomatic than its preceding synonym.

The next point I wish to raise is that of the excessive use of the same common word in a particular rhyme ending. Such words are often attached to semi-formulaic phrases and are again only filling the line. My investigation of a select list of these words shows that, numerically at least, if not always proportionately, there are some differences between Juan Ruiz and other *cuaderna vía* poets. For instance, Juan Ruiz has less recourse than either the *Alexandre* or Berceo to lines and phrases ending in *de grado, nada, vegada, mal, lugar, manera, dezir, sazón,* etc. There are, further, scarcely any such words which Juan Ruiz uses to a greater extent than the other poets; this would seem to favour the notion that he was making an effort. if not always successfully, to break away from previous tradition.

I should like at this stage to mention the effect of rhyme on Juan Ruiz's syntax as this has a definite bearing on his composition. To begin with, we can only accept Aguado's findings with the strongest reservations, since, however correct they may be in syntactical defini- tion, they tend to treat each instance as of linguistic rather than styl- istic significance. Such infringements and oddities, many of which appear exclusively in rhyme, must come into the category of 'ballad syn- tax' and its cognates.

Hence, several of the periphrastic expressions (Aguado, p. 71), and other paraphrases are once more in rhyme. In rhyme also are virtually all the examples of syllepsis (Aguado, p. 80) and «intercalación de pa- labras o frases» (Aguado, p. 85). Likewise the «infinitivo oracional» (Aguado, p. 88). We should consider, too, the effect such instances have on the rest of the work, for once the particular poet or poets in general resort to 'ballad syntax', it seems likely that this could influence composition in general and exceed the original motivation which the rhyme set off.

A further point of interest is the extensive use of the present sub- junctive in rhyme in the *Libro de buen amor.* Aguado (p. 68), dealing with some odd substitutions of subjunctive for indicative and vice- versa, gives several examples nearly all of which are in fact demanded by the rhyme. I would add to this several instances where Juan Ruiz's choice of rhyme means that there are scarcely any words left in the language, other than present subjunctive forms, which will fit. Exam- ples where Juan Ruiz uses this solution are: 940 *—ardan (padan/gra- dan);* 467 *— aga (faga/yaga);* 1239 *— amen (desamen/llamen);* 904 *— ançe (alcançe/lançe/trançe);* 444 *—andes (demandes/andes);* 1195 *—arta (par- ta);* 1457 *(parta);* 1529 *(parta);* 293 *—ema (tema);* 939 *—enga (manten- ga/venga/tenga);* 976 *—idas (comidas,* because of the elaborate rhyme); 755 *—ienda (defienda);* 864 *(entienda);* 155 *—ive (abive/esquive);* 956 *—oge (enoje/moje/despoje);* 619 *—ondas (rrespondas);* 926 *—orra (corra/acorra);* 73 *—ueva (mueva);* 114 *—urra (aburra).*

The use of such forms in rhyme gives rise to the syntactical problem of fitting in a suboıdinate clause or exhortative or shade of doubt or futurity which the sense may not necessarily require. In this way a further body of clumsy lines is created, although some of the exhorta-

tions may add incidental vigour to a particular passage. It is nevertheless unfortunate that many of the rhymes concerned are precisely
those which are not much adopted by other poets, and of which Juan
Ruiz is so proud. While Juan Ruiz was clearly being clever, we have
seen that he often runs into trouble. It is also conceivable that some
of the *cuaderna vía* poets, particularly Berceo, saw the dangers and
preferred simplicity or even monotony to doggerel.

The last item I wish to deal with in this section is Juan Ruiz's use
of names. The appearance of a host of specific and apparently humorous place and personal names in the *Libro de buen amor* does much
to liven up the work as a whole. While I could not contend that the
reason for their appearance is in every case merely technical, it is
surprising how many of them are found exclusively in rhyme. This
could support the point I raised earlier, namely that the rhyme word
might occupy a position of special emphasis. However, several names
in the *Libro de buen amor* not only have endings for which there are
not too many words available, but further, are not called upon until
lines *c* or *d*. Thus, although the result may be humorous or graphic
or picturesque, the initial motive may well be technical. We can compare here some of Juan Ruiz's examples of word play, though clearly
not all, which may also originate for reasons of rhyme, e. g. *mal va/mal-
va*, 104, or *aburra/burra/burla*, 114. Examples of names used in this
way, where the rhyme is very difficult to fill, are: *Visagra*, 1306*d*, *Rron-
çesvalles*, 1209*c*, *Alarcos*, 1110*d* (ms. *G*)., *don Aly*, 1088*c*, *Ortiz*, 881*d*,
Boloña, 1517*b*, *Moya*, 972*d*, *Calataut*, 582*c*. Thus, however well contrived some of these may be, e. g. *don Aly* and *Ortiz* above, Juan Ruiz is
often primarily concerned with getting out of difficulty and draws on
names as a stock of additional items when words fail him. Surprisingly
enough, several other significant names appear first in rhyme, though
not exclusively so later, e. g. *Rrama* 812*c* (though Corominas regards
this as a noun), *Urraca* 919*c* and even *Ruiz* 19*b*. Yet it would clearly
be extravagant to take this theory too far. It could, for example, easily
be argued that, even if *Ruiz* is a fictitious name, the line in question
was composed together with line *a* of the strophe. This line ends in
raíz and is an example of the type of *interpretatio* mentioned on p. 24.
The similarity between *Ruiz* and *raíz* is obvious and Juan Ruiz clearly
associates the two deliberately, but it would seem quite likely in this
instance that line *a* was composed with line *b (Ruiz)* in mind and not
vice-versa. [22]

[22] A comparison can be made here with certain humorous verse forms in

Conclusions

Not only is the variety of rhyme terminants in the *Libro de buen amor* extensive, but also the work is enhanced by the frequent use of elaborate rhyme beyond the basic requirements. Thus, we have seen that a very considerable portion of the *Libro de buen amor* is affected by one or other of these features. The figures for other *cuaderna vía* writers are nothing like as significant, especially when mere coincidence is allowed for.

Yet, despite Juan Ruiz's conscious departures from previous practice, he defeats his own purpose to a degree in that he imposes new restrictions upon himself by the often limited range of vocabulary available for a particular rhyme. We could also add that the choice of the *cuaderna vía* stanza was contributory to this problem, since the poet is obliged to find no less than four words in the same terminant on each occasion. Thus, over the whole work, the vocabulary proliferates, but within a given stanza, the choice is somewhat restricted. In the lyric poems of the *Libro de buen amor,* however, the problem is not so acute, since the exigencies of rhyme are not usually as great. I have, then, based my main arguments on the parts of the *Libro de buen amor* written in *cuaderna vía.* It would nevertheless be totally erroneous to take the theory so far as to pretend that Juan Ruiz's work was nothing more than the product of a medieval computer. The ingenuity of the poet, however stretched at times, is often highly original and successful.

I have not been able to show any considerable relationship between rhyme and the structure of the *Libro de buen amor,* with one or two exceptions. It is clear at the same time, from a study of the rhyming devices, that Juan Ruiz wrote both the *cuaderna vía* portion and the remainder of the work. As for the link between rhyme and humour, it is possible to suggest that the effect is in part accidental, several of the associations being inevitable for a poet who is determined to be «uno de trobadores mill» (65*d*).

Finally, it has been my purpose in this article not to denigrate Juan Ruiz, but rather to place his work in a realistic context. I have

which the initial choice of rhyme is deliberately directed towards hilarity; a case in point is the limerick, which usually begins with a difficult place-name. For instance, I have it on good authority that a Cambridge fellowship awaits the poet who can complete the poem «There was a young fellah from Samothrace, who put all he had on a mammoth-race...»

tried to come to grips with the practical problems of composition which all poets have to resolve, whatever their quality. I have been concerned too with the reservations which must be made before the *Libro de buen amor* can be considered as a linguistic document. The whole of my argument has been based on one consideration, that of rhyme, which I consider of the utmost importance. There are obviously kindred topics, such as rhythm, stress and caesura which are not restricted to rhyme. These too clearly play their part, but I suspect that similar conclusions would emerge.

Addendum

My attention has only recently been drawn to a new contribution to *Libro de buen amor* studies which is relevant in part to some of the points I have made above. This is Margherita Morreale's «Glosario parcial del *Libro de buen amor:* palabras relacionadas por su posición en el verso», published in *Homenaje, Estudios de Filología e Historia Literaria Lusohispanas e Iberoamericanas, publicados para celebrar el tercer lustro del Instituto de Estudios Hispánicos, Portugueses e Iberoamericanos de la Universidad Estatal de Utrecht* (La Haya, 1966).

Morreale is aware of rhyme as a factor in the choice of vocabulary employed by Juan Ruiz (see p. 391 'el metro, el ritmo y la rima...' or p. 392, note 1, '...rima, con las trabas que esto supone, en un metro como el de la cuaderna vía.') However, no special treatment is given to rhyme and its influence on composition. Certain pertinent points in this new study should be mentioned in connection with some of my own findings. For example, the reference to glosses, 'generalmente enfáticas o ripiosas' (p. 391) or the mention of *variatio* and *amplificatio* (p. 397). Further, in a number of the examples quoted by Morreale, rhyme is not given the necessary emphasis; this applies, for example, to gula/tragonía (p. 397), *derramar* (p. 401) and to some of the pairs of synonyms on pp. 398-399.

Trinity College,
Dublin

JANET A. CHAPMAN

Juan Ruiz's «Learned Sermon»

Since both the identity and occupation of Juan Ruiz have been called
into doubt by Criado de Val and L. G. Moffatt, [1] it cannot be stated
with any certainty that the author of the *Libro de buen amor* received
the education of a priest in the cathedral school of Toledo, as Lecoy
has suggested. [2] Nevertheless, it may be assumed that he had at least
studied the *trivium* —grammar, rhetoric and logic— in common with
all who had received an elementary education in the Middle Ages, [3] and
that he was acquainted with the theories of pulpit oratory. Although
the art of preaching did not form part of the medieval school curricu-
lum, treatises on the subject were available to both priesthood and educated laity: in England Chaucer adhered rigidly to their precepts in
the Parson's Tale, and it has recently been suggested that an appreciat-
ion of sermon structure might help the scholar better to understand
Piers Plowman. [4] While no Spanish sermon collections comparable to

---

[1] M. Criado de Val, *Teoría de Castilla la Nueva* (Madrid, 1960), pp. 158-159.
   L. G. Moffatt, «The Evidence of early Mentions of the Archpriest of Hita or
of his Work», *MLN*, LXXV (1960), 33-43.
[2] F. Lecoy, *Recherches sur le Libro de buen amor de Juan Ruiz, Archiprêtre
de Hita* (Paris, 1938), pp. 337-340.
[3] The most useful general studies on medieval education for a background
to this essay are:
   L. J. Paetow, *The Arts Courses at Medieval Universities with Special Reference to Grammar and Rhetoric*, University of Illinois Studies III, no. 7 (Ur-
bana-Champaign, 1910);
   F. M. Powicke, *The Christian Life in the Middle Ages and other Essays* (Oxford, 1935);
   M. A. Galino, *Historia de la educación. Edades antigua y media* (Madrid,
1960).
   Two studies of use for a knowledge of clerical education in medieval Spain
are:
   V. Beltrán de Heredia, «La formación intelectual del clero según nuestra
antigua legislación canónica (siglos XI-XV)», *Escorial*, VII (1941), 289-298;
   — «La formación intelectual del clero en España durante los siglos XII, XIII
y XIV», *Revista española de teología*, VI (1946), 313-357.
[4] A.C. Spearing, *Criticism and medieval Poetry* (London, 1964), pp. 68-95.

those of Middle English exist or have been published, [5] arts of preaching and other aids to the composition of sermons are still extant or existed in medieval Spanish libraries, [6] and Juan Ruiz could have been as well acquainted with any of them as his English contemporaries, without necessarily being in holy orders. His prose prologue to the second, expanded, version of 1343 of the *Libro,* represented by ms. *S,* while neither such a perfect nor such a tedious example of the application of the theories of learned pulpit oratory as the Parson's Tale, is still the outstanding proof to date that these theories were applied to sermons in the vernacular language in Castile.

The sermon was not a uniform creation throughout the Middle Ages: [7] different kinds of sermon were preached to differing congregations, but a rough division into popular and learned may be made. The popular sermon, lively and direct, and appealing more to the emotions than to the reason, was delivered to lay congregations in the vernacular language. The preacher could speak either on a text, or on the festival of the day, drawing on *exempla* —moral tales— and *sententiae* or *auctoritates* —apothegms either of a proverbial nature or attributed to some source of wisdom — to illustrate his teaching; sometimes he might refer to his own experiences or at least claim direct acquaintance with the stories or events chosen. He made personal appeals to repentance to his flock, and often drew on material concerned with their daily lives. His style was often at its best in descriptions of sins and of the torments of hell; he clearly hoped to frighten his congregation into virtue and heaven if he might not persuade them thither. In many ways his sermons resembled those of the more

[5] W. O. Ross, *Middle English Sermons* (Oxford, Early English Text Society, 1940).

[6] Arts of preaching and other aids to sermonising still in Spanish libraries have been catalogued by:

Th-M. Charland, *Artes Praedicandi: Contribution à l'histoire de la rhétorique au moyen âge* (Paris and Ottawa, 1936);

H. Caplan, *Medieval Artes Praedicandi: a Hand-list* and *Medieval Artes Praedicandi: a supplementary Hand-list,* Cornell Studies in Classical Philology, XXIV (1934) and XXVI (1936).

A. D. Deyermond, in his review of the second edition of Owst's *Literature and Pulpit in Medieval England* in *Estudios Lulianos,* VII (1963), 233-235, notes that the lists given by the above two authors are incomplete and gives other examples of both arts of preaching and of *compendia* for the use of preachers.

[7] For accounts of pulpit oratory in the Middle Ages see:

Charland, *Artes Praedicandi;* Ross, *Middle English Sermons;* Spearing, *Criticism and medieval Poetry;* and

E. Gilson, «Michel Menot et la technique du sermon médiéval», *Les idées et les lettres* (Paris, 1932), pp. 93-154;

G. R. Owst, *Preaching in medieval England* (Cambridge, 1926);

— *Literature and Pulpit in medieval England* (Cambridge, 1933).

exuberant modern evangelists albeit his command of language was considerably more forceful and picturesque. Although it is possible that the popular sermon influenced both the style and content of the *Libro de buen amor* as a whole as much as it did the Pardoner's Tale, nevertheless in a study of the prose prologue to the *Libro* it is the learned sermon which is of concern.

The learned or «university» sermon was a more formal and impersonal creation than the popular sermon. It followed certain rules concerning structure and content as laid down in innumerable arts of preaching which were accessible throughout western Europe. On the whole it appealed more to the mind than to the emotions, although in sermons with an admixture of popular material emotional appeals were not wanting. The arts of preaching were composed in Latin, but the learned sermon could be delivered either in Latin or in the vernacular language, in spite of the fact that the possibilities of stylistic ornamentation were more limited in the latter. A learned sermon could be preached to an assembly of priests or other religious, or to an educated lay congregation who might appreciate some aspects of the formal development while not being aware of all the structural intricacies. Not all preachers observed the rules to the letter, especially when preaching in the vernacular language, but the arts of preaching give us an impression of the nature of the ideal sermon, and this must be used as a basis for judging Juan Ruiz's excursion into learned preaching.

The learned sermon could begin with the recitation of a biblical text, called the *thema,* which should be appropriate to the message which the preacher wished to deliver. A further quotation from Scripture, called the *prothema,* could be added. It had to be verbally related to the *thema,* and its principal purpose appears to be that of leading up to an opening prayer. If a *prothema* were included, then the *thema* must be repeated after it, probably for the benefit of latecomers who had not heard it the first time. Then followed the discussion of the *thema,* in which the preacher sought to make the purpose of his sermon clear, and to attract the attention again of his congregation in the event of its already wandering. The *thema* was then divided into its component parts, usually two or three, the latter being preferable since the very use of the threefold division honoured the Trinity. The divisions of the *thema* must be natural ones, and must not modify or corrupt the sense of the text as a whole. In a complex sermon, the main divisions of the *thema* could be further subdivided, but in a simpler form the basic divisions could be discussed in turn without subdivision, and this discussion or analysis of the *thema* constituted the body of the sermon. Each part of the discussion could be amplified and developed by various means, including the use of *auctoritates,* usually from biblical or patristic sources, which should be related by word or sense to the particular division of the *thema;* if the relation was by word only it was known as «verbal concord»; if by sense, as «real concord». The arts of preaching disapproved of purely verbal concord, accepted real concord alone, but approved most highly of a combination of real and verbal concord. The preacher might also draw on *exempla* apposite to his argument. The art of illustrating the divisions of the *thema* by the use of *auctoritates* was known as *divisio intra,* and that of illustrating them with *exempla* was known as *divisio extra.*

The use of rhetorical «colours» or figures of speech was advocated, but not for purely ornamental purposes: they had a suasory function, in that elegances of style might both attract and sway the mind of the listener. The use of «colours» was taught as part of the elementary education of the Middle Ages, and both classical and late Latin and early medieval arts of rhetoric contained lists of these «colours», together with examples of their use. Medieval names and definitions of figures of speech were largely based on the pseudo-Cornifician treatise *Ad Herennium* of the first century B.C., and it is therefore convenient to follow in this article the nomenclature and definitions of this work for the figures used in the prose prologue of the *Libro.* [8]

The schematic representation on p. 51 together with a brief summary of the prologue will show that although Juan Ruiz's argument may not appear to be logical he nevertheless makes an attempt to link by various means one section to another as he progresses from his *thema* to his conclusion.

The *thema* of the sermon is the tenth verse of Psalm 31 : [9] «Intellectum tibi dabo et instruam te in via hac qua gradieris, firmabo super te occulos meos» (3, i). [10] Juan Ruiz states that this verse refers to three qualities of the soul: understanding, will and memory, which bring with them three results: consolation to the soul, prolonged physical

[8] *Ad C. Herennium Libri IV,* with an English translation by H. Caplan (London, Loeb Classical Library, 1954).
[9] In the quotations of biblical *auctoritates,* I have retained Juan Ruiz's orthography in his versions and have given the full reference with corrected orthography from the *Biblia Sacra juxta Vulgatae,* ed. A. C. Fillion (Paris, 1887).
[10] When quoting from the prologue I have used Arabic numerals for Ducamin's page number and Roman numerals for the line number.

life, and a good reputation (3, v-xi). He links the three qualities with a threefold division of the *thema:* «intellectum tibi dabo»; «et instruam te»; and «in via hac qua gradieris, firmabo super te occulos meos». The qualities of the soul are each discussed in turn with quotations, usually from Holy Writ, to support the argument. (Only one *auctoritas* —a quotation from the fourth century *Disticha Catonis*— is not biblical). By understanding, man knows good and evil; man, understanding good, will fear God, this fear being the beginning of wisdom; therefore understanding is in those who fear God. All this is to be understood in the first division of the *thema* (3, xi-xxiv). In the second instance, the instructed soul which is to be saved is led to love and desire *el buen amor de Dios* and to hate the sin of *el loco amor de este mundo.* [11] Thus follows the second division. Thirdly, when the soul, with understanding, will and memory, chooses *el buen amor de Dios,* good works, by which man is saved, will follow. And thus the text concludes (4, xiv-xxi). On the occasions that man sins, the desire to sin comes not from the three qualities of the soul but from certain failings: human weakness, lack of understanding and poor memory, and man's inclination towards evil rather than towards good (4, xxi-5, x). Since the first and last of these failings are virtually the same, the list of human frailties may be placed in opposition to the three qualities of the soul. Therefore books of laws, advice and customs, and pictures and sculpture are made as aids to the memory; for perfect memory is divine, a property more of the immortal soul than of the mortal body (5, v-xxv). And thus the *Libro* has been composed as a reminder of what is good, and in order to expose *el loco amor.* Those of good understanding will choose the good; those of poor understanding will respect their own reputations and will love themselves more than sin, for true charity begins at home. They will reject *el loco amor,* which brings about the condemnation of the soul, shortens life, and brings ill fame and harm to the body (5, xxv-6, xvi). [12] But because it is human to sin, the *Libro* contains some indications of how to do so for those who wish to persist in *el loco amor.* Thus all may benefit from the book, and may well repeat the words of the *thema* (6, xvi-

---

[11] Since any translation of *buen amor* and *loco amor* is bound to be inadequate, owing to the ambiguity of the terms in the *Libro,* I have considered it preferable not to translate them in this discussion of the prologue. See B. Dutton's essay in this volume.

[12] Compare Richard of Thetford's list of the results of lechery: loss of good name, corruption of body and soul (Quoted by Ross, p. li). This combination of results may be a commonplace of medieval preaching.

xxiv). All should bear in mind the three qualities of the soul. Finally, the moral as well as the poetic intentions of the work are emphasised (6, xxiv- 7, xi). The prologue ends with an invocation to the Trinity.

At the beginning of the prologue Juan Ruiz disobeys one of the precepts of the learned sermon, that the preacher should not modify or corrupt the sense of the *thema* by the way in which he divides it, for the first and second parts of his threefold division have the same sense, the second being a rhetorical amplification of the first, while the first part of the third division —«in via hac qua gradieris»— should be associated with the first two phrases. It is possible that Juan Ruiz deliberately contravenes the rules for comic effect, but this would assume a greater erudition in him than would be justifiable to expect. The comic effects of the prologue are obtained by other means. [13]

The argument of the prologue is developed in two main sections, which I have called developments A and B in the schematic representation. The first deals with the good qualities of the soul and the actions which spring from them (3, xi-4, xxi). The second section deals with the sins and their resulting actions which are in contrast with the good qualities and actions of the soul; with God's perfection and the necessity of aids to devotion; and finally with the threefold purpose of the *Libro:* to turn its audience from the sin which it exposes; to demonstrate certain kinds of sin to recidivists; and to exemplify different forms of poetry (4, xxii-7, xi). At this point it is clear that though Juan Ruiz may be using sermon technique he is not composing a serious sermon, since the ending, from «enpero por que es umanal cosa el pecar» (6, xvi), could call into question the seriousness of all that precedes it. The change to the comical is possibly heralded in the earlier part, by the word-play on *acordar-desacuerdo,* and by the preacher's protestations of ignorance (5, xxvi). The various meanings of *desacuerdo* —wrong kind of remembering, forgetfulness, variance— introduce the possibility of ambiguity into the apparently serious remarks on memory, and by extension into the remarks on understanding and will, whilst Juan Ruiz's pleas of ignorance, although a medieval commonplace, may be warning his audience not to accept unreservedly what is to follow.

The schematic representation of the prose prologue indicates that there is some structural symmetry, and throughout the prologue can be

---

[13] See, for example, A. D. Deyermond's essay in this volume.

found balanced concepts and phrases which give it a semblance of logical development and of adhering to the precepts of the learned sermon. The *thema* introduces the sermon according to rule, and is followed by the introductory formula for the division of the *thema*: «en el qual verso entiendo yo tres cosas», which is the equivalent of the Latin «in quibus verbis tria tanguntur», [14] and the Middle English «I vndirstonde in this teme dyvers thinges». [15] This formula is followed by the division of the thema (3, v-xi). Of the two possible methods of division Juan Ruiz has chosen the more learned, *divisio intra,* generally drawing on biblical authorities to support his argument. The headings under which the divisions are to be expounded —understanding, will, memory— are not clearly related to the three parts of the *thema* as the arts of preaching require:

> In any division the preacher merely expresses some legitimate ideas suggested to him by the theme. The ideas are legitimate only when they are based upon a proper comprehension of the passage which he is dividing. [16]

The three qualities of the soul bring three things to man —consolation, longer life and honour (3, ix-xi). In my schematic representation, development A consists of a discussion of each of the division headings in turn, and a connection between them and the corresponding part of the *thema* is established or sought by means of *auctoritates,* one word of which is related to one of the words of the *thema* by real and verbal concord. Four *auctoritates* support the first division, two support each of the remaining two divisions. The quality of understanding is first discussed without reference to the other two qualities (3, xiii-xxiv). At the beginning of the second section there may be a reference to understanding in the adjective *informada* (3, xxv). Both understanding and will are linked with the quality of memory at the beginning of the third section of development A (4, iii).

Development B of the schematic representation, which is linked to the above sections by the reiteration of the topic of understanding, will and memory, is divided into two principal parts. In the first Juan Ruiz contrasts human failings with divine perfection, mainly in terms of poor and perfect memory (4, xxi-xxv). The discussion of human

---

[14] Charland, *Artes Praedicandi,* p. 151.
[15] Ross, *Middle English Sermons,* Sermon 3, p. 13, 1.27.
[16] Ross, *Middle English Sermons,* p. xlvi.

4

failings bridges the first and second sections, for it is argued that since human memory is poor, aids to memory are needed, and thus the *Libro* has been written «in memory of good» (5, xxv-xxxi). The three intentions of the author in composing the work are given (5, xxxii-7, xi). The second and third intentions are stated simply; only the first is subdivided: the effects of the *Libro* will differ for those of right understanding and for the ignorant; the resultant actions of these two sorts of people are described; turning from evil will lead to hatred of sin (6, xxiv). There is a further subdivision dealing with the three results of sin (6, xiv-xvi), which are contrasted with the three gifts brought by memory, understanding and will (3, ix-xi). This contrast, spanning such an extensive passage, is evidence that Juan Ruiz took some care in constructing the prologue, although the second group of results appears in a subdivision of development B, while the first group appears in the main division of the *thema*.

The first and second intentions of the *Libro* are linked retrospectively by a return to the *thema* (6, xxiv), the repetition of which is not required at such a point by preaching precept, and by an exhortation to hold to the three qualities of the soul, which is followed by a commonplace of pure intention (6, xxiv-7, viii), such as is found in 909*b* of the poem. The third intention is briefly stated, and the *clausio* (7, xii) introduces the main body of the *Libro*, since the Latin words which conclude the sermon are repeated in Castilian at the beginning of the prayer for aid (st.11). The poem is not mentioned until the second section of development B (5, xxxi), although the subject of poor memory has earlier introduced the need for books as reminders to holiness. Although the argument is not always clear, Juan Ruiz is attempting to direct the sermon towards the introduction of the subject of the poem and to link the work, through its aims, to the *thema*. The fact that he does not constantly adhere to the rules of learned sermon structure does not argue for a partial ignorance of the rules; many learned sermons in Middle English depart from the rules at times, although their authors were well acquainted with the arts of preaching. [17]

Juan Ruiz usually creates divisions in his arguments by taking a significant word from his *thema* and using it as a basis for a section of the sermon. He obeys the rule of giving chapter and verse for the *thema*, but only book or author references for the texts within the sermon. All *auctoritates* but one are to be found in developments A

---

[17] Ross, *Middle English Sermons*, p. liv.

and B. The three divisions of the thema are each supported by *auctoritates,* the first —«intellectum tibi dabo»— by four:

> Da michi intellectum (Ps. 118, xxiv: Da mihi intellectum, et scrutabor legem tuam, et custodiam illam in toto corde meo.)
>
> yniçium sapiençie timor domini (Ps. 110, x: Initium sapientiae timor Domini.)
>
> Intellectus bonus omnibus façientibus eum (Also Ps. 110, x, which continues: intellectus bonus omnibus facientibus eum; laudatio ejus manet in saeculum saeculi.)
>
> qui timet dominum façiet bona (Eccl. 15, i: Qui timet Dominum, faciet bona, et qui continens est justitiae apprehendit illam.)

The second division —«et instruam te»— is suported by two *auctoritates:*

> E meditabor in mandatis tuis que dilexi (Ps. 118, xlvii: Et meditabor in mandatis tuis quae dilexi.)
>
> qui diligitis dominum, odite malum (Ps. 96, x: Qui diligitis Dominum, odite malum; custodit Dominus animas sanctorum suorum, de manu peccatoris liberabit eos.)

The third division —«in via hac qua gradieris...»— also has two supporting *auctoritates:*

> Beati mortui qui in domino moriuntur, opera enim illorum secuntur illos (Apoc. 14, xiii: Beati mortui qui in Domino moriuntur. Amodo jam dicit Spiritus ut requiescant a laboribus suis; opera enim illorum sequuntur illos.)
>
> tu redis *(sic)* unicuique justa opera sua (Ps. 61, xii: Semel locutus est Deus; duo haec audivi: Quia potestas Dei est, et tibi, Domine, misericordia: quia tu reddes unicuique juxta opera sua.)

The first section of development B falls into three subsections, each of which has its supporting *auctoritates,* the first and second having two each:

> Nemo sine crimine vivit (*Disticha Catonis,* Book I, Distich 5: Si uitam inspicias hominum, si denique mores,
> Cum culpas alios: nemo sine crimine uiuit.) [18]

---

[18] Cato (Pseudo-), *Disticha Catonis. The Distichs of Cato. A Famous Medieval Textbook,* translated from the Latin with an introductory Sketch by Wayland Johnson Chase. *University of Wisconsin Studies in the Social Sciences and History,* VII (1922).

> quis potest fazere mundum de imudo (*sic*) conçeptum se-
> mine (Job 14, iv: Quis potest facere mundum de inmundo con-
> ceptum semine?)

and

> cogitaciones hominum vane sunt (Ps. 93, xi: Dominus scit
> cogitationes hominum, quoniam vanae sunt.)
> Nolite fieri sicut equs e mulus in quibus non est intellectus
> (Ps. 31, ix: Nolite fieri sicut equus et mulus, quibus non est
> intellectus.)

The third subsection, like the first section of development A, has four
auctoritates:

> Anima mea illius vivet, querite dominum e vivet anima ves-
> tra (This is a combination of two verses. Ps. 21, xxxi: Et
> anima mea illi vivet; et semen meum serviet ipsi; and Ps. 68,
> xxxiii: Videant pauperes et laetentur; quaerite Deum et vivet
> anima vestra.)
> breves dies hominis sunt (Job 14, v: Breves dies hominis
> sunt; numerus mensium ejus apud te est; constituisti terminos
> ejus, qui praeteriri non poterunt.)
> homo natus de muliere, breves dies hominis sunt (Here
> there is a confusion between Job 14, v and Job 14, i; Homo
> natus de muliere, brevi vivens tempore, repletus multis miseriis.)
> Anni nostri sicut aranea meditabuntur (Ps. 89, x: Anni
> nostri sicut aranea meditabuntur; dies annorum nostrorum in
> ipsis, septuaginta anni.)

The second section of development B contains only one reference
to a biblical *auctoritas* —«veni veritatis». The correct quotation would
lead naturally back to the *thema.* [19] (Ps. 118, xxx: Viam veritatis elegi;
judicia tua non sum oblitus.)

Juan Ruiz employs different means of relating the *auctoritates*
to each other, and to the division of the *thema* and quality of the soul
which they purport to illustrate. Only in the first section of development A are the *auctoritates* and the *thema* in real and verbal concord, and only here do they approach being a proof of the argument
by which the preacher seeks to clarify the meaning of the division
in question. The word *intellectus* appears in the first and the third
auctoritates, and also in the division of the *thema.* The second and

[19] G. Chiarini, *Libro de buen amor* (Milan-Naples, 1964), p. 7, also notes
this error.

fourth, which expand the first and third, contain the corresponding phrases *timor domini-timet dominum;* the first and second are
linked by synonym, or real concord —*intellectus-sapientiae;* the third
and fourth by the verbal and real concords *bonus-bona* and *faciet-
facientibus.* The argument of this first section has an order lacking
in the other two sections: understanding leads to knowledge, knowledge leads to fear of God, therefore understanding is in those who fear
God. All *auctoritates* are apposite, although the fourth is not used
in the argument but to support the other three.

In the second section Juan Ruiz tries by other means to connect
the division of the *thema* with those *auctoritates* which should demonstrate the results of divine instruction: it is only after the soul is made
to understand and is instructed that it desires *el buen amor de Dios.*
Juan Ruiz attempts to establish a real concord between the division
of the *thema,* the quality of the soul it supposedly illustrates, and the
auctoritates, with the word *diligere* by which the *auctoritates* are in
verbal concord with each other. But the relationship of the concept
of will with the division of the *thema* and with the *auctoritates* is not
made clear. The concept of instruction is both a starting point for
this section and a conclusion, but there is no obvious reason for introducing it at all.

The argument of the third section of the first part has even less
order, and the connection between division, quality of soul and *auctoritates* is still less clear than in the second section: good memory,
with the other two qualities, helps the soul to remember *el buen amor
de Dios* and inspires the body to good works; and from this final
result hang the *auctoritates,* related to the argument and to one another
by the word *opera.* «Obras sienpre están en la buena memoria»
(4, xv) is the phrase intended to establish the relationship, and upon
this phrase depends the relevance of the *auctoritates.* In this section, Juan Ruiz builds the supposed link between division and *auctoritas* in the vernacular: «buenas obras» translates the concording
word; «la carrera de la salvaçión» is implicit in the phrase «in via
hac qua gradieris»; and «firma sus ojos sobre él» renders in the third
person the second half of the third division of the *thema.* The *auctoritates* of the divisions of the *thema,* with the exception of those
in the first division, do nothing to clarify the *thema* nor to advance
the preacher's argument.

The remaining Latin *auctoritates,* with the exception of «viam veritatis...», are to be found in the first section of development B. Their

distribution is uneven, though they are found in groups of two, two and four, so that their grouping corresponds inversely with that of the *auctoritates* of development A.   This section deals with the origins of human sin: human weakness and sinful nature, lack of understanding and poor memory.   The statements on weakness and lack of understanding are supported by two *auctoritates* each; the statement on poor memory has no *auctoritas*.   The concluding remarks on perfect memory, the immortal soul, imperfect memory and the mortal soul have four *auctoritates*, the first of which alone refers to immortality, while the other three refer to the brevity of life.

The first group of two *auctoritates* —«nemo sine crimine vivit» and «quis potest facere mundum...»— are related to the theme of human weakness which leads to sin; the relationship between statement and *auctoritas* is created by the words *crimen-inmundus*.   In both this and the second group of two *auctoritates*, the concord is real but not verbal.   The second group of two, supporting Juan Ruiz's statement that «omne piensa vanidades de pecado» (4, xxxi) —«cogitationes hominum...» and «nolite fieri sicut equus...»— are, respectively, an affirmative statement, in real and verbal concord with the Castilian —*vanidades-vanae*— and a negative command with real and verbal concord, by the word *intellectus*, to the first division of the *thema*. The third group consisting of four *auctoritates* —«anima mea...», «breves dies...», «homo natus...» and «anni nostri...»— have a very slender relation with the subject they should illustrate.   Having said that perfect memory is a property of divinity, Juan Ruiz then links the statement to the term «the memory of the soul»; the first *auctoritas* illustrates the immortality of the soul, with the real and verbal concord of *alma-anima*.   Much the same method is used to introduce the second, third and fourth *auctoritates*, which correspond with each other, the second and third by real and verbal concord, and the third and fourth by real concord: after the statement that perfect memory does not belong to the body, which is mortal, follow the three *auctoritates* on the subject of mortality.   The author's inability to sustain even the appearance of a carefully developed argument is more obvious in this section than in any other, both in the weakness of the link between argument and *auctoritas* and in the inaccuracy of two of the four quotations. [20]

The final Latin *auctoritas* —«viam veritatis...»— is concerned with

[20]   It is possible that the inaccuracy is due to scribal error, as in the case of the misquoting of Ps. 118, xxx.

the choice of the wise who have elected good works; it is in verbal concord with the *thema* by the words *via-viam*. It does not concord with any other *auctoritas*.

The prologue contains vernacular references to other authorities, all but the last two of which appear in development B, and which with one exception are non-biblical. Most of these vernacular authorities can be taken as loose translations from the Latin, and cannot be considered as important as the Latin *auctoritates* for the advancement of the argument. It is even possible that Juan Ruiz, in order to give weight to his own words at certain points (some of these *auctoritates* have a proverbial character) has attributed them to a known authority such as Gregory IX or Gratian, just as in the versified part of the *Libro* he attributes various *sententiae* to an unidentified *sabio*.

The first three vernacular *auctoritates* are attributed to Gratian's *Decretum*. This was the first systematic compilation of the papal Decretals —letters resolving points of canon law— and was composed by Gratian in the twelfth century. (Otis Green, however, has come to the conclusion that these quotations cannot be traced in the *Decretum*.)[21]

> la natura umana que más aparejada e inclinada es al mal que al bien, e a pecado que a bien (5, viii-ix).
> la memoria del omne deslezandera es (5, xiv-xv).
> tener todas las cosas en la memoria e non olvidar algo, más es de la divinidat que de la umanidad (5, xv-xvii).

All of these *auctoritates* are followed by the phrase «eso dize el decreto» (5, x, xv, xvii). The first two are repetitions of previous statements made by Juan Ruiz (4, xxv-xxvi and 5, iv-vii), and the third amplifies the second.

The first and third *auctoritates* of the next group are attributed to common law, the second to the *Decretum*, and the fourth to Saint Gregory.[22]

> ca mucho es cruel quien su fama menospreçia, el derecho lo dize (6, ix-xi).
> la ordenada caridad de si mesmo comiença, el decreto lo dize (6, xii-xiii).

---

[21] Otis H. Green, *Spain and the Western Tradition. The Castilian Mind in Literature from El Cid to Calderón*, Vol. I (Madison, 1963), p. 51.

[22] Chiarini, *Libro de buen amor*, p. 8, identifies this *auctoritas* as coming from Gregory the Great —«Minus enim iacula feriunt, quae praevidentur».

> segund derecho las palabras sirven a la intençión e non la intençión a las palabras (6, xxix-xxx).
>
> dize sant Gregorio que menos firién al onbre los dardos que ante son vistos, e mejor nos podemos guardar de lo que ante hemos visto (7, vi-viii).

The first *auctoritas* corresponds by the word *fama* with the preceding statement (6, iv-ix) and constitutes a comment on those of poor understanding who should learn from the exposure of their conduct not to despise their honour. The third also corresponds verbally, by the word *palabras,* with the preceding statement (6, xxvi-xxviii) which it amplifies. The second is linked to the previous statement by real concord of the words *amar-caridad* (6, xi) and expands it. The fourth supports a preceding statement of Juan Ruiz's (7, iii-v).

The last two vernacular *auctoritates* appear in the *clausio* (7, xii-xvii) and are in fact two in appearance only. They have both been taken from the first sentence of the first Decretal of Pope Clement V. Clement's Decretals, called the *Clementinae,* were promulgated in 1317, after his death. Clement's opening words are: «Fidei catholice fundamento propter quod teste apostolo nemo potest aliud ponere firmiter inherentes aperte cum sancta matre ecclesia confitemur unigenitum dei fili uni in hiis omnibus in quibus deus pater existit unacum patre eternaliter subsistente et partes nostre nature simul unitas.»

Juan Ruiz has perhaps wished to give an added air of erudition to his final remarks by attributing only the first *auctoritas* to Clement V: «toda buena obra es comienço e fundamento Dios e la fe cathólica, e dize lo la primera decretal delas crementinas» (7, xii-xiv); and the second to «el apóstol»: «do este non es çimiento non se puede fazer obra firme nin firme hedifiçio, segund dize el apóstol». This second *auctoritas* is simply a gloss of the allusion in the first Decretal to 1 Cor. 3, xi:

> Fundamentum aliud nemo potest ponere, praeter id quod positum est... Christus Jesus.

These two *auctoritates* show that when quoting in the vernacular, Juan Ruiz is not concerned with the same verbal accuracy or numerical balance as he is with the Latin *auctoritates.*

Juan Ruiz's prologue contains several examples of the more elementary rhetorical devices allowed for the ornamentation of the medieval sermon. Apart from *auctoritas* or *sententia* —«oratio sumpta de vita quae aut quid sit aut quid esse oporteat in vita breviter ostendit» (*Ad Herennium,* IV, xvii)— the following figures appear most frequently in the sermon:

> *Expolitio* —«est cum in eodem loco manemus et aliud at-que aliud dicere videmur. Ea dupliciter fit: si aut eanden plane dicemus rem, aut de eadem re» (*Ad Herennium* IV, xlii).

An almost identical figure is *interpretatio:*

> «est quae non iterans idem redintegrat verbum, sed id commu-tat quod positum est alio verbo quod idem valeat» (*Ad Herennium* IV, xxviii).

Both *expolitio* and *interpretatio* consist of saying the same thing in two or more different ways, and the examples given in the *Ad Herennium* of these figures are very similar, and it will be convenient to group all examples of this kind of repetition under the same heading of *expolitio.*

> *Annominatio* —«est cum ad idem verbum et nomen acce-ditur commutatione vocum aut litterarum, ut ad res dissimi-les similia verba adcommodentur.» (*Ad Herennium* IV, xxi).

This figure is easier to use with elegance in Latin, involving as it does the introduction of different cases of the same word or repetitions of a word-root, but nevertheless it is used with frequency in vernacular languages.

> *Contentio* —«est cum ex contrariis rebus oratio confici-tur» (*Ad Herennium* IV, xv); «est per quam contraria referen-tur» (*Ad Herennium* IV, xlv).

The pseudo-Cornificius gives two kinds of this antithesis: the first definition refers to the simple contrasting of words, the second to an opposition of actions or concepts.

Juan Ruiz uses different kinds of repetitions, but the most frequent kind to be found in the prologue is *conduplicatio* —«est cum ratione amplificationis aut commiserationis eiusdem unius aut plurium verbo-rum iteratio». This figure does not demand the repetition of a word at a particular point in each succeeding phrase, as do other sorts of figures of repetition. A well-known example of this figure in English is the lament of Lady Capulet and the Nurse over the supposed corpse of Juliet (*Romeo and Juliet,* Act IV, Scene v) in which the word «day» is repeated again and again with a variety of epithets.

A figure which is strangely not listed by the pseudo-Cornificius, although its opposite is, and although it is a common feature of medieval poetry and prose, is polysyndeton. In this figure conjunctions are repeated between every phrase of a sentence, often together with a repetition of prepositions.

In the prose prologue the examples of *expolitio* are of the simplest kind, in which a statement is repeated in other terms only once:

> dan le onrra con pro e buena fama (3, x-xi)
> pónelo en la çela de la memoria por que se acuerde dello (4, v-vi)
> tener todas las cosas en la memoria e non olvidar algo (5, xv-xvi)
> mi poquilla çiençia e ... mucha e grand rrudeza» (5, xxvi)
> fiz esta chica escriptura ... E compuse este nuevo libro (5, xxxi-xxxii)
> la mi entençión por que lo fiz (6, xxvii).

These examples of *expolitio* have slight differences, for while the first, second and last are simple repetitions of the same idea, the third reiterates a positive concept in negative terms, and the fourth example is related to this affirmative-negative form of the figure. Ross's collection of Middle English sermons shows a similar liking for *expolitio,* with a preference for the simple repetition of one concept, as in the prologue to the *Libro de buen amor:*

> hiȝ myȝthe and infinite powere (Sermon 39, p. 225, 1.33).
> Lat vs all, than, hate synne and vnclene lyvynge (Sermon 43, p. 284, 1.33).

Sometimes the affirmative-negative *expolitio* appears in more style-conscious preachers:

> chese vertew, and leue synne and wrechednesse (Sermon 6, p. 26, 11.20-1)
> euerlastynge peyne withowte anny reste other ese (Sermon 6, p. 29, 11.23-4)
> let vs somwhat of kyndenes qwyte hym aȝeyn, leste that we be fonde vnkynde to-hymward (Sermon 7, p. 31, 11,12-13).

Annominatio usually appears in the *auctoritates* introduced by Juan Ruiz into his prologue, but there are a few examples of his own of the kind «por el buen entendimiento, entiende onbre el bien» (3, xi-xii), and there are similar elementary examples in the Middle English sermons :

> For oure Lorde is ryghtwysnes, and ryght-wysily shall deme
> (Sermon 46, p. 302, 11.11-12).

Contentio is an almost automatic choice of figure when a preacher is contrasting sinner with virtuous man, and a series of *contentiones* describes the different kinds of people who may benefit from a reading of the *Libro:*

> a todo omne o muger, al cuerdo e al non cuerdo, al que entendiere bien e escogiere salvaçión e obrare bien amando a Dios, otrosí al que quisiere el amor loco, en la carrera que andudiere (6, xx-xxiii).

The Middle English preachers found a similar need to write of good and evil using *contentio:*

> Ther on the othur side ther loue and charite was wonte to be amonge hem and euery man to stond and maynten othur, now is envi and wrouthe reynyng, euery man to accuse othur of treson and falsenes (Sermon 47, p. 313, 11.2-5).

Repetitions are a constant feature of Juan Ruiz's sermon : *entendimiento, voluntad, memoria* appear many times; *buen amor* and *loco amor* are referred to throughout the sermon. In these cases the *conduplicatio* is combined with *contentio,* since *buen amor* and *loco amor* are always contrasted. Other combinations of rhetorical figures can be found in the prologue. Polysyndeton appears most frequently in lists which exemplify *expolitio:*

> los libros de la ley e del derecho e de castigos e constumbres e de otras çiençias (5, xi-xii)
> maneras e maestrías e sotilezas
> trobas e notas e rrimas e ditados e versos (7, x).

In the following example polysyndeton is combined with *contentio:*

> pienssa e ama e desea omne el buen amor de Dios e sus mandamientos. ... E otrosí desecha e aborresçe el alma el pecado del amor loco deste mundo (3, xxvi-xxx).

These phrases could also be considered as an example of affirmative-negative *expolitio*.

The presence of these figures in Juan Ruiz's prologue does not necessarily prove that he has deliberately set out to adorn his style with rhetorical «colours». He may be imitating other preachers or simply be composing under the influence of biblical style, itself full of rhetorical devices. It is not the place here to argue for Juan Ruiz's ignorance or first-hand knowledge of rhetorical theory, but merely to point out how like his sermonising style is to that of other medieval preachers in this and other respects.

Juan Ruiz, like an English contemporary, feels it necessary to put himself in good standing with his audience or congregation by a display of humility; unwilling to be held entirely responsible for what he says, he speaks of his «poquilla çiençia ... e mucha e grand rrudeza» (5, xxvi). A Middle English preacher uses a similar commonplace of affected modesty:

> And ther-fore with the grace of God I will thise day teche you aftur myn sympull connunge... But notwithstondynge, it is full herde for me, for I knowe my-selfe vnabull and not sufficiente for to do this dede (Sermon 37, p. 207, 11.20-1).

In Juan Ruiz's treatise on confession (1128-1160) he again protects himself with a display of trepidation and confession of ignorance:

> Es me cosa muy grave en tan grand fecho fablar,
> es piélago muy fondo, más que todo el mar;
> só rrudo e syn çiençia, non me oso aventurar. (1133*a-c*)

This commonplace is not confined to pulpit oratory, but like another commonplace in the prologue —the declaration of the author's purity of intention (6, xxx-7, iii)— it is to be found also in secular literature.

The language of the prose prologue is not popular: there are no colloquialisms, unless the semi-proverbial style of the vernacular *auctoritates* be counted. This is remarkable in the light of the style of the remainder of the *Libro* where, in spite of the abundance of rhetorical usage, the style is frequently colloquial. It is possible that the sermon was intended to be something of a private joke: the impersonal approach of the learned sermon in which the congregation is never directly addressed increases the humour, but the sermon would have a greater appeal as a joke to a clerical or a learned lay audience; a popular audience might apprehend the humour of the author's intentions, but would be less likely to appreciate as a joke the structure of the prologue.

Juan Ruiz uses the first person singular in his prologue, and thus it serves not only as an introduction to the subject matter of the *Libro de buen amor* but also as an indication of the form the work will take, that of a first person narrative. But the sermon is in no way autobiographical. The author is following the common medieval practice, customary in the pulpit orator and the poet, of speaking of himself, of his own understanding of a particular biblical passage, or of his hopes that the congregation will take to heart what he has said and is about to say. During the greater part of his prologue he is speaking as a preacher, and his use of the first person singular can only be related to passages in the main body of the work where the preacher can be heard again, for instance in the treatise on confession. The medieval English preacher used the first person singular in the same «impersonal» manner as does Juan Ruiz in his sermon:

> And I sey who-so lyvith in this synne, he stondeth not stedfastely in the ryghtwisnes of is soule. And so I may shewe to you be story and also be ensampull of kende... I drede me thise dayes that suche maner of pride reyneth now meche amonge mankeende (Sermon 37, p. 208, 11.15-18, and p. 209, 11.25-7).

After the transition to the clearly humorous part of the sermon, Juan Ruiz presents himself as the author of the *Libro* and as the exponent of various kinds of versification; he then becomes more closely identified with the male protagonist of the work, in that both lover and preacher claim to have composed the lyric passages. However, the preacher cannot be identified entirely with the lover, but only with the author who has discarded his pseudo-autobiographical character in order to introduce a work he has previously written. Juan Ruiz's afterthought of composing an introduction to his work in the form of a learned sermon adds one more complication to our interpretation of the «yo» of the *Libro*. This may well be a complication of the modern critic's making, and not one that would have troubled the medieval audience. Marshall McLuhan has pointed out that the consistent attitude of an author is a product of a print culture and not a manuscript culture:

> ...the author felt little pressure to maintain a single attitude to his subject or a consistent tone to the reader. ... Instead

of homogeneity there was heterogeneity of tone and attitude, so that the author felt able to shift these in mid-sentence at any time, just as in poetry. It was disturbing to scholars to discover in recent years that Chaucer's personal pronoun or his «poetic self» as narrator was not a consistent *persona*. The «I» of medieval narrative did not provide a point of view so much as immediacy of effect. [23]

This statement is of course relevant not just for a consideration of the prologue of the *Libro de buen amor* but for the work as a whole. Juan Ruiz's audience might well be amused by the shifts of attitude and point of view of the «yo». They would not be so surprised as we. [24]

ADDENDUM

Not until this essay was completed did I read Pierre L. Ullman's article «Juan Ruiz's Prologue», *MLN, LXXXII* (1967), 149-170, and as a result I have been unable to incorporate some of his discoveries into my study. This article is clearly of great importance in its analysis of the Augustinian features of the prologue to the *Libro de buen amor*, but I can only comment briefly on a few points, and leave to those better qualified the discussion of St. Augustine's influence on Juan Ruiz.

I do not believe that Ullman has convincingly proved that the «sermon» proper ends at the word *breve*, nor that the first ten stanzas of the later redaction of the *Libro* are an integral part of the «sermon» as Ullman sees it. Admittedly there appears to be some kind of *volte face* after the word *breve*, but I think that this is explained both by Marshall McLuhan's words, previously cited, and by Otis H. Green's comments on medieval laughter (*Spain and the Western Tradition*, vol. I, pp. 53-4): dirty jokes or blasphemous jokes were not indications of godlessness to the medieval mind, and a sudden switch from the apparently serious to the humorous would not be surprising in the fourteenth century. I hope that I have shown in my analysis that in spite of the *volte face* at the point Ullman indicates, Juan Ruiz has been leading up to his joke.

Ullman does not offer any evidence of poetry being used prothemi-

[23] Marshall McLuhan, *The Gutenberg Galaxy* (University of Toronto Press, 4th edition, 1967), p. 136.

[24] I should like to express my gratitude to A. D. Deyermond of Westfield College for his assistance at various stages of this essay.

cally in the Augustinian homily prior to Juan Ruiz, and I know of no contemporary English sermons which start in this way, though the rhymed sermon in Latin is not unknown. If the presence of similar themes and like words in the first ten stanzas and in the prologue offer proof of their being an integral whole, should not the argument be extended to prove that the prologue and the rest of the work are an integral whole, since the Latin words that end the prologue are repeated in Castilian at the beginning of stanza 11? Ullman seems to believe that the fact that the prologue did not appear in the first redaction of the *Libro,* represented by mss. *G* and *T,* proves that it is not integral to the work, because it is not «initiatory». But Ullman, as a scholar, must know that the majority of introductions are written when the rest of the work is finished. Moreover, if the delay in adding the prologue to the *Libro* proves it to be adventitious, how must we look at the later additions to the main body of the work? Are they somehow less «integral» to the work than some of the items in the earlier hodge-podge? The implication of Ullman's remarks is that the rest of the work *is* an integral whole.

All scholars till Ullman have assumed that the division of the *thema* in the prologue is intrinsic rather than extrinsic, and I am not yet convinced that because Juan Ruiz uses Augustinian terminology to prove his argument he is therefore dividing his *thema* extrinsically. If Juan Ruiz is as learned as Ullman's article would have us believe, then he would almost certainly have used *divisio intra* for his sermon. Contrary to what Ullman asserts, *divisio intra* was not generally reserved for the *Latin* sermon, but for the *learned* sermon, and there are abundant examples of *divisio intra* in learned vernacular sermons in England.

Ullman does not appear to have noted that Juan Ruiz slightly modifies the meaning of the *thema* by his divisions; indeed, his comments indicate that he has not thought of any more appropriate division:

> In the first and second *razones* man was shown standing still, endowed with understanding and taught the commandments. *Now he is on his way.* (p. 159. My italics.)

But the point of the verse used for the *thema* is that man is being taught as he goes along, he is not standing still until he is sufficiently filled with understanding. Juan Ruiz, therefore, has modified the original meaning of the verse.

I have noted a few small points which Ullman could perhaps have clarified, though they may not be directly relevant to his central thesis:

In his footnote no. 33 on p. 161, Ullman mentions «Cato» as «a lay writer from antiquity». As I have shown, the *auctoritas* «nemo sine crimine vivit» is taken from the pseudo-Catonian *Disticha* which were composed in the Christian era as far as is known, not later than the fourth century.

Ullman does not consider the possibility of Juan Ruiz's confession of «poquilla çiençia...» being a topic of modesty, devised to dispose his audience kindly towards him.

At the end of the article, Ullman refers to the «medieval reader» (p. 170). The term «medieval audience» would be more appropriate until more is known of Juan Ruiz's public.

Finally in rejecting Lecoy's admittedly incorrect term of «sermon joyeux» for the prologue, Ullman appears to believe that he has largely excluded the comical possibilities of the prologue. In the course of the article, Ullman reminds us that it is necessary to «divest ourselves of our modern prejudices» (p. 165) and I am inclined to believe that the failure to see the funny side of Juan Ruiz is as much the result of modern prejudice as the failure to see the Augustinian implications of the prologue.

Westfield College,
University of London

SCHEMATIC REPRESENTATION OF THE PROLOGUE

THEMA (3, i-ii)

Intellectum tibi dabo et instruam te in via hac qua gradieris // firmabo super te occulos meos

DIVISION OF THEMA (3, v-vi)

enel qual verso entiendo yo tres cosas
(3, viii-xi)

1. Understanding:
   Consolation to soul

2. Will
   Longer life

3. Memory
   Good reputation

DEVELOPMENT A (3, xi-4, xxi)

1. Understanding:
   Argumentation to conclusion and author-
   ities.
   Intellectum tibi dabo. (3, xi-xxiv)

2. Understanding and instruction linked:
   Argumentation to conclusion and
   authorities
   Et instruam te.   (3, xxiv-4, iii)

3. Three qualities of soul together:
   Argumentation to conclusion and author-
   ities.
   In via hac..occulos meos. (4, iii-xiv)

Further argumentation with vernacular version of third division to justify authorities and combination of the two phrases of the third
division. (4, xiv-xxi)

DEVELOPMENT B (4, xxi-7, xi)

(4, xxi-5, xxv)   (5, xxv-7, xi)

1. *Human imperfections*

   Forgetting to do good comes not from good
   understanding, will and memory, but from:
   i) human weakness
   ii) lack of understanding
   iii) poor memory and sinful nature

   Reasons for books, pictures, etc.

Perfect memory divine: Imperfect memory human:
                          mortal body
                          immortal soul

2. *Intentions*

   moral aim
   leads   ignorant
   wise
   to   hatred
   good   of sin
   works

   ii) textbook of sins

   Therefore
   Intellectum tibi dabo,
   etc.

   Results of sin:
   i) lost soul
   ii) short life
   iii) ill fame (5, xxv-6, xvi)

   Further protestation of
   pure intention (6, xvi-
   7, viii)

   iii) examples of lyric poetry (7, viii-xi)

CLAUSIO (7, xii-xxi)

Invocation

A. D. DEYERMOND

Some Aspects of Parody in the 'Libro de buen amor'

One of the most solid advances in *Libro de buen amor* criticism of the past three decades has been the recognition that parody plays an important part in the work. It was once possible not merely for a mediocre commentator like Julio Puyol y Alonso to write an *Estudio crítico* on the Archpriest with only an occasional censorious comment on the poet's irreverence in one or two of the more obvious parodies, [1] but even for Menéndez y Pelayo to overlook the question in the chapter of the *Antología de poetas líricos castellanos* that he devotes to the *Libro*.[2] Successive statements of Menéndez Pidal's views have laid increasing stress on the parodic element, [3] but an even greater share of the credit must go to Félix Lecoy, whose *Recherches* (ch. 8-9) deal at length with the Archpriest's Goliardic-type parodies and with the Cuaresma-Carnal conflict.

In the past ten years, it has been increasingly recognized that parody is not confined to some episodes but is, in some sense (there is, as yet, no agreement on detail), a central feature of Juan Ruiz's art. G. B. Gybbon-Monypenny suggested in 1957 that the *Libro* is a parody of the courtly genre that he identifies as the erotic pseudo-autobiography, and that the parody is intended to demolish the pretensions of Courtly Love. [4] In the following year, Otis H. Green studied one of the main

---

[1] *El Arcipreste de Hita, Estudio crítico* (Madrid, 1906). One such comment may be found on p. 349.

[2] Ch. 5. He recognizes in passing the existence of one parody (Edición nacional, Madrid, 1944-45, i, 274), but in discussing the Archpriest's relation to the Goliards (i, 295) he does not even mention parody.

[3] The most recent formulation is in *Poesía juglaresca y orígenes de las literaturas románicas* (6th ed. [of *Poesía juglaresca y juglares*], Madrid, 1957), 204-207.

[4] «Autobiography in the *Libro de buen amor* in the Light of Some Literary Comparisons», *BHS*, XXXIV (1957), 63-78. More recently, Pierre Le Gentil has also maintained that the *Libro* is essentially a parody of worldly love: «A propos des *Cánticas de Serrana* de l'Archiprêtre de Hita», *Wort und Text: Festschrift für Fritz Schalk* (Frankfurt, 1963), 133-141.

parodies in some detail, and he subsequently extended his study to the
book as a whole, seeing in it an example of medieval laughter in which
parody played a major part. [5] In Anthony N. Zahareas' recent book
we have the most explicit and detailed recognition so far of parody as
an essential and characteristic feature of the *Libro*. [6]

There is, therefore, little point in setting out to prove either that
parody is present in the Archpriest's work, or that it is extremely important. Whatever the disagreement about details, the main point
seems by now to be generally accepted. [7] Nor is it necessary to stress
either the nature or the importance of parody as an element in medieval
culture, for these have been amply studied in Paul Lehmann's authori-
tative book, *Die Parodie im Mittelalter*. [8] Lehmann has two main categories (recognizing, of course, that they overlap): parody whose purpose
is criticism, dispute and triumph, and parody which is primarily entertaining and cheerful (both types are to be found in the *Libro*). The aim
of the present article is thus a more restricted one: I propose, with a
brief enumeration of the major «set-piece» parodies in the *Libro*, to
consider in more detail the Archpriest's use of multiple parody, his
simultaneous parodying of more than one thing; to study some examples
of his incidental parody, the brief and perhaps instinctive passing parodies that abound in the book; and finally, with the caution appropriate
to any interpretation of this complex and elusive poet, to draw some
conclusions from the assembled evidence. It will be seen that the set-
piece parodies are for the most part extended developments of some
type of literary or ecclesiastical text, which is parodied throughout,
whereas the incidental parodies are more often the apparently serious
use of a traditional topic or literary device which is, by a last-minute
incongruity (what María Rosa Lida de Malkiel describes as a zigzag),
devalued and shown to have been absurd from the start.

I should briefly explain the sense in which I use the word «parody»

[5]   «On Juan Ruiz's Parody of the Canonical Hours», *HR*, XXVI (1958), 12-
34. *Spain and the Western Tradition. The Castilian Mind in Literature from El
Cid to Calderón* i (Madison, Wisconsin, 1963), ch. 2.
[6]   *The Art of Juan Ruiz, Archpriest of Hita* (Madrid, 1965).
[7]   It is accordingly possible for Giorgio Chiarini to take it for granted in the
introduction to his critical edition: «la musa segreta del *Libro* è l'ambiguità...
come ambivalenza programmatica nell'ordine significativo, come doppio registro
tonale, come controcanto parodistico...» (Juan Ruiz, Arcipreste de Hita, *Libro
de buen amor*, edizione critica a cura di Giorgio Chiarini [Documenti di Filolo-
gia, 8, Milano-Napoli, 1964], p. lxxii).
[8]   First published 1922; 2nd ed. Stuttgart, 1963. There is also much valuable material on late medieval parody in P. Le Gentil, *La Poésie lyrique espagnole et portugaise à la fin du Moyen Age*, i (Rennes, 1949).

in this article. Parody, for my present purposes, includes also the sub-division of humour that some literary theorists classify as burlesque, as well as that classified by all theorists as parody. In other words, it includes the cruder as well as the more subtle and sophisticated mani-festations of this type of humour; it includes the humorous effects ob-tained by deliberate incongruity between style and matter, by the em-ployment of literary conventions in a wholly inappropriate setting, and by the apparently serious use of a genre or *topos* in which the author shows, at the last minute, that his tongue was in his cheek, thereby devaluing what has gone before. Most parody is of literary texts, genres, themes or techniques, but it is also possible to parody liturgical or other ceremonies, musical forms and popular entertainments; the essen-tial requirement is, of course, that the thing parodied should be familiar to the audience to whom the parody is addressed, for without this familiarity, the audience cannot grasp the comparison which is at the base of all parody. Parody, like any literary category, overlaps other categories. Much parody is also satirical, and much is also ironic, but this means simply that parody may be used for a variety of pur-poses. This variety is illustrated by the examples given in the pres-ent article, but parody, irony and satire are not thereby rendered identical. I do not seek to convince the reader that the sense in which I use «parody» is the only, or even the best, sense, and any elaborate theoretical justification would be out of place. I wish only to ensure that the reader knows the meaning I attach to the term.

I should perhaps make it clear at this stage that the present article does not purport to be either comprehensive or wholly novel. A full treatment of all the cases of parody in the *Libro* would be far too long for a single article, and in any case would be hampered by the lack of agreement on whether some parts of the book are parodic or «straight». Nevertheless, this profusion of parodies and possible par-odies is in itself a significant pointer to the Archpriest's literary tastes, and I hope that the examples discussed here will provide enough evi-dence on which to base a judgment. As to originality, all of the set-piece and some of the incidental parodies have been noted by previous students of the *Libro;* I give references below to some of the most signi-ficant commentaries on the relevant passages, and further bibliography will be found in the works cited. All I can hope to do here is to list the major parodies, to re-examine some of those already known, adding fresh information or re-interpreting the text, and to point to some paro-dies that have hitherto been overlooked.

A. Set-piece parodies

1. The prose sermon (Ducamin, pp. 3-7). See Janet Chapman's article in this volume. Not all critics accept that this prologue, which (as Miss Chapman clearly shows) takes the form of a learned, or *divisio intra,* sermon in the vernacular,[9] is parodic. The point is, however, noted in passing by several scholars, is clearly established by Green (*Spain,* i, 46-53) and is reinforced by the observations of Zahareas (*Art,* 21-24), even though he does not use the words 'sermon' or 'parody'. It is, as Green, Zahareas and others point out, hard to take seriously the Archpriest's statement that

> por que es umanal cosa el pecar, si algunos, lo que non los conssejo, quisieren usar del loco amor, aquí fallarán algunas maneras para ello.

Even more dangerous to anyone who wishes to take this sermon seriously is the next sentence, on which Zahareas (*Art,* 22-23) also comments:

> E ansí este mi libro a todo ome o muger, al cuerdo e al non cuerdo, al que entendiere el bien e escogiere salvaçión e obrare bien amando a Dios, otrosí al que quisiere el amor loco, en la carrera que andudiere, puede cada uno bien dezir: intellectum tibi dabo e cetera.

The *intellectum* which provided the sermon's *thema,* or opening quotation, and which consequently underlies its whole structure, turns out to be a true understanding of God, or a skilful technique for seduction; the reader may please himself. This may be compared with stanza 1627, discussed below.

After this article was completed, Pierre L. Ullman published his study, «Juan Ruiz's Prologue».[10] Ullman argues that the Archpriest's prose prologue is not a parodic sermon, since (*a*) other medieval parodic sermons are obvious burlesques throughout, and differ in form from the *Libro* prologue; (*b*) it refers, by its emphasis on *entendimiento* and

---

[9] Use of the vernacular for a learned sermon is unusual, but is not in itself parodic: for a perfectly serious *divisio intra* sermon in Spanish by Pedro de Luna (Pope Benedict XIII), see *BH,* XLIX (1947), 38-46 and L (1948), 129-146.

[10] *MLN,* LXXXII (1967), 149-170.

voluntad, to the medieval epistemological controversy between Augustinian voluntarists and Thomist intellectualists; and (c) the passages
cited above are to be taken seriously. None of these arguments seems
to me to establish Ullman's case. The first shows merely that the
Archpriest's parody is a subtle and individual one. It was imprudent
of Lecoy to label it a *sermon joyeux* when that was the name used for
a different type of parody, but a demonstration of Lecoy's mistake
in nomenclature does not affect the central question of whether the
Archpriest's prologue is a parodic sermon (Ullman accepts that it
has the form of a sermon). Secondly, Ullman's interesting and important discussion of the voluntarist-intellectualist controversy clari-
fies further the kind of sermon that is being parodied, and makes it
still more obvious that this must have been intended for an educated
clerical public, but it again does not affect the issue of whether this
particular sermon is a parody. In order to determine the issue, we
must examine the text in detail in order to see whether it is parodic
or wholly serious. Ullman discusses (on pp. 169-170 and 165-166, respectively) the two sentences quoted above, but although his comments
on the second refer to a double use of *intellectum,* they do not deal
with the particular ambiguity that impedes a wholly serious interpretation of the passage. In commenting on the first of the sentences
quoted, Ullman comes very close to admitting (p. 169, n. 52) that the
Archpriest's tongue is in his cheek, but suggests that «Perhaps he
whets the appetite of the sinner with the ulterior motive of awaken-
ing him to his interior teacher.» But even if this is true (and Ullman's
supporting evidence is drawn not from learned, but from popular, or
divisio extra, sermons), it establishes the purpose of the parody rather
than casting doubt on the parody's existence. In short, the case for
regarding the prose prologue as a parody of a learned sermon still
stands: the parodic note appears only at the end, but it retrospectively
tinges the remainder, for it changes the reader's attitude to what has
gone before.

2. The Greeks and the Romans (st. 44-70). [11] This seems to be a
fourfold parody:

(a) of the formal academic disputation, at that time a standard

[11] See Lecoy, *Recherches,* 164-168 and 365-368; Zahareas, *Art,* 53-59. I have
discussed some aspects of this story in «The Greeks, the Romans, the Astrologers and the Meaning of the *Libro de buen amor*», RomN, V, no. 1 (Autumn
1963), 88-91. For a different interpretation, see Ian Michael's article in the
present volume.

feature of university training. [12] The Archpriest's parody casts doubt both on the validity of such disputations as a means of arriving at the truth or even of exchanging views (each of the adversaries totally misunderstands the other — see sts. 59-63), and on the significance of higher degrees. The Roman yokel is dressed up in doctoral robes (st. 53), but remains a yokel underneath; in terms of the common medieval formula, his *corteza* is learned, his *meollo* is that of a country bumpkin. He is delighted with his new clothes, *catando sus vestidos* (56d). But worse is to come, for the learned Greek is also impressed by the robes of his adversary, and does not think to ask how he came by them. Moreover, the Greek has the same robes as the Roman, even though he came by them honestly, and this similarity of *corteza* is increased by their identical actions in mounting the *cathedra:*

> Vistieron lo muy bien paños de grand valía,
> como si fuese doctor en la filosofía;
> subió en alta cathedra, dixo con bavoquía:
> «d'oy mays vengan los griegos con toda su porfía».

> Vino ay un griego doctor muy esmerado,
> escogido de griegos, entre todos loado;
> sobió en otra cathreda, todo el pueblo juntado,
> e començó sus señas, como era tratado.

(53-54)

And, most subversive of all, we are left with the feeling that *meollo* as well as *corteza* is very similar, since the Greek proves to be as foolish as the Roman. The parody of university degrees and their ceremonial trappings is probably as old as the degrees themselves, and it continues today (for instance, in Bergman's film *Wild Strawberries*), but the Archpriest's use of it is unusually effective.

(b) of sign-language. Signs of this sort were known in classical antiquity, and such a language was well developed in twelfth-century Cluny. Some of the signs are remarkably constant, being found with similar meanings in medieval books, [13] in Mediterranean countries today, and among Red Indians. They were, of course, particularly valu-

---

[12] For some of its literary connections, see Hiram Peri (Pflaum), «Die scholastische Disputation», *Romanica et Occidentalia. Etudes dédiées à la mémoire de Hiram Peri (Pflaum)*, ed. Moshé Lazar (Jerusalem, 1963), 349-368. The Archpriest's familiarity with the disputation as an educational instrument is attested by 1133cd, as Mrs. Hamilton has reminded me.

[13] See G. Van Rijnberk, *Le Langage par signes chez les moines* (Amsterdam,

able in medieval monasteries, where speech was forbidden at some times of day by all Orders, and permanently by a few Orders. The Archpriest parodies sign-language by employing it in a situation where it has no universally accepted meaning, so that the same signs mean different things to different people, and a kind of visual Babel ensues. Such a parody of a monastic convention would, as previous commentators have noted, be especially attractive to the secular clergy.

(c) of the *translatio studii*. The concept of *translatio* —transfer of political authority or of intellectual dominance to a new people when the old one had become unworthy— was familiar and influential in the Middle Ages. [14] *Translatio imperii* was a useful weapon of political propagandists, [15] and *translatio studii* (from Athens to the West) was almost as important. Juan Ruiz shows us this *translatio* taking place under highly formalized conditions, but in an absurd way, leading to the acceptance of a ludicrously unqualified people as worthy inheritors. It may be significant that there really were disputations in the twelfth and thirteenth centuries between representatives of the Greek and Roman churches, and that on at least one occasion these were explicitly linked to the *translatio studii*: a fragmentary Latin text recording a disputation in 1112 represents the Byzantine Emperor, who was present, as complaining that his champions had been worsted, and that whereas Greeks had once carried wisdom to the West, a Latin was now able to bring it to the East. [16] It should be noted that the earliest analogues found by Lecoy for the Archpriest's story date from this period.

(d) of scriptural exegesis. It is fairly well known that the medieval insistence on *corteza* and *meollo* is connected with the tradition of seeking a hidden meaning in Biblical texts. At its fullest development, this tradition of exegesis uncovered four layers of meaning in the text. The application of this exegetical technique to the interpretation of medieval literature is a matter of acute controversy, [17] but

---

1954), and Mário Martins, «Livros de Sinais dos Cistercienses Portugueses», *BdF*, XVII (1958[1960]), 293-357.

[14] See E. R. Curtius, *European Literature and the Latin Middle Ages* (trans. W. R. Trask, London, 1953), 28-30.

[15] Walter Ullman, *A History of Political Thought: The Middle Ages* (Harmondsworth, 1965), 61, 67 and 108.

[16] Kenneth M. Setton, «The Byzantine Background to the Italian Renaissance», *Proceedings of the American Philosophical Society*, C (1956), 1-76, at pp. 21-23; see also p. 33. I am indebted to Professor Otis H. Green for this reference.

[17] The leading exponent of this method is D. W. Robertson; see, for example, his *A Preface to Chaucer. Studies in Medieval Perspectives* (Princeton, 1963). A balanced account of the controversy may be found in *Critical Ap-*

there can be no doubt that the exhortation to the reader or hearer to disregard the *corteza* and attend only to the *meollo* was a commonplace of medieval writing, prose and verse, sacred and secular. Such exhortations occur frequently in the *Libro,* but this does not prove that the Archpriest meant them seriously. They might be merely a device to protect him against criticism, or they might —and in some cases, I believe that they do — have a comic purpose. It has been shown that scriptural exegesis could be used for satire, [18] and that the misapplication of *sententiae* and *exempla* could be an important feature of a medieval poet's comic art. [19] In view of these other comic uses of didactic techniques, there is nothing startling in the suggestion that the Archpriest might parody such techniques. I have argued elsewhere that in the story of the Greeks and the Romans, the Archpriest can hardly be serious when he tells us to seek the correct meaning of his book, and it is unnecessary to repeat the details of the argument here. [20] He seems, in fact, to be parodying the *meollo/corteza* tradition, and this view is reinforced by one further consideration. It was commonly accepted in the Middle Ages that prophecies and portents could be correctly interpreted only by those who had faith in the true God, and that those who lacked this faith blundered into misunderstandings that were either ludicrous or disastrous. Thus, in the *Auto de los Reyes Magos,* Herod's rabbis are unable to interpret the prophecies of the Nativity, and in Berceo's *Vida de San Millán,* Abderrahman's wise men misread the signs of God's wrath as a promise of victory. [21] In both these cases, the faithful are correct in their interpretations, and attain their objectives. The contrast between this traditional pattern and what happens in the Archpriest's story of the Greeks and the Romans is strongly marked, and the result is undeniably comic.

proaches to Medieval Literature, ed. Dorothy Bethurum (New York, 1960), 1-82. For an application of the method to the *Libro,* see Thomas R. Hart, *La alegoría en el Libro de buen amor* (Madrid, 1959).

[18] G. R. Owst, *Literature and Pulpit in Medieval England* (2nd ed., Oxford, 1961), 63. There is, of course, no suggestion in this case that the method itself is parodied.

[19] Zahareas, *Art;* Donald MacDonald, «Proverbs, *Sententiae* and *Exempla* in Chaucer's Comic Tales: the Function of Comic Misapplication», *Speculum,* XLI (1966), 453-465.

[20] See the article cited in note 11, above. Joan Corominas, in his commentary on this passage (Juan Ruiz, *Libro de buen amor,* edición crítica de Joan Corominas [Madrid, 1967], p. 88), also concludes that no single meaning is intended by the Archpriest, but he does not consider the question of parody.

[21] *Auto de los Reyes Magos,* 135-147 (in D. J. Gifford & F. W. Hodcroft, *Textos lingüísticos del medioevo español,* 2nd ed., Oxford, 1966, p. 42). *Vida de San Millán,* sts. 400-405 (in B. Dutton, *La vida de San Millán de la Cogolla de Gonzalo de Berceo. Estudio y edición crítica* [London, Tamesis, 1967]).

Thus, in this episode, Juan Ruiz parodies academic disputation, sign language, *translatio studii,* and exegetical method. Zahareas' comparison of the Archpriest's treatment of the story with its analogues confirms that his version has more parodic elements than any other. The story of the Greeks and the Romans is not the only instance of multiple parody in the *Libro,* but it is the most striking, and it helps us to realize the extent to which the Archpriest's mind turned automatically to parody. It may even be —though I advance this view very tentatively— that the fourfold parody contained in an apparently simple episode is a parodic counterpart of the fourfold exegesis of the Bible.

3. The trial (st. 321-371). Its parodic nature has been adequately discussed by Lecoy (*Recherches,* pp. 129-30) and Lida de Malkiel (*Masterpieces,* pp. 36-37); Lecoy emphasizes that there is a much fuller comic development in Juan Ruiz's version than in any of the analogues. The only point to require special comment is the parody of notarial style in st. 326 and 348-366 (compare the letters exchanged by Doña Cuaresma and Don Carnal, which are described as parodic by Lida de Malkiel, *Masterpieces,* p. 43; there are exact parallels for these in thirteenth-century Latin, as Kemlin Laurence notes in her article in the present volume).

4. The canonical hours (st. 374-387). Discussed by Lecoy (*Recherches,* pp. 214-229), Green («On Juan Ruiz's Parody», and *Spain,* i, pp. 53-60), Zahareas (*Art,* pp. 93-99), and Corominas (commentary, 162-174). Corominas agrees that this is a primarily parodic section, but dissents from Green's view that most of it is obscene. His surprising statement (162) that this is a *Misa de Amor* is not substantiated.

An interesting comparison may be made with the Goliardic *Confession* of the Archpoet. [22] The Archpoet is, of course, writing wholly in Latin, whereas Juan Ruiz here writes macaronic verse. It should be noted that his gloss on the *Ave Maria* (sts. 1661-67) is also macaronic, and that his poem on the Crucifixion (sts. 1049-58) is, like this account of the amorous cleric's activities, based on the time-scale of the canonical hours. Thus Juan Ruiz is able to use the same techniques for parody and for genuine religious emotion. It is also worth recalling that Cejador points out in his note on this passage that 375b, *en*

[22] F. J. E. Raby, *A History of Secular Latin Poetry in the Middle Ages,* ii (Oxford, 1934), 183-186.

alta boz a cantar, is a reminiscence of the rubric in Missal and Breviary; in other words, not only the services themselves but also the prescribed procedure for them contribute to this parody.

Finally, there is the important additional parody contained in sts. 376-378:

> Desque sientes a ella, tu coraçón espaçias;
> con la maytinada cantate, en las friurias laçias;
> laudes aurora lucis, das les grandes graçias;
> con miserere mey, mucho te le engraçias.
>
> En saliendo el sol, comienças luego prima;
> deus in nomine tuo, rruegas a tu saquima
> que la lieve por agua e que dé a todo çima,
> va en achaque de agua a verte la mala esquima.
>
> E sy es tal que non usa andar por las callejas,
> que la lyeve a las uertas por las rrosas bermejas;
> ssy cree la bavieca sus dichos e conssejas,
> Quod eva tristis trae de quicunque vult rredruejas.

This is, of course, a dawn-poem: the services concerned —lauds and prime— are just before and just after dawn; the words *aurora* (376c) and *salyendo el sol* (377a) make the point explicit; and the context is an erotic one. The lovers are not, however, youth and maiden, nor even romantic adulterers, but a lecherous priest and his compliant parisioner. Juan Ruiz has, therefore, not only written a dawn-poem much earlier than the Castilian poems collected in *Eos;* [23] he has also parodied the *alborada* (poem of a dawn greeting) while at the same time parodying the canonical hours. [24]

5. The *serrana* episodes (sts. 950-1042). Discussed by Le Gentil, [25] Hart (*Alegoría,* pp. 67-92), Zahareas (*Art,* pp. 147-52) and by R. B. Tate in this volume. Zahareas, surprisingly, dismisses the view that these are parodies (*Art,* p. 147, n. 152) on the grounds that *pastourelles* often

---

[23] *Eos. An enquiry into the theme of lovers' meetings and partings at dawn in poetry,* edited by Arthur T. Hatto (The Hague, 1965). The Iberian chapter (pp. 299-343) is by E. M. Wilson & S. M. Stern.
[24] All of the Galician-Portuguese dawn-poems in *Eos* are earlier than the *Libro,* and most of them are *alboradas;* the volume also illustrates the extent of the tradition in medieval Latin, Provençal and Old French. There was thus, as in the case of the *serrana* poems, discussed below, plentiful material for the Archpriest to parody, even if it was not in Castilian.
[25] *La Poésie lyrique,* i, 543-50; «A propos des *Cánticas*» —Le Gentil refers specifically to parody on p. 136,

contain sensual elements. This is, of course, true, but the parody does not depend on sensuality. There are five parodic elements in these episodes, and, while most of them have been pointed out by previous students of the *Libro,* they should be briefly noted here:

(*a*) The setting is winter, not (despite 996*c*) the spring which is the traditional setting for *pastourelles* and for much of medieval love-poetry in general.

(*b*) Woman is the pursuer, man the pursued. This exchange of rôles is emphasized by the next element:

(*c*) The description of Alda, the fourth *serrana* (sts. 1010-20), is a point-by-point antithesis of that of the ideal lady (sts. 431-435). [26] This antithesis of beauty is traditional, [27] though it is often contrasted with the appearance of the same person when younger. Alda is, however, not merely contrasted with the ideal lady, but is also shown to be very similar to the Juan Ruiz described by Trotaconventos (sts. 1485-90). Moreover, if one accepts Kane's view that the description of Juan Ruiz is carefully constructed to emphasize his virility, [28] it follows that Alda's characteristics are those of male sexual potency.

(*d*) The exchange of rôles is further stressed by the fact that, while three of the *serranas* want sexual satisfaction, and the fourth wants marriage, the male protagonist is interested only in a good square meal. It is food, not women, that receives sensuous emphasis (sts. 968-969).

(*e*) The protagonist addresses the second *serrana* in flattering terms (st. 989), hoping that this will release him from his difficulties, but the only result is a sudden blow that sends him sprawling down the hillside. He has followed the approved procedure, but it has had the opposite effect to what he intended. [29]

In the *serrana* episodes, then, the Archpriest appears to parody the

---

[26] María Rosa Lida, «Notas para la interpretación, influencia, fuentes y texto del *Libro de buen amor*», *RFH* II (1940), 105-150, at pp. 123-124.

[27] See Edmond Faral, *Les Arts poétiques du XIIe et du XIIIe siècle. Recherches et documents sur la technique littéraire du Moyen Age* (Bibliothèque de l'École des Hautes Études, CCXXXVIII, Paris, 1924), 76-77; Italo Siciliano, *François Villon et les thèmes poétiques du Moyen Age* (Paris, 1934), 383-96. A further example may be found in the *Roman de la Rose,* ed. Félix Lecoy (Classiques Français du Moyen Age, 92, Paris, 1965), lines 339-60.

[28] Elisha K. Kane, «The Personal Appearance of Juan Ruiz», *MLN*, XLV (1930), 103-9. See also Peter Dunn's article in the present volume.

[29] I do not know of other cases in medieval literature where the use of such language to a peasant girl leads to physical violence, though Marcabru —followed by many later Provençal poets— shows its use provoking a rebuff: see William T. H. Jackson, «The Medieval Pastourelle as a Satirical Genre», *PQ*, XXXI (1952), 156-70, at p. 165.

pastourelle and courtly love-poetry in general, and his technique is generally one of reversal.

It would, of course, be quite wrong to suggest that all features of the Archpriest's *serrana* poems are unprecedented. Women in the medieval lyric sometimes express sexual desire openly, as in the *kharja* «¡Alba de meu fogore!»; in *cantigas d'amigo* by Joam Servando, «Fui eu a San Servando», and Juião Bolseiro, «Aquestas noites tan longas»; in the anonymous pastourelle «Quant voi la flor nouvele»; or in Guido Cavalcanti's *pastorella* «In un boschetto trova' pasturella.» They may even take the initiative, and the man may be helpless and ridiculous, as in the *vers* of Guilhem IX, «En Alvernhe, part Lemozi.» Finally, the grotesquely ugly woman may be addressed in courtly fashion, as in the anonymous *porquiera*, «Mentre per una ribiera.»[30]. Yet the only cases that approach the spirit of the Archpriest's poems are the last two, and even so one would have to combine them in order to create something like the effect achieved in the *Libro*. With the Archpriest's *serranas,* the reversal of rôles is total, and extends even to the violence which Andreas Capellanus advises the nobleman to use should he unfortunately desire a peasant woman, and which is here used against the narrator by the *serrana.*[31]

6. The battle of Cuaresma and Carnal, with the triumph of Don Carnal and Don Amor (sts. 1067-1314). Discussed by Lecoy (*Recherches,* pp. 244-288), Lida de Malkiel (*Masterpieces,* pp. 43-44), Green (*Spain,* i, pp. 61-62), Corominas (commentary, 410-492), and in Kemlin Laurence's article in the present volume. The principal objects of parody are the epic, in the first part of the section, and the religious

[30] The texts are to be found in E. García Gómez, *Las jarchas romances de la serie árabe en su marco* (Madrid, 1965), no. 4; J. J. Nunes, *Cantigas d'amigo dos trovadores galego-portugueses* (Coimbra, 1926), nos. 374 and 405; Richard Aldington, *Fifty Romance Lyric Poems,* 2nd ed. (London, 1948), pp. 40-42 and 50; André Berry, *Anthologie de la poésie occitane* (Paris, 1961), pp. 1-3; and Jean Audiau, *La Pastourelle dans la poésie occitane du Moyen Age* (Paris, 1923), no. 24. I owe many of these references to Professor T. R. Hart and Mrs. Jane Hawking. It is necessary to recall here the warning of the *Leys d'Amors* that Provençal examples of the genre are sometimes far from idealistic: «E deu tractar d'esquern per donar solas. E deu se hom gardar en aquest dictat maiormen, quar en aquest se peca hom mays que en los autres, que hom no diga vils paraulas ni laias, ni procezisca en son dictat a degu vil fag...» (*Les Troubadours,* ii, *Le Trésor poétique de l'Occitanie,* ed. R. Nelli & R. Lavaud, Bruges, 1965, p. 620).
[31] Si vero et illarum te feminarum amor forte attraxerit, eas pluribus laudibus efferre memento, et, si locum inveneris opportunum, non differas assumere, quod petebas et violento potiri amplexu (*De amore libri tres,* ed. A. Pagès, Castelló de la Plana, 1930, p. 137).

procession, in the second part. Zahareas (*Art,* p. 136) says that the digression on confession is parodic, but this does not seem to be the case, as Rita Hamilton's article in this volume shows. The parody of the procession is too well known for comment here, but it may be appropriate to comment on the use of epic style. No Spanish epic extant or traceable in the chronicles is a parody, but examples are to be found elsewhere in medieval Europe, as in the twelfth-century French *Audigier* and *Le Pèlerinage de Charlemagne à Constantinople,* and the early fifteenth-century German-Swiss poem *Der Ring;* in the Renaissance, of course, this genre was widely favoured. Even in a «straight» epic, the poet can exploit a disproportion betwen heroic style and unheroic content, as in *Cantar de Mio Cid* 2745-46, where the squalid and cowardly crime of the Infantes de Carrión is implicitly condemned by being described in a style appropriate to deeds of valour on the battlefield. In the Archpriest's parody, the effect is of pure comedy, not of censure. He uses some of the stock motifs of medieval epic, which are rendered absurd when the combatants are fish and joints of meat: a messenger delivers challenges (1068-76), a *plazo* is fixed (1081*a*), there are comparisons with Alexander the Great (1081*d*) and the Battle of Alarcos (1110*d*), the army is enumerated (1082-93), the battle begins with a series of single combats (1102-09) [32] and turns into a general slaughter (1113-23), and some of the infidel prisoners are hanged (1125-26). To heighten the comedy, the fate of some combatants is carefully adjusted to their normal treatment on the way to the table: castration of capons (1107*b*), hanging of sides of bacon (1125*d*). Some, but not all, of these parodic features are present in the analogues described in Kemlin Laurence's article, and these contain other parodic elements that the Archpriest does not use. The parodic procession is, however, found by Mrs. Laurence to be the Archpriest's original contribution.

7. The lament for Trotaconventos (1520-78). Discussed by Lecoy (*Recherches,* 200-212), Green (*Spain,* i, 62-67), Zahareas (*Art,* 209-217) and Rafael Lapesa, «El tema de la muerte en el *Libro de buen amor*», *Estudios dedicados a James Homer Herriott* (University of Wisconsin, 1966), pp. 127-144. They disagree on how much of the lament is parodic and how much serious, but it is not necessary to decide this question

---

[32] Corominas, commentary, 426, points out that Juan Ruiz skilfully combines the enumeration of Cuaresma's army with the narrative of single combats, whereas the analogous French text has two enumerations before the battle begins. For the parodic use of epic motifs, see also B 15, below.

here. [33] The final section of the lament — the epitaph composed by the protagonist for the go-between's tomb (1576-78) — will, however, repay further study. It is generally recognized (for example, by Zahareas, *Art*, 131) that this is a parodic epitaph, but it has not, so far as I know, yet been pointed out that it parodies one particular epitaph, that of Achilles in the *Libro de Alexandre:*

Fallo entre los otros
    un sepulcro ondrado
todo de buenos uiessos
    a derredor orllado
quieno uersifico
    fue ome bien letrado
ca puso grant razon
    en poco de ditado

Achildes soe que iago
    so este marmol cerrado
el que ouo a Ector
    el troiano domado
matome por la planta
    Paris el periurado
a furto sin sospecha
    seyendo desarmado. [34]

ffízele un pitafio
    pequeño con dolor,
la tristeza me fizo
    ser rrudo trobador,
todos los que lo oyeren,
    por Dios nuestro Señor,
la oración fagades
    por la vieja de amor.

«Urraca só que yago
    so esta sepultura,
en quanto fuy al mundo
    ove vyçio e soltura,
con buena rrazón muchos casé,
    non quise locura,
cay en una ora
    so tierra del altura.

Prendióme syn sospecha
    la muerte en sus rredes,
parientes e amigos
    aquí non me acorredes,
obrad bien en la vida,
    a Dios non lo erredes,
que byen como yo morí
    asy todos morredes.» (1575-77)

[33] It may be noted in passing, as a literary curiosity, that W. B. Yeats wrote a poem on a similar theme: *John Kinsella's Lament for Mrs. Mary Moore*, with the refrain «What shall I do for pretty girls / Now my old bawd is dead?» (*The Collected Poems*, London, 1950, 383-384).

[34] *Libro de Alexandre*, ed. R. S. Willis (Elliott Monographs in the Romance Languages and Literatures 32, Princeton-Paris, 1934), sts. 330-331 in Willis's composite numbering. The quotation is from MS. *O. Alexandre* has long been presented by students of the *Libro* as the Archpriest's only Castilian source, and a number of specific debts have been noted. Yet, despite Corominas' statement in the prologue to his edition (p. 8) that he carried out «Un cotejo total y a fondo, verso por verso, palabra por palabra, del texto de Juan Ruiz, en todos sus aspectos, con... el *Libro de Alexandre* y demás fuentes menores», there still remains work to be done in the comparison of the two texts. There is also a need for more investigation of the Archpriest's vernacular sources, since the *Alexandre* is not the only one: see A. D. Deyermond and Roger M. Walker, 'A Further Vernacular Source for the *Libro de buen amor*', BHS XLVI (1969), 193-200. The further source referred to is the *Libro del cavallero Zifar*.

There may be a reminiscence of the *Alexandre* in the introductory stanza: the author of Achilles' epitaph was a great poet, while sadness turned the Archpriest into a *rrudo trobador*. In the epitaph itself, the debt is obvious: *Libro* 1576a is almost identical with *Alexandre* 331a; *Libro* 1576bc, like *Alexandre* 331b, sums up the deceased's career on earth; *Libro* 1576d and *Alexandre* 331c deal with the moment of death; and *Libro* 1577a and *Alexandre* 331d complain that the death was not only sudden but treacherous, *syn sospecha*. The main point of this is, I suspect, the Archpriest's joy in a literary parody, but he probably intended the equation of a go-between with a great warrior to shed an ironic light on the go-between's activities. It may also be that here, as in the battle between Cuaresma and Carnal, he wished to encourage a more sceptical attitude to military glory than that displayed by the epic poets or the *Libro de Alexandre*.

B. *Incidental parodies*

What follows is only a partial list, and any reader will be able to add further examples of his own. Juan Ruiz's taste for the incidental parody is, however, sufficiently illustrated by the examples given here. The parodic nature of some of these passages has already been pointed out by previous students of the *Libro*.

1. Parodic application of a scriptural text (105-6):

> Como dize Salomón, e dize la verdat,
> que las cosas del mundo todas son vanidat,
> todas son pasaderas, van se con la edat,
> ssalvo amor de Dios, todas sson lyviandat.
>
> E yo, desque vi la dueña partida e mudada,
> dixe: «querer do non me quieren ffaría una nada,
> rresponder do non me llaman es vanidad provada.»—
> partí me de su pleito, pues de mí es rredrada.

The text is given first, with apparent seriousness, but the next stanza reveals that it is to be heeded only when bad luck in love makes any other course impossible. See Zahareas (*Art of Juan Ruiz*, pp. 16-17).

2. Sententious style devalued (111):

> Una fabla lo dize que vos digo agora,
> que una ave sola nin bien canta nin bien llora;
> el mastel syn la vela non puede estar toda ora,
> nin las verças non se crían tan bien sin la noria.

The proverb in 111*b* and the comparison in 111*c* provide a rising stylistic level, which is rendered absurd by the bathos of 111*d,* with its equation of woman with cabbage. Yet, although the content of 111*d* can only be comic, its form is the same as in 111*c*.

3. Comic use of ecclesiastical comparison (242*c*): the defeated war-horse has *rrodillas desolladas, faziendo muchas prizes.* [35]

4. The *Ubi sunt? topos* applied to an incongruous subject (243-244):

> Los quadriles salidos, somidas las yjadas,
> el espinazo agudo, las orejas colgadas;
> vídolo el asno nesçio, rrixo bien tres vegadas;
> diz: «conpañero sobervio; ¿dó son tus enpelladas
>
> ¿Dó es tu noble freno e tu dorada silla?
> ¿dó es tu sobervia, dó es la tu rrenzilla?
> sienpre byvrás mesquino e con mucha manzilla,
> vengue la tu sobervia tanta mala postilla». [36]

5. Parodic use of the inexpressibility *topos* [37] (421-422):

> Plázeme byen, te digo, que algo non te devo;
> eres de cada día logrero e das a rrenuevo;
> tomas la grand vallena con el tu poco çevo.
> Mucho más te diría, salvo que non me atrevo.

[35] See María Rosa Lida de Malkiel, «Nuevas notas para la interpretación del *Libro de buen amor*», *NRFH,* XIII (1959), 17-82, at p. 26.

[36] Lecoy, *Recherches,* pp. 125-126, points out that this parody is already present in the Archpriest's source. For this *topos* in general, see Étienne Gilson, *Les Idées et les lettres* (Paris, 1932), pp. 9-38; and for Spanish, see Anna Krause, *Jorge Manrique and the Cult of Death in the Cuatrocientos* (Berkeley, 1937). This passage is discussed by Zahareas, *Art,* pp. 213-214.

[37] See Curtius, *European Literature,* pp. 159-162.

> Porque de muchas dueñas mal querido sería,
> e mucho garçón loco de mi profaçaría;
> por tanto non te digo el diezmo que podría;
> pues cállate e callemos, Amor, vete tu vya.

The Archpriest makes the *topos* doubly comic: his reason for not giving a full account of the subject is not the usual one, the subject's greatness, but rather the author's fear of retaliation; and this fear is itself absurd, since he has already said more than enough to make enemies.

6. The Spring love-lyric devalued by sordid detail (463):

> «Yo era enamorado de una dueña en Abryl;
> estando delante ella, sossegado e muy omyl,
> vyno me desçendimiento a las narizes muy vyl:
> por pereza de alympiar me perdy la dueña gentil.»

The April setting and the lover's humility before his lady conjure up the atmosphere of many medieval courtly lyrics, such as the *Razón de amor* or the English *Alison,* composed not long before the Libro. [38] The violent incongruity between the first and second halves of this stanza, between the implied promise of undying courtly devotion and the actual failure to perform even a minimal act of courtesy, parodies this genre and casts doubt on all courtly protestations. [39] The Spring love-lyric is parodied in a different way in the episode of the *Clérigos de Talavera* (B15, below). More conventional use of it is found at the beginning of the triumph of Don Amor and Don Carnal, where the return of these *dos emperadores* is greeted by sunshine, trees and birds (1210-11), though even here there is a disconcerting change of stylistic level in the next stanza, with *triperas* joining in the welcome. [40]

7. Statement of a Courtly Love principle turned into an attack on women's character (467-469):

Stanza 467 concludes the *exemplum* of the lazy wooers, and states

[38] See James J. Wilhelm, *The Cruelest Month. Spring, Nature and Love in Classical and Medieval Lyrics* (New Haven, 1965). *Alison* is in R. T. Davies, *Medieval English Lyrics. A Critical Anthology* (London, 1963), pp. 67-68.
[39] This passage is discussed by Zahareas, *Art,* 84-85, but he believes that it, like the rest of the *exemplum,* is a parody of epic style.
[40] For this shift of emphasis from sex to food, cf. A5d, above.

a principle of Courtly Love: never be lazy or unmannerly in serving
your lady:

> «Buscad con quien casedes, que la dueña non se paga
> de perezoso torpe nin que vileza faga».—
> por ende mi amigo, en tu coraçón non yaga
> nin tacha nin vyleza de que dueña se despaga.

The following stanzas, however, subvert the principle while pretend-
ing to amplify it:

> Ffaz le una vegada la verguença perder,
> por aquesto faz mucho sy la podieres aver;
> desque una vez pierde vergüença la muger,
> más diabluras faze de quantas omne quier.

> Talente de mugeres, ¿quién le podría entender,
> sus malas maestrías e su mucho mal saber?
> Quando son ençendidas e mal quieren fazer,
> alma e cuerpo e fama todo lo dexan perder. (468-469)

That is, the true argument against laziness in love is that a display of
energy will not only overcome any woman's resistance, but will so
stimulate her sexual desire and sexual adventurousness that they know
no bounds.

8.   Another Courtly Love principle subverted (485):

> Por ende te castiga, non dexes lo que pides;
> non seas Pitas Pajas, para otro non errides;
> con dezires fermosos a la muger conbydes;
> desque te lo prometa, guarda non lo olvides.

But the reason given for the generally accepted principle that a lover
should never leave his lady is —as the preceding story of Pitas Payas
makes clear— that a woman left on her own will sleep with the first
man to approach her. [41]

---

[41] The story is discussed by Lecoy, *Recherches,* pp. 158-160; L. G. Moffatt,
«Pitas Payas», *South Atlantic Studies for Sturgis E. Leavitt* (Washington, 1953),
pp. 29-38; and Zahareas, *Art,* pp. 85-91. None of these discussions, however,
deals with the parody considered here.

9. Parody of rhyme-scheme (487):

> Dyz la muger entre dientes: «otro Pedro es *aqueste,*
> más garçón e más ardit qu'el primero que *ameste;*
> el primero apost *deste* non vale más que un *feste,*
> con *aqueste* e por *este* faré yo, sy Dios me *preste».*

Occasional internal rhyme is a well-known poetic device, but its excessive use in the second half of this stanza (the rhyme words are italicized) makes the convention break down in breathless absurdity. The Archpriest is, as Zahareas shows, always serious about his own artistic merits, but this seriousness need not exclude a demonstration that his mastery of his medium extends to an ability to draw comic effects from it.

10. Parodic baptism (776, 778):

> La puerca, que se estava so los sauzes loçanos,
> fabló contra el lobo, dixo dechos non vanos;
> diz: «señor abbad compadre, con estas santas manos
> bautizat a mis fijuelos, por que mueran cristianos...»

> Abaxóse el lobo ally so aquel sabze
> por tomar el cochino que so la puerca yaze;
> dióle la puerca del rrosto, echóle en el cabçe;
> en la canal del molino entró, que mal le plaçe.

This is so well known, and so generally recognized as a parody, that further comment would be superfluous.

11. The ass as *juglar cazurro* (894-900). This episode is discussed by Lecoy (*Recherches*, pp. 140-142); see also Ian Michael's article in the present volume. The main point of the story is that the ass annoys the sick lion, escapes, is lured back and killed; the lion then terrorizes the other animals into offering him the largest share of the ass's body. Parody is to be found, not in this plot, but in the incidental description: the ass is a *juglar* (894*a*, 899*d*) — in fact, a *juglar cazurro* (*sus caçurias*, 895*a*), who plays the drum (894*c*, 895*c*, 898*b*, 899*d*), and sings and dances (899*b*). [42]. He is gullible, and is easily taken in by *la gulhara*

---

[42] See Menéndez Pidal, *Poesía juglaresca*, pp. 232-233.

juglara (896*d*), who praises him for the *solaz* he gives (897*c*, 898*a*). [43]
Thus the *juglar cazurro* is shown to be ludicrously unaware of his
offence, and foolishly ready to listen to praise of his art. And, of
course, he is literally an ass. There is no need to assume that this is
a hostile parody —after all, the Archpriest wrote songs for *juglares
cazurros,* and it seems much more likely that he is, as in many other
parts of the book, merely revelling in an absurd spectacle. [44]

12. The musical goat (1218*cd*):

al cabrón que está gordo el muy [mal] gelo pynta,
faze[l'] faze[r] : ¡ve! valando en bos e doble quinta.

[*S:* faze faze]

As with the previous case, the parody lies in the perfomance of the
professionally correct actions (here expressed by the technical vocabulary of music) by an absurdly incongruous perfomer.

13. The final advantage of *dueñas chicas* (1617):

Ssyenpre quis muger chica más que grande nin mayor,
non es desaguisado del grand mal ser foydor,
del mal tomar lo menos, dízelo el sabidor,
por ende de las mugeres la mejor es la menor.

This is discussed by Lida de Malkiel (*Masterpieces,* pp. 48-49). In
stanzas 1606-16, Juan Ruiz has used only direct praise and simile, and
has omitted *sententia,* which was a common device in eulogies. In
the final stanza, *sententia* is used, and it devalues and renders absurd
all that has gone before.

[43] The normal meaning of *solaz* in this kind of context is the pleasure to
be derived from poetry of high quality, as in *Libro de Alexandre,* 3*b,* though
the poetry need not be learned: see Corominas, commentary, 348, and cf. *Libro,*
1633*b,* and *Libro de Apolonio,* ed. C. C. Marden (Elliott Monographs, 6 and
11-12, Princeton-Paris, 1917-22), 428*a.* This seems to be the meaning here,
though the Archpriest elsewhere uses the word to mean pleasure in general
(e.g. 1342*b,* 1375*d,* 1381*b,* 1402*b,* 1609*b*).
[44] There seem to be reminiscences of this parody in 1405*c* and 1440*d* (and,
in general, sts. 1437-41).

14. The book's moral effectiveness subverted (1627):

> Buena propiedat ha do quier que sea,
> que si lo oye alguno que tenga muger fea,
> o sy muger lo oye que su marido vil sea,
> fazer a Dios serviçio en punto lo desea.

The Archpriest appears to make, in the first and fourth lines of this stanza, the conventional claim that his book will turn people to love of God and to good works (which are listed in 1628). The conditions on which it will do so are, however, given in the second and third lines: the book will turn people to the love of God only if the unattractiveness of their sexual partner gives them no incentive for anything else. This subversive parody of the *topos* of good intentions may be compared with A1, A2 and B1, above; it is discussed by Américo Castro, [45] Zahareas (*Art*, 40-42) and Corominas (commentary, 598-600).

15. Parody of epic and of courtly literature in the opening stanzas of the *Clérigos de Talavera* (1690-93):

> Allá en Talavera, en las calendas de abril,
> llegadas son las cartas del arçobispo don Gil,
> en las quales venía el mandado non vil,
> tal que si plugo a uno pesó más que a dos mill.

> Aqueste açipreste que traya el mandado,
> bien creo que lo fizo más con midos que de grado;
> mandó juntar cabildo, a prisa fue juntado,
> coydando que traya otro mejor mandado.

> Ffabló este açipreste e dixo bien ansy:
> «Sy pesa a vos otros, bien tanto pesa a mí;
> ¡ay! ¡viejo mezquino! ¡en qué envegeçí!
> ¡en ver lo que veo e en ver lo que vy!»

> Llorando de sus ojos, començó esta rraçón,
> diz: «el papa nos enbía este constituçión,
> he vos lo a dezir, que quiera o que non,
> maguer que vos lo digo con rravia de mi coraçón.»—

---

[45] *España en su historia. Cristianos, moros y judíos* (Buenos Aires, 1948), p. 427.

The episode as a whole has been frequently discussed —for example, by Menéndez Pidal (*Poesía juglaresca,* pp. 205-207), Lecoy (*Recherches,* pp. 229-236) and Zahareas (*Art,* pp. 105-112). As is well known, it is an adaptation of the *Consultatio Sacerdotum,* to which the Archpriest adds many individual touches. Among these is the parodic element. Zahareas (*Art,* p. 108) says that «The dolorous style resembles that of the epics and *romances* in describing loss.» It is, I think, possible to go further than this, and to find in the first four stanzas other reminiscences of epic tradition which are used for a parodic purpose.

The arrival of a messenger bearing a letter of challenge is a widespread epic motif [46] (and, of course, it occurs elsewhere, especially in Arthurian literature). In 1690*b* and 1691*a,* the message delivered by an archpriest is from the Archbishop, but the clerics of Talavera treat it as a hostile challenge. Another epic motif, frequently associated with that of the receipt of letters, is the council or assembly. [47] Here, the Archbishop's letters, conveying the Pope's command, are delivered to a specially-summoned chapter-meeting (1691*c*). This use of epic motifs in the context of clerical concubinage parodies the epic and implies a caustic comment on the priests of Talavera. The wording also seems to derive from the epic tradition: the antithesis of *plazer* and *pesar,* designed to emphasize antagonistic groupings of characters, is an effective and much-used device in the *Cantar de Mio Cid,* and here it is found in 1690*d* and 1692*b.* 1691*b, más con midos que de grado,* closely resembles *CMC* 84, and there is some reason to believe that this is a traditional formula in Spanish epic. [48] Even clearer debts to this tradition are *llorando de sus ojos* (1593*b*), which is frequent in *CMC,* and the archpriest's lament (1692*cd*), which is very close to the wording of laments in the *Siete Infantes de Lara* and *Roncesvalles.* [49] It is hard to believe that so many resemblances concentrated in a few stanzas are mere coincidence, and deliberate parody seems a much more likely explanation.

The epic tradition is not, however, alone in providing material for this section of the *Libro.* The Treasurer's comparison of his and his

---

[46] Albert B. Lord, *The Singer of Tales* (Harvard Studies in Comparative Literature, 24, Cambridge, Mass., 1960), pp. 82-83.

[47] Lord, pp. 68-81. For the two motifs together, see Lord, p. 96.

[48] See my *Epic Poetry and the Clergy. Studies on the Mocedades de Rodrigo* (London, Tamesis, 1969), p. 168. On the traditional formula, see Lord, ch. 3.

[49] This is the resemblance pointed out by Zahareas. The near-identity of wording at this point between the two epics is probably due to common use of a tradition, not to direct borrowing; see my «The Singer of Tales and Mediaeval Spanish Epic», *BHS,* XLII (1965), 1-8, at p. 3,

mistress Teresa's love with that of Blancaflor and Flores, and with that of Tristan, is very well known, but, though it is intended to shed an ironic light on clerical behaviour —and perhaps on Courtly Love fiction—, it is not really parodic. Parody of secular love-literature is, nevertheless, mingled with that of the epic: indeed, it serves to introduce the whole episode. A medieval reader (or hearer) confronted with *Allá en Talavera, en las calendas de abril* would almost certainly expect a love-poem to follow; the expectations aroused by this line would be less specific than those aroused by 463*ab* (see B6, above), since less detail is given, but they would not be radically different. April[50] is in the medieval lyric —even more than in everyday life— the time for the return of joyous sexual love, and Juan Ruiz acknowledges this earlier in the *Libro* when he describes the defeat of Cuaresma by Carnal, and the triumphal procession of Carnal and Amor. Yet these expectations are quickly disappointed in the present episode, for April brings not the return of love but its sudden prohibition. In stanza 463, the spring love-lyric was parodied by juxtaposition with revolting physical detail; here it is parodied by sudden reversal.[51]

C. Conclusions

Most of the Archpriest's parodies considered above fit into one of two categories: either the object parodied is ecclesiastical, or it is a form of secular literature, and often of love-literature.[52] In the first category come the learned sermon (A1), monastic sign-language (A2*b*), scriptural exegesis (A2*d* —and cf. the *topos* of good intentions, B14), the canonical hours (A4), a scriptural text (B1), kneeling at prayer (B3), and baptism (B10). The parody of the genres and techniques of secular literature covers the dawn-song (A4), the *pastorela* (A5), the spring love-lyric (B6, B15), two principles of Courtly Love (B7, B8), the epic

[50] Or the end of March: *Alison* is set «Betwene Mersh and Averil». Thus it makes no difference whether we interpret *en las calendas* as meaning April or the end of March. The beginning of March —*dia de Sant Meder* (951*a*)— does not have the same connotation.

[51] It may be noted that in the first eleven and a half lines of the General Prologue to the *Canterbury Tales,* Chaucer similarly arouses expectations of a spring love-lyric, only to change course without warning in the second half of line 12. Clearly, this question, especially as it is complicated by the association of sexual love and pilgrimages, cannot be dealt with here, but I propose to discuss it elsewhere.

[52] The exceptions are disputation and degrees (A2*a*), the *translatio studii* (A2*c*), and legal procedure and notarial style (A3).

(A6, B15), a hero's epitaph (A7), sententious style (B2 — and cf. B13), *Ubi sunt?* (B4), the inexpressibility *topos* (B5), and internal rhyme (B9). With this list may be associated the *juglar cazurro* (B11) and music (B12).

In general, it may be said that the Archpriest has two favourite methods of parody: reversal, as in A5 or B15, and incongruous association, as in A4 or B6. Either of these methods may be combined with that of multiple parody, which is seen at its most ambitious and complex in A2, but which also occurs in several other cases, as with A4.

The main purpose of this article has been to shed further light on the nature and the extent of parody in the *Libro,* rather than to use the evidence of parody to settle such general problems as the Archpriest's intentions in composing the book. Nevertheless, a little attention must be given to the point just mentioned. It can certainly not be assumed that Juan Ruiz's parodies of religious texts and practices imply hostility to religion.[53] Such parodies may, on the contrary, develop most freely within a secure framework of belief —thus we find that some of the most daring goliardic parodies are the work of eminent churchmen whose orthodoxy is unquestioned. Green («On Juan Ruiz's Parody», pp. 12-24, and *Spain,* i, pp. 37-38) supplies a great deal of evidence from a wide variety of sources to show that parody need not involve hostility or rejection, and we have just been reminded of this point by the reissue of Iona and Peter Opie's *The Lore and Language of Schoolchildren:*

> Parody, that most refined form of jeering, gives an intelligent child a way of showing independence without having to rebel... [They] are not necessarily irreverent. It is just a thing they do. It is as if children know instinctively that anything wholly solemn, without a smile behind it, is only half alive.[54]

Moreover, parody —including parody of religious objects— can have a moral or even a mystical purpose.[55] Is parody in the *Libro,* then, a weapon of morality? This view is suggested by Gybbon-Mony-

---

[53] Among those who rightly make this point is Lida de Malkiel, *Masterpieces,* p. 9. Its formulation by Pierre Le Gentil, *La Poésie lyrique espagnole,* i, pp. 454-458, is more detailed, but slightly exaggerated.

[54] Oxford Paperbacks, 1967 (first published 1959), p. 87.

[55] For examples, see Raby, *Secular Latin Poetry,* ii, 215-219; M. O'C. Walshe, *Medieval German Literature. A Survey* (London, 1962), 285-286; Peter Dronke, *Medieval Latin and the Rise of European Love-Lyric,* i (Oxford, 1965), 62; and Bruce W. Wardropper, *Historia de la poesía lírica a lo divino en la Cristiandad occidental* (Madrid, 1958).

penny («Autobiography») when he argues that the book is a parody of the erotic pseudo-autobiography, and it is generalized by Le Gentil («A propos des *Cánticas*», 139), who believes that Juan Ruiz parodies everything connected with *loco amor*. This is entirely possible, and there are certainly some parodies in the *Libro* that have a moral point. Yet we must be careful. If parodies of religious observances need not imply hostility to religion, then parodies of the dawn-song or the spring love-lyric need not (though they may) imply hostility to Courtly Love or to any secular love.

Finally, we have seen that the Archpriest delights in multiplying parodies, and in displaying his linguistic and conceptual inventiveness in this way as in others. He is as likely to parody the *topos* of good intention, or the elaborate techniques of interpretation, as to choose anything else as victim. This prevalence of parody should intensify the caution with which we would in any case approach any attempt to extract a consistent overall meaning from such a diverse work —and one probably composed over such a long period— as the *Libro*. It should, in particular, make us hesitate to assume that because the Archpriest is deeply serious in some sections of his work, he is always serious in his statements about the work as a whole; equally, we should be unwise to conclude that because he very often indulges in parody, he can never be serious. The only conclusions that can safely be drawn from the evidence assembled above are that parody is to Juan Ruiz not merely a convenient device, but a way of looking at the world, and, perhaps, that this parodic vision of the world —inherited from the goliardic tradition but going beyond it— may account for some of the ambiguity and shifting planes of reality that have sometimes been attributed to Arabic or Hebrew influence. [56]

Westfield College,
University of London

---

[56] Parody is not, of course, confined to the Western European tradition, and María Rosa Lida de Malkiel rightly points out («Nuevas notas», 24-5) that parodies of sacred and profane texts are to be found in the *maqāmat*, and specifically in the *Book of Delights*. However, the sources and analogues that have been discovered for individual parodies in the *Libro* have been Western, and usually goliardic; and the goliardic tradition would be familiar to the Archpriest through his training and profession. Thus there is no need to look beyond that tradition, which, unlike the *maqāmat*, relies heavily on parody, when we are considering the origin of the Archpriest's parodic vision.

This article, like all the others in the present volume, has benefited greatly from the comments of the editor, Gerald Gybbon-Monypenny, and of other contributors who read the typescript (in this case, Janet Chapman and Roger

POSTSCRIPT

Carmelo Gariano, *El mundo poético de Juan Ruiz* (Madrid, 1968), published while the present article was in press, contains a chapter entitled «La sonrisa del Arcipreste» (pp. 87-119). Part of this (101-107) deals with parody. Gariano's work adds very little to what has already been published on this subject, and it does not make necessary any revision of the article, but it may be helpful to note here the parodies that he discusses. Of those that I have labelled «set-piece parodies», he deals with the trial (pp. 100, 102), the canonical hours (104-105) and the Carnal-Cuaresma episode (102-104). The story of the Greeks and the Romans is discussed as a comic situation (107-108), but with only a passing reference to parody. One of the *serrana* episodes is presented as an example of grotesque visual caricature (113-115), but literary parody is not considered. There is no discussion in this chapter of the prose sermon or of Trotaconventos' epitaph. Of the incidental parodies, only two are mentioned by Gariano: B 6, the lazy lover (p. 112), and B 10, the mock baptism (p. 106). In the first of these cases, Gariano does not recognize any parodic element.

Walker). I have had the additional advantage of having my typescript read by Professor T. R. Hart, of the University of Oregon, and his comments have saved me from a number of errors and omissions. I need hardly add that none of these friends can be held responsible for the views that I have expressed.

PETER N. DUNN

'De las figuras del arçipreste'

The 'personal fallacy' which for so long enveloped the *Libro de buen amor* like a fog, flattening the perspectives and creating strange shadows has, fortunately, dissipated itself. The autobiography of the Archpriest is seen for the fiction that it is, not as a scandalous exhibition by a wolf in priest's cloth. It is true that the air sometimes becomes clouded, at his mention of 'esta prisión', but this is of small importance. The *Libro* is a poem, a thing made, and we may suppose that, like other artefacts, it has been shaped by the interplay of invention and judgement, a sense of the whole imposing some —however little— restraint upon the parts. This is where our difficulties start. It is still open to us to debate what the fiction means, how the varied and unpredictable structure moving from narrative to song, from personal adventure to allegorical vision, can be shown to entail a meaning. And Juan Ruiz clearly willed the debate, though he would be surprised by some of the contributions to it. I do not propose to contribute directly to it, except insofar as the examination of certain details and their relation to a context suggests a response which may be found to be relevant in a broader sense.

Elisha Kane broke new ground in 1930 with his article on «The Personal Appearance of Juan Ruiz», [1] where he showed that stanzas 1485-89 are not the portrait of an individual taken from life, and that we cannot expect to discover in them the true appearance of the author. Rather, they present the picture of a tall, handsome, vigorous, gay young man, who would make the girls' hearts flutter. «*L'altezza è mezza bellezza;* the old bawd is merely outlining, after the conventional pattern, a physically perfect lover» (p. 104). Kane then goes on to explain the discordant features: the long nose, the large ears, thick neck

---

[1] Elisha K. Kane, «The Personal Appearance of Juan Ruiz», *MLN*, XLV (1930), 103-109.

79

and lips, as traits having an erotic significance. Nose and ears, in popular jokes and stories, are a visible index to the size and vigour of what is hidden from view, and Kane cites some piquant examples to establish his point. Abundance of hair is still recognizable masculine plumage, and deep voice requires no footnotes. Kane thus leaves us with the generalized portrait of an attractive man, with some sexual innuendoes. I propose to re-examine this passage in the light of the medieval science of physiognomy, so as to discover what its separate details signify, the small as well as the large. We shall discover contradictions which underline certain motifs in the narrator's career; it is also, I think, an intimate part of the intricate convergence of three fascinating figures, —Trotaconventos, the Archpriest, and Doña Garoça. (For convenience I refer to the fictional narrator as the Archpriest, and to the author of the book as Juan Ruiz).

But first, let us assume the present status of the portrait, and examine the context in which it is presented. This means observing Trotaconventos's use of it as a phase in her persuasion of Doña Garoça, and also her stance before the reader or audience. Later, after scanning the features of the Archpriest, we shall return to the matter of Trotaconventos's motives, discuss how the narrator's temperament is revealed in his amorous career, and attempt an answer to the perplexing questions: why does Doña Garoça accept him, and then on so different a footing from that which he had hoped? and why did he endure so spiritual an association?

Following Kane's observations, we would have to say that in her presentation of the Archpriest, the go-between is speaking in character, but in two distinct ways. First, she is insinuating herself in ways which her talent, her profession, and her role in the book all demand that she should. Speaking to the lonely and (to Trotaconventos's mind) deprived nun, she baits Doña Garoça's fancy with this picture of a dream-lover, tall, dark, striding and singing: «Sodes las monjas guarrdadas, deseosas, loçanas...» (1491a). She presumes to touch the woman's hesitant and concealed inclinations, enticing them to the level of intention. Seeming to respect the nun's scruples, like the smith who damps the fire in order to confine and concentrate its heat she adds, «mas yo non vos conssejo eso que vos creedes» (1480b). She disguises with suave advocacy the cloven hoof which was, so bluntly, the theme of Doña Garoça's last *exemplum,* the robber who sold his soul to the Devil (stanzas 1454-79). Having in mind this wily circumspection, this foxy encirclement of the victim with soft assurances, we may wonder whether the coarseness which Kane detected is conveyed to Doña Garoça, and she alert to it, or whether it is an innuendo to be picked up by the more broadly tuned ear of the listener or reader. If Doña Garoça catches the sexual hint, will Trotaconventos be risking her success in this delicate suit by indicating facial members which point to those below the Archpriest's belt? No, the nun is no fool, she has known the old bawd before, whose mere presence announces her business. In the battle of the *exempla* the nun scores some palpable hits — or does she protest too much, as a prelude to stepping gaily into the pit? No, Doña Garoça's resistance is firm and shrewd, and we can see later that she has been a match for Trotaconventos, since she is equal to herself. Doña Garoça is not a demure girl to be frightened by Trotaconventos's insinuations. Trotaconventos knows this is so, and by her former association, which she recalls as they meet (1344-46), she exerts some kind of moral blackmail, presuming upon past intimacies. Secondly, if Trotaconventos's part in the presence of Doña Garoça is to entice and coax, to make the worse appear the better reason, we may also reasonably expect a bawd to be bawdy. If the Archpriest had a long nose, why should she not mention it? — good looks are not everything! This is a joke between Trotaconventos and the *Libro*'s public. The narrator is involved, too, and on more than one plane. Trotaconventos was talking about him, and he is now telling us. The Archpriest does not appear dissatisfied with his portrait. «Es ligero, valiente, byen mançebo de días...» (1489a) is a fine affirmative phrase to end a testimonial, and it confirms the opinion he has of himself. But Trotaconventos must be a crafty composer of testimonials, and it is legitimate to ask ourselves whether this one, like many a character-reference, also covertly implies what it conceals. We think of what we know of the narrator: his infinite capacity for being outwitted; the comic distance which is maintained between desire and performance; his conviction of being ruled by Venus — a destiny which obstinately evades him.[2] Is the portrait, then, a simple irony, like that of the failed entertainer who continues to believe his publicity manager's 'image' of him? Or is the 'image', perhaps, as ambiguous as the reality?

[2] I am not convinced that Don Melón has to be understood as a transformation or continuation of the Archpriest, making the episode of Doña Endrina the culmination of the Archpriest's career. However, the matter is admittedly open to argument. Cf. Fernando Lázaro, «Los amores de Don Melón y doña Endrina. Notas sobre el arte de Juan Ruiz», *Arbor* 62 (1951), 210-236; Roger M. Walker, «Towards an Interpretation of the *Libro de buen amor*», *BHS*, XLIII (1966), 1-10.

Up to this point I have indicated how the context of the portrait raises questions of itself. These questions are about directions in which Kane's study did not go, because his interpretation did not lead him there. To repeat Kane's argument in brief, the description is a conventional portrait of a physically attractive man, sexually vigorous, and the aesthetic defects have a colloquial sense which reaffirms its meaning, but on a coarser level. That the portrait is conventional has been affirmed repeatedly since Edmond Faral studied the prescriptions of medieval *artes poeticae* and word-portraits based on them.[3] Personal descriptions in late antique and medieval literature are stylized representations of beauty or ugliness, and their aim is persuasive force, not factual accuracy. The part played by convention can be seen in the set order which writers followed, starting at the head, and finishing at the feet. Faral made his point with abundant literary evidence, and it is now generally assumed that Trotaconventos's picture of the Archpriest is one more example of this literary tradition.[4] To suggest that a medieval word-picture must be 'rhetorical', however, is to go beyond Faral, and leaves two matters out of consideration. First, the choice of details. When a portrait is not merely a case of beauty or ugliness, a praise or a denigration, but a *characterization* (as the portraits of the *Canterbury Tales* certainly are), what is to be attributed to the features, separately and together? How does physique express the inner man? and by what criteria of correspondence? Such criteria can scarcely be literary in their origin. A literary convention may convey what is, essentially, a mode of moral judgement, but it must be sustained by a conviction, on other grounds, of the validity of the correspondence. Second, why does the rhetorical mode, the orderly enumeration, have such tenacity? Is it simply order for order's sake?

The answer to these questions lies in the medieval acceptance of physiognomy as a science which established the relations between the physical and the moral characteristics of persons. This was not an innovation of medieval Europe. Physiognomy had flourished as a branch of medicine, and also as a branch of astrology since ancient times, and one of the earliest separate treatises on the subject was

[3] Edmond Faral, *Les arts poétiques du XIIe et du XIIIe siècle* (Paris, 1924), pp. 75-82.
[4] See, for example, María Rosa Lida, «Notas para la interpretación, influencia, fuentes y texto del *Libro de buen amor*», *RFH*, II (1940), pp. 122-125; Leo Spitzer, «En torno al arte del Arcipreste de Hita», in *Lingüística e historia literaria*, 2nd ed. (Madrid, 1961), pp. 121-123; Anthony N. Zahareas, *The Art of Juan Ruiz* (Madrid, 1965), pp. 144-147.

attributed, inevitably, to Aristotle. [5] The theory of the humours, located in different parts of the body and forming the basis of personality; the effect of a man's stature on the distribution of the 'vital heat', whereby an over-large man would be more sluggish than a small man of the same temperament (and small women more lively than others; see stanzas 1606-17); the medieval synthesis of cosmology and physiology, which gave each planet dominion over an organ or a member; [6] such were the broad foundations in medieval science for this medical psychology which could read character in features, bodily proportion and movement. The grounding of physiognomy in anatomical theory and in astrological medicine gave it universal credence. The abundance of expositions on this subject, [7] and its frequent incorporation into manuals of natural philosophy show how it once filled the need for a general theory of personality. But the treatises stress the practical value also. The physician must know the temperament of the patient and his dominant humour, as well as the conjunctions of the stars and planets, before he chooses his course of treatment. The man of affairs, in assessing his colleagues, rivals, or strangers, the rich householder in choosing his slaves and servants, the merchant his subordinates, the king his advisers, could not do better than to have a thorough knowledge of this guide to character. The *Secretum secretorum*, which contained a section on physiognomy, and was supposedly a book of advice written by Aristotle for Alexander, was the starting-point for all those late medieval treatises *De regimine principum*. [8] It is strange that Hispanists have paid little heed to this subject. The late María Rosa Lida de Malkiel, in a short section of a long article, noted the Archpriest's sanguine temperament, [9] but she relied heavily on the

[5] The pseudo-Aristotelian *De physiognomia*, in the Latin translation by Bartholomeus de Messana, is included in [P.] Richardus Foerster, *Scriptores physiognomonici graeci et latini*, 2 vols. (Leipzig, 1893), together with other ancient and medieval texts which will be referred to in their place.   This edition will be cited as «Foerster».

[6] Jean Seznec, *The Survival of the Pagan Gods* (New York, 1953), ch. II, and W. C. Curry, *Chaucer and the Mediaeval Sciences* (New York, 1926; 2nd ed. 1960) have ample bibliographies on this matter.

[7] e. g., Vincent of Beauvais, *Speculum maius*; Bartholomeus Anglicus, *De proprietatibus rerum*, and Roger Bacon's uncompleted *Scriptum principale*.

[8] See the Introduction by Robert Steele to his edition of Lydgate and Burgh's *Secrees of old Philisoffres* (London, 1894).   Latin texts of *Secretum* (or *Secreta*) *secretorum* are given in Foerster and by Robert Steele in *Opera hactenus inedita Rogeri Baconi*, fasc. 5 (Oxford, 1920).

[9] «Notas..., p. 125.   The editor of this volume has also brought to my attention the doctoral dissertation of André S. Michalski, *Description in Mediaeval Spanish Poetry* (Princeton University, Ph. D., 1964; University Microfilms Reprint, Ann Arbor, 1967).   Attention is given in this work to the use

7

Archpriest of Talavera, who exaggerates the sexual and erotic aspects of every temperament, and is hardly a model of sober disinterest when he pursues his favourite subject.

Trotaconventos begins her description with his *cuerpo bien largo*. [10] Size, so long as proportion is maintained, is not significant, and in a sanguine man it is in keeping with his temperament. On the whole, however, a middle stature is preferred, «qui est non nimis longus nec nimis brevis». [11] The *cabeça non chica* is the first of several ambiguous features: the neck is not over long, and the mouth is not small. The cunning Trotaconventos absolves the Archpriest of the faults of a small head (slyness) and so on, but will not say unequivocally that these features are in perfect proportion. If the head is large, says pseudo-Aristotle, «Quicunque autem habent magnum caput, sensitivi, referuntur ad canes» (cap. lxiv; Foerster II). The physiognomists agree that if the forehead is large, the man is slow, lazy, with a tendency to anger and resentment (pseudo-Aristotle, cap. lxv; Rhazes, [12] cap. xxxi, in Foerster, *Script. phys.* II). Dark hair signifies «rectitudinem et amorem justicie» (*Secretum,* cap. iii) and, taken with the swarthy complexion, suggests the influence of Saturn, a detail to which we shall return. If the neck is not merely 'not too long', but 'short', «Qui vero habet collum breve valde est callidus, defraudator, astutus, et dolosus» (*Secretum,* cap. xi); «callidus et ingeniosus» (Rhazes, cap. xxxix; Vincent of Beauvais, *Spec. nat.,* lib. XXVIII, cap. lxxxvii). The large ears, «qui habet auriculas magnas est valde fatuus, hoc excepto quod erit bone memorie et retencionis» (*Secretum,* cap. ix); «magnae vero ac prominentes stoliditatem et garrulitatem [signant]» (Vincent of Beauvais, *Spec. nat.,* XXVIII, li). *Cejas apartadas:* Kane indicated that joined brows may signify homosexuality, but it is not clear why Trotaconventos should be concerned to deny that the Archpriest is homosexual. In fact she could be exonerating him from other sexual deviations associated with this trait. [13] Since the Ancients, and the Eastern physic-

of physiognomy in some of Juan Ruiz's portraits (especially on pages 68-101). Dr Michalski's thesis is the examination of mediaeval poetic texts for their presentation of, or deviation from, the rhetorical precepts of *descriptio*.

[10] Since the portrait is brief, I shall not refer every feature to its place in the text of the *Libro*.

[11] *Secretum secretorum,* cap. xvii, ed. Steele (see n. 8, above). All quotations from *Secretum* refer to this edition.

[12] *Abubecri Rasis ad Mansorem De Re Medicina Liber II translatus ex arabico in latinum a Gerardo Cremonense,* in Foerster II, 163-179. Rhazes (or Rhases, Rasis al-Rāzī) was the great Persian scholar and practitioner who was physician to the hospital in Baghdad until his death in 925. This work is known in the original as *al-Kitāb al-Manṣūrī*.

[13] «Mettant en équations le proverbe *turpe senilis amor,* la tradition est à

ians from whom the physiognomists' material derives, had no prejudice against joined brows, the medieval writers say nothing, or offer
only vague innuendoes: «Supercilia quibus porriguntur in rectum, mol-
les signat» (Vincent of Beauvais, *Spec. nat.*, XXVIII, lxxxviii). The
upright gait and measured tread is interpreted by Trotaconventos herself; *de buena rraçón,* which is the kernel of what the experts said
(see, for example, *Secretum,* caps. ii, xvi). As to noses, the physiognomists classify with reference to length, breadth, direction, fleshiness,
and many other variations. A nose that is merely *luenga,* then, may
have the bawdy sense which Kane suggested, but note Vincent of
Beauvais: «Narium extremitas longa et subtilis festinationem, stulti-
tiam ac levitatem [significat]» (XXVIII, lii). The redness of the gums
is evidence of the sanguine temperament, and the sonorous voice a
sign of bravery and eloquence (*Secretum,* cap. x; Polemon, *De phy-
siognomonia,* in Foerster, I). On the other hand, small eyes are a bad
sign, indicating a small heart (pseudo-Aristotle, cap. lxiii) or «homo...
malus et stultus» (Rhazes, cap. xxviii), and of the other facial signs,
Secretum says, «Qui vero habet latum os, est bellicosus et audax, et
est loquax et saepe gulosus. Qui habet labia grossa stultus est» (cap.
viii). Big shoulders, of course, always signify courage, and we shall
comment on these contradictions shortly. The color *baço* is rendered
by Chiarini in his recent edition of the *Libro* (Naples, 1964) as 'olivas-
tro', and the greenish tinge is a sure sign, the astrologers say, of the
influence of Saturn in one of his aspects. [14] The *pechos delanteros* are
interpreted in forceful language by a Middle English version of *Secretum:* «tho that haue ribbis bocchynge owtwardes like as they weryn
y-swolle, bene yanglours [i.e., vain talkers], and folis in wordys, and
bene like frusshes and toodes». [15] The *piernas cumplidas* may be well
formed or long, but in neither case does the phrase appear to indicate
any excess. Small feet, however, may be variously interpreted. Thus
Vincent (XXVIII, 104) following Rhazes, says, «Pedes... parvi et pul-

peu près unanime à attribuer à Saturne les amours 'honteux'... 'sales'», A.
Bouché Leclercq, *L'astrologie grecque* (Paris, 1899), 436, n. 1. In the Roman
world it was believed that Saturn was worshipped by the Jews, since their Sab-
bath falls on *Saturni die.* Later, he was regarded as the patron of Muslims, and
Stephanus of Alexandria gave wide currency to the idea that Mahomet was
born under a conjunction of Venus and Saturn (Leclercq 318, 371). Hence, dis-
sidence, heresy, and ultimately, self-destruction may be provoked by Saturn.
More precise references to sexual unorthodoxy promoted by Saturn may be
found in the *Tetrabiblos* of Ptolemy.
[14] Curry, pp. 134-135.
[15] James Yonge, *The Gouernaunce of Princes,* in Robert Steele (ed.), *Three
Prose Versions of the Secreta Secretorum,* vol. I (London, 1898), p. 227.

chri fornicationem et iocosum innuunt», but *Secretum* has «duriciem» (cap. xv), and Yonge, «febill and feynte, and like to women» (Steele, *Three Prose Versions,* p. 226). Finally, stanza 1489 gives the signs of a sanguine man, as María Rosa Lida made clear in the article referred to. In a note on p. 125, she quoted a Latin couplet from an «autor desconocido», Albert of Trebizond: «Largus, amans, hilaris, ridens, rubeique coloris, / Cantans, carnosus satis, atque benignus». In fact these lines were already familiar to Vincent of Beauvais (to whom Juan Ruiz is indebted for a great deal of material) who cites them, with similar verses on the other three 'complexions' — choleric, phlegmatic, melancholic — in his treatise on anatomy (*Spec. nat.,* XXXI, lxx).

It is excessively clear, from this array of features, that we must respect the prime injunction of the physiognomist, to judge as a whole, and not by one sign alone (*Secretum,* cap. xvii; Vincent of Beauvais, *Spec. nat.* XXVIII, cxv). The sceptical reader may wonder at this point: why can we not accept the sanguine nature by itself, since it is Trotaconventos's business — in the physiognomists' sense — to put the best complexion on the Archpriest, and leave the rest aside as picturesque detail? The answer would be that where the human form is concerned, medieval art does not know the picturesque, nor the realist notion that the details must appear complete, whether they signify anything or not. The outer man may conceal the inner, to the ignorant eye, but to the knowledgeable eye the outer reveals the inner; isn't this what Juan Ruiz says about his book? In particular, there are deviations from the sanguine type; the Archpriest is notably not *rubei coloris,* but *un poquillo baço.* And when we compare the attributes of the sanguine man with the narrator's achievements there is some disparity; he may have been formed with a natural complexion which is *hilaris,* but his joviality is constantly checked by disappointment, and this in spite of his measured tread which proclaims him master of his destiny, «Cujus passus sunt lati et tardi prosperabitur in omnibus operibus suis et factis» (*Secretum,* cap. 16). Has Trotaconventos, the cynical counterfeiter of 'images', slipped in some of the discordant features in order, more cynically perhaps, to show how she sees the truth about this tiresome client? The short answer is that the dominant humour may be overruled by planetary influence and the zodiac at nativity. Thus, he may be *valiente* («audax») and have big shoulders, yet his eyes will reveal that his initiative fails him when he most needs it. He may well be endowed with the gift of words, and carefree ingenuity; he is also careless enough to lose a lady by confiding in false friends (93-94), he alienates another by giving songs instead of presents (171), and a careless word earns him the resentment of the indispensable Trotaconventos (920-921). A «yanglour», in fact, as his barrel-chest and big ears confirm. He has a fine flow of angry rhetoric which he aims at Don Amor, but the anger is truly against his own failure, not against the god of love. If the *cabeça non chica* is a litotes, it would indicate a bull-like trait, «iracundus», and complement the short neck («callidus»), the thick lips («stultus») in representing what lies behind the carefree countenance: the obstinate and puzzled commitment to a concept of personal destiny which is comic to the extent that it is futile. We recall how he ascribed his amorous personality to the influence of Venus in his horoscope, with no more evidence than his belief that it must be so (stanza 153). This contrasts significantly with the brief but precise horoscopes by which Chaucer objectively characterizes such figures as the Wife of Bath, or Palamon and Arcite, without robbing them of humanity. The Archpriest, though, is his own narrator, his own justifier, the pleader in his own cause, and in ascribing his amorous itch to Venus he has said nothing which deserves to be read seriously as a statement on the human condition or on the power of the will. The irony of it is that he persists in his own reading of his fate, whereas the portents, as revealed by Trotaconventos's portrait, are a much more adequate reflection of the truth. It is true that in the sanguine type, as Vincent of Beauvais expresses it, «sanguis facit boni voti simplices, blandos, hilares, et semper amorosos» (*Spec. nat.* XXXI, 70), but given a favourable horoscope, such a man would also be sharp, alert, and self-sufficient which the Archpriest is not. If the *trotera*'s only indication of his character were in this mention of sanguine temperament, the astute nun might well wonder why such a man should approach her, and why a man of such self-reliance as this should have Trotaconventos continually on call. But the sanguine humour is no guarantee of amorous success. The influence of Venus, on the other hand, means that the subject is attractive to the other sex, endowed with grace, elegant height and bearing, slender, round-face, fair-skinned, with flowing auburn hair (Curry, 108-110). In his appeal to Nature, that is to say. Nature-as-instinct (71-76), he shifts his ground from a special plea to the general one of the average sensual man. It is less blatantly at odds with fact, but no more morally tenable. But then, we do not expect the central character in a comedy to take up an attitude which is morally tenable, unless he has a compensating credulity which allows him to be imposed upon by rogues. Or, unless he is a hypocrite, or is self-deluded, and as Anthony Zahareas has rightly maintained, the 'morality' of the Archpriest's attack on Don Amor is questionable indeed. [16]

I return to the signs of Saturn. The stocky build, the heavy arms, the swarthy hue and black hair all denote the influence of this god. His baleful effect on the Archpriest's career is clearly apparent, for he most commonly frustrates or perverts men's natural inclinations, blunts their talents. [17] So, though the Archpriest is gregarious by nature, he is repeatedly left lamenting his loneliness; being of a trusting disposition, he is cheated; he has the gifts of verse and song, but they fail to move women as they ought; even the tutelage of Don Amor and Doña Venus leaves him where he was before, since he already knew it all. But, for some fatal reason, he cannot practise what he knows. His is a case of *quiero y no puedo,* during most of the game: «¿quál fue la rraçón negra porque non rrecabdé?» (577d). Even the great powers of Trotaconventos can do little for him. The women refuse, or quickly lose interest. The widow —the one who is most satisfyingly infatuated— dies, we suspect, of the aphrodisiacs administered by Trotaconventos (941-943). It need hardly be said that the rough-and-tumble in the mountains with the *serranas* emphasises rather than detracts from my argument. Thus the unflattering features denoting folly, garrulity, petulance, are not random traits, but linked with the Saturnine influence.

This interpretation is confirmed by another fourteenth-century poet, John Gower, in the *Confessio Amantis:*

> Ovide ek seith that love to parforne
> Stant in the hond of Venus the goddesse,
> But whan sche takth hir conseil with Satorne,
> Ther is no grace, and in that time, I gesse,
> Began mi love, of which myn hevynesse
> Is now and evere schal, bot if I spede:
> So wot I noght miself what is to rede.

(Book VIII, 2273-2279, ed. G. C. Macaulay.)

[16] A. N. Zahareas, «Parody of the Canonical Hours: Juan Ruiz's Art of Satire», *MP*, LXII (1964-5), 105-109.
[17] «Its occupation is any one which requires much work and which yields little reward... It denotes... wandering... humiliation... and it does not meet with success in any undertaking.» Abraham Ibn Ezra, *The Beginning of Wisdom,* ed. by Raphael Levy and Francisco Cantera (Baltimore, 1939), p. 194.

In this work, too, the author represents himself as a lover who is urged on by Nature, but is denied fulfilment.   (I have not found any reference in Ovid to the hindrance by Saturn; perhaps Gower meant to ascribe only the first part of his statement to the author of the *Ars amatoria*.)

Thus we can see that the portrait is of a man whose temperament promises success, but who is rendered helpless by some contrary influence. A cynical clown who stumbles over himself, and who can blame his fate for the falls. But the situation is complex, since the provision of the physiognomonical details by which the reader can appreciate the Archpriest's career is not Trotaconventos's prime purpose. In this respect it is an aside to the audience in which, perhaps, she shows that she, the infallible procuress, has had difficulty enough with this client.   In showing by these physical details that he is capable of ruining his own best chances, we may notice a petulant concern for her professional reputation. But whatever her pique (and here we note a parallel with the Archpriest, who once spoke truth to Don Amor, despite himself, and would glady retract for the assurance of success), there is work to be done. The portrait ends with the wholehearted praise of the sanguine man. It is easy to read the old bawd's intention : if a man who is given the most cunning help and brilliantly managed introductions spoils it all with his ill-luck, let us try to fix him up with a nun. She may give him what he wants, but there is ample possibility for the ambiguities of poetic —or goliardic— justice in this affair of priest and nun. If she listens, she will at least be kind. And if his fate cheats him again of his prize, who could better exemplify its fatuity? Quevedo, a sort of seventeenth-century goliard, was also to combine the extreme futility of hopeless langours with the sacrilegious love of nuns, in the *Buscón* (II, ix). But it remains for us to ask why Doña Garoça should agree to receive the Archpriest, after her long and shrewd resistance. She is well past the precarious age, as we see from Trotaconventos's mention of their previous association : «Yo la serví un tiempo, moré y byen diez años» (1333*a*). She is not a weak or careless girl, but a grown woman *de seso bien sano* (1347*a*), old enough and wise enough, even if she had not been a nun, to know that this Devil's advocate cannot persuade her to anything to which she does not already consent inwardly. It would be incongruous, then, to suggest that she is bowled over by a picture of gay sensuality; incongruous, that is, with what we already know of her, and also with the way she conducts herself with the Archpriest (1503-04, especially 1504*d* : «en locura del mundo nunca se tra-

bajava»). I submit that she is as well able to read the signs which
the old bawd has put into the portrait as Trotaconventos herself, and
knows that his urge to achieve amorous successes is a mirage in
which he has lost himself. He does not bear the marks of a desecra-
tor of nuns, and her good sense can tell her that a bawd is more likely
to represent a timid or hopeless amateur than an accomplished amorist.
Doña Garoça responds 'with a love rooted' in charity to a nature which
is at odds with itself. The Arabic origin of the name Garoça ('aru-
sa = 'betrothed', hence 'bride of God') [18] sets the tone of the episode,
but does not entirely explain it. Moreover, what are we to understand
by Trotaconventos's hints of a former association with the nun? Is
this Juan Ruiz's delicate way of way of telling us that she is a Magdalene, formerly in the old procuress's company, or that she was once
a victim of her persuasions? Is her *alto cuello de garça* (1499c) intended to link her in our mind with the fate of Doña Endrina, who
was presented with the same evocative phrase (653b)? In what way
did Trotaconventos, a master of euphemism, 'serve' Doña Garoça (1344a,
1346c)? Doña Endrina remedied her fall by marrying Don Melón;
was Doña Garoça's spiritual marriage the result of a similar experience? The parallels, and the divergences, of the two episodes are sug-
gestive. If Doña Endrina is the case of 'once bitten', could not Doña
Garoça be the case of 'twice shy', except that to characterize it thus
would be a vulgarity more in keeping with the mind of the go-between
than with that of the author. The previous history of the passionate
nun is left in twilight, and rightly so. To fill it in would be a vulgar
pedantic realism. The hints, tenuous though they are, are strong
enough to bear the weight of the episode, and to enable us to see how
she understands the Archpriest from the depth of her human experience, a wretched soul in need of solace rather than the 'solaz' that
he imagines. Eros is many, but in *agape* it becomes one. Whatever
his cynicism, the Archpriest is moved by her love, and sees, after the
event, the greater love which contained it:

> Rescibióme la dueña por su buen servidor,
> ssyenprel' fuy mandado e leal amador,
> mucho de bien me fizo con Dios en lynpio amor,
> en quanto ella fue byva, Dios fue mi guiador.   (1503) [19]

[18] See María Rosa Lida de Malkiel, «Nuevas notas para la interpretación
del *Libro de buen amor*», *NRFH,* XIII (1959), pp. 63-64.
[19] In his recent edition of the *Libro de buen amor* (Madrid, 1967), Professor Joan Corominas claims that the Archpriest's account of his relations with

So we begin to see the old landscape as it appears from a new bend in the road. After the death of Doña Garoça he searches desperately for a new union. Trotaconventos dies, Solomon's *Vae soli* can be heard in the silences, and the Archpriest is headed, in spite of himself, towards reality as time, decay, and death press in upon him. The blemishes of the portrait contribute to maintaining the artistic distance between the reader and the Archpriest; it is of a piece with the diatribes against Don Amor and the later immoderation (1520-1568) before a deceptive world shot through with mortality, a world which he has courted to the top of his bent. Expressed in another way, the portrait is one of many points at which the reader is expected to use the *intellectus* which he has. Far from being rhetorical in the sense that Faral confers on this word —that is to say, exciting praise or blame (*Les arts poétiques...*, p. 76), as far as the reader is concerned its effect is of a different kind. The procuress, ostensibly epideictic, to be sure, has inserted barbs of truth against the obstinate fantasy of sexual prowess. The character is set before a mirror — the ruthless scrutiny of Trotaconventos — and the reader looks over his shoulder at this mixture of ambitious self-regard and puzzled mediocrity.

It is clear that the portrait is decidedly not 'rhetorical' if by this is meant that the poet has followed a purely literary procedure, a convention of the *artes poeticae,* whether it be claimed that he blindly followed or creatively renewed it. The image of the Archpriest is a physiognomonic key, certainly accessible to the poet's audience, and scientific in its origin: «Cum itaque fuerit anima superans corpus et dominans et ei preponderans, et virtus flammea existens in corde non desinat inter ipsam virtutem vitalem existentem in cerebro, tunc sublimatur et augmentatur et declaratur intellectus secundum mensuram... Scias ergo quod oportet te querere signa et vestigia cum pulcritudine nature, scilicet, sciencie phisonomie que est sciencia magna...» Thus says *Secretum secretorum* (cap. i) in its general introduction, in terms which are too commonplace to excite comment. As for the ordering of the details, this too has its scientific reason, for certain parts of the body reveal the character more powerfully than others. The signs to be judged first are those about the head; second, the breast and the shoulders; third, the limbs and their extremities; finally, the abdo-

Doña Garoça is full of euphemisms, and that it all has to be taken in a carnal sense (notes on pp. 558, 560). These are delicate matters of interpretation for which there is no adequate place here. It is undeniable that a bawdy construction can be put upon words in this passage (sts. 1502-1505), but the value and intent of the bawdy have yet to be debated.

men. [20] It is this last section which Trotaconventos leaves blank, with mock pedantry: «dél non vy mas» (1488*d*). Juan Ruiz keeps closely to this order, but with observations on the Archpriest's size, stature and gait, inserted into the early part of the catalogue. Since the treatises on physiognomy frequently do this, it simply confirms the dependence of our author on these works. We can see, at the same time, that the poetic theorists who prescribed the order in which personal features should be listed, did so for precisely the same reason. The literary framework is not rhetorical and arbitrary, an example of a meaningless 'authority' which has to be followed for authority's sake, but a scheme which was held to be scientifically valid, based on the distribution of the humours and the movements of the vital heat. [21]

This would not be the place to discuss at greater length the relation of the Archpriest's love for Doña Garoça to the *Libro* as a whole. But it is clearly of crucial importance; it is the one moment when the frustrated amorist, striving for success, falls, not from *buen amor,* but into it, and finds the worldly love of woman dignified by divine love. After this, the amorous career is virtually, though not virtuously, at an end. The portrait occurs here rather than elsewhere, I think, because of the unique quality of this episode in the Archpriest's story: the laughing, singing, sensual, but strangely disappointed and unsatisfied everyman (we all have our contrary star) who finds his —everyman's— destiny in unsolicited love of a different kind. But, to return to the matter of physiognomy, and especially its relation with astrology, I am sure that this will suggest to some readers that Juan Ruiz is tipping the scale against the freedom of the will. One could reply by pointing to the story, common in the Middle Ages, and found in all versions of the *Secretum secretorum,* of how Polemon, the ancient master of the skill of physiognomy, was put to the test. Hippocrates' disciples made a portrait of their master and took it to Polemon, and asked him to interpret it. Polemon, on studying it, said: «Iste homo luxuriosus est, deceptor, amans coitum.» When Hippocrates' disciples, angered by this, wished to kill Polemon, he said he knew that the picture was of the great physician, but that he had judged by the signs, according to science. When Hippocrates was told, he defended

---

[20] This is common to the treatises on physiognomy; see, for instance, Vincent, *Spec. nat.,* XXVIII, cxv.

[21] Since Frances Yates's brilliant book *The Art of Memory* (Chicago and London, 1966), it is clear that much of what we have accepted as being rhetorical (i.e., affecting the hearer) will have to be referred to «places of memory», (i.e., as aiding the speaker in his exposition).

Polemon: «Certe verum dixit Philimon (*sic*), nec pretermisit unam litteram. Verumptamen ex quo ego respexi, consideravi hec turpia esse et reprobanda, constitui meam animam regem supra ipsam, et retraxi eam ab eis, et triumphavi super retencionem concupiscencie mee» (cap. i). In Juan Ruiz's story, the astrologers of the King Alcaraz foretold how the prince would die, not what kind of life he would lead. Our nature is complex, and astrology and physiognomy allow for this complexity in the infinite permutations and combinations which they provide. Considered as aspects of Divine Providence, it is clear that the heavenly bodies and the inborn temperament cannot, on any orthodox view, eliminate the moral life. The moral life is not a matter of denying one's nature, but of co-operating with some part of it. Such a question, however, applied to the *Libro,* seems to me as futile as it is irrelevant. The concept of Nature-as-destiny is here deployed by an artful priest, who wishes to convince himself and us that his life is predestined to go thus, and no other way. We have already noted the comic hollowness of this. The Archpriest's choice, justified by naturalistic bits of Aristotle (possibly lifted out of Vincent of Beauvais, [22] where they figure as part of the theological and moral scheme of the sciences), tendentious astrology, and so on, leads him along the road of low comedy where Love is God, and Trotaconventos («llamatme buen amor») is its saint.

To conclude, I hope that this article will succeed in rectifying some small matters of fact in the *Libro de buen amor.* The placing of the portrait in a tradition which was not literary but medical, does not imply that it was any less intelligible to Juan Ruiz's readers. It can be shown, moreover, that the female types in the *Libro* are also drawn from the same range of sources, and I hope to deal with this subject elsewhere. There is little point in talking of «Arabic sensuality» when Arabic, Persian, Hebrew, Latin and Greek writers agreed on the signs of sensuality; when Vincent had read Rhazes, and Rhazes had read Aristotle.

University of Rochester,
Rochester, N. Y.

---

[22]   e. g., *Spec. nat.,* caps. **XXIX, XXX**; *Spec. doct.,* Lib. L, cap. XIII.

BRIAN DUTTON

'Buen amor':
Its Meaning and Uses in Some Medieval Texts

This study is basically a reworking of a previous article on the same theme. Since my earlier paper on the meaning of the title of the *Libro de buen amor,* [1] I have examined the use of the term *bon' amors* in Provençal texts and it now seems fitting to expand my previous work as it is now possible to give rather more precision to my earlier findings. It appears that there are three essential kinds of *buen amor,* reflecting the traditional *agape, philos* and *eros,* and that these three senses occur in both Provençal and Castilian. This study aims to show that Juan Ruiz knew and used the term in all three senses, but for the first time to our present knowledge, to mean any or all of the three, with a direct purpose and frequently with an intentionally contrived ambiguity. For the sake of completeness I shall quote all the relevant passages in full from both the *Libro de buen amor* and the other texts concerned.

The best study of the term *buen amor* to date is that by G. B. Gybbon-Monypenny. [2] His classification of the opinions of other critics is as follows:

      a) it means courtly love, as it did in Provençal (Menéndez Pidal, [3] F. Lecoy, [4] H. J. Chaytor); [5]

---

[1] «'Con Dios en buen amor': A semantic analysis of the title of the *Libro de buen amor*» *BHS,* XLIII (1966), 161-176. I am grateful to the Editor of the *Bulletin of Hispanic Studies,* Professor G. W. Ribbans, for permission to use the material in that article.

[2] «Lo que buen amor dize con rrazón te lo prueuo», *BHS,* XXXVIII (1961), 13-24.

[3] R. Menéndez Pidal, «Título que el Arcipreste de Hita dio a sus poesías», *RABM,* II (1898), 106-109, reprinted in *Poesía árabe y poesía europea* (Austral, no. 190), Buenos Aires, 1946, 109-114.

[4] Félix Lecoy, *Recherches sur le 'Libro de buen amor'* (Paris, 1938).

[5] H. J. Chaytor, «Provençal influence on the *Libro de buen amor*», *MHRA,* XVIII (1939), 10-17.

b) it means the love of God (J. Cejador, [6] L. Spitzer, [7] Ulrich Leo, [8] T. R. Hart); [9]

c) it means either, according to the context (M. R. Lida, [10] W. Kellerman, [11] G. B. Gybbon-Monypenny). [12]

There are three other studies worthy of note. F. Capecchi [13] considered *buen amor* to mean divine love, used as cover for a book about profane love. G. Sobejano [14] also considered the meaning of the term, and came to the conclusion that it is impossible to establish what *buen amor* means, but suggests that the most likely interpretation is that *buen amor* is either divine love or honourable human love, while *loco amor* is simply lechery. The latest study, by F. Márquez Villanueva [15] in 1965, closely links *buen amor* with courtly love, in the Provençal tradition, but unfortunately returns to the by now discredited theory that there was a connexion of some kind between the *Libro* and Ibn Hazm's *Collar de la Paloma*. [16] The links, if any, with *'Udhrí* love must be those that link it with the Provençal tradition. One further critic, A. N. Zahareas, has stressed the way in which Juan Ruiz uses the term with deliberate ambiguity. [17]

There are several occurrences of the term *buen amor* in Old Spanish texts, and these will be considered first. The first three are already widely known and quoted. The earliest of these appears to be stanza

---

[6] J. Cejador, ed. *El Libro de buen amor* (*Clásicos castellanos,* nos. XIV and XVII); see note to stanza 933.

[7] Leo Spitzer, «En torno al arte del Arcipreste de Hita», in *Lingüística e historia literaria* (Madrid, 1955).

[8] Ulrich Leo, *Zur dichterische Originalität des Arcipreste de Hita* (Frankfurt, 1958).

[9] T. R. Hart, *La alegoría en el Libro de buen amor* (Madrid, 1959).

[10] María Rosa Lida de Malkiel, «Nuevas notas para la interpretación del *Libro de buen amor*», NRFH, XIII (1959), 17-82.

[11] W. Kellerman, *Zur Charakteristik des «Libro de buen amor»,* ZRP, LXVII (1951), 225-254.

[12] *Art. cit.*

[13] F. Capecchi, «Il *Libro de buen amor* di Juan Ruiz, Arcipreste de Hita», CN, XIII (1954), 135-164 and XIV (1954), 59-90.

[14] Gonzalo Sobejano, «Escolios al 'buen amor' de Juan Ruiz», *Studia Philologica, Homenaje a Dámaso Alonso,* III (Madrid, 1963), 431-458.

[15] F. Márquez Villanueva, «El buen amor», RO, 2.ª época, III, no. 27 (June, 1965), 269-291.

[16] See Claudio Sánchez Albornoz, «Originalidad creadora del Arcipreste, frente a la última teoría sobre *El buen amor*», CHE, XXXI-XXXII (Buenos Aires, 1960), 275-289 and *España, un enigma histórico,* vol. I (Buenos Aires, 1956), pp. 451-533 for the grounds for refuting Américo Castro's theory, for which see Castro's *España en su historia* (Buenos Aires, 1948), pp. 371-469, revised in *La realidad histórica de España* (México, 1954), pp. 378-442.

[17] Anthony N. Zahareas, *The Art of Juan Ruiz, Archpriest of Hita* (Madrid, 1965), chapter II.

629 of the *Poema de Fernán González* (=*PFG,* ed. A. Zamora Vicente, «Clásicos castellanos», Madrid, 1954):

> «Buen conde —dixo ella— esto faz buen amor,
> que tuelle a las duennas vergüença e pavor;
> olvidan los parientes por el entendedor,
> de lo que él se paga, tiénenlo por mejor.»

These words are spoken by Doña Sancha when she helps the Castilian count to escape from her father's prison. In the prosified version of the *PFG* in the *Primera Crónica General,* she says «...esto faze fazer el grand amor, ca es la cosa del mundo que más tuelle a las duennas pavor et verguença de quantas cosas son...» These words have been taken to mean Courtly Love, though such expressions of it were not quite to be expected of women in the courtly code. However, in stanza 627 Doña Sancha states: «quiero contrra el conde una cosa fazer, / al su fuerte amor dexarme yo vençer», which is prosified in the *Crónica* as: «Et quiero fazer una cosa esquantra éll, et vencerme á agora el so grand amor que ell a de mí et el gran bien que me quiere.»[18] In this sense there would be no difficulty in interpreting *buen amor* as Courtly Love.

The other previously known occurrences are in its fairly general use in the fifteenth and sixteenth centuries as an endearment:

> Buen amor, no me deis guerra,
> que esta noche es la primera...[19]

> ...encontré a mi Buen amor...
>
> (*Antología,* no. 92).

> Buscad, Buen amor,
> con qué me falaguedes...
> ...y vos, Buen amor,
> con otra holgando...
>
> (*Antología,* no. 118).

---

[18] The *Crónica* is quoted at the foot of pp. 186-187 of the A. Zamora Vicente edition of the *Poema de Fernán González* (Clásicos castellanos, no. 128).
[19] Dámaso Alonso and J. M. Blecua, *Antología de la poesía española: poesía de tipo tradicional,* 2nd. ed. (Madrid, 1964), no. 60; also *Cancionero musical de los siglos XV y XVI,* ed. Asenjo Barbieri (Madrid, 1890), no. 424. For the *Libro de Alexandre* I have used the edition by R. S. Willis (Princeton-Paris, 1934) using ms. *O* and Willis' composite numbering. The Berceo quotations are from my own tentative editions. All other quotations, unless otherwise stated, are from BAE, volume LVII.

Ya cantan los gallos,
Buen amor, y vete,
cata que amanesce...

(*Cancionero Musical,* no. 413).

The last example quoted also occurs in the *Antología,* no. 78, taken from another source, with the variant *amor mío* for *Buen amor,* which makes the meaning of the endearment and its value quite plain.

The most widely known use of the term is in the expression *de muy buen amor,* equivalent to *de grado:* 'willingly, gladly'.

Yo te quitaría de muy buen amor.

(*Libro de Apolonio,* 497d, BAE, vol. 57).

Todo lo fará él, de muy buen amor.

(Berceo, *Milagros de Ntra. Sra.,* 798d).

Aprendré lo que dixieres muy de bon amor.

(*Alex,* 49c).

Beurién agua de río de bon amor

(*id.* 2.149d)

Respondiéronlle todos: «De muy buen amor.»

(*id.,* 402d).

The meaning of this expression is made quite clear by a parallel line in Berceo's *Vida de San Millán,* 431d: 'Respondiéronli todos: «Sennor, de muy buen grado.»' The two are combined in *Alex.* 1883b: 'Yo os daré auondo muy de grado e d'amor.'

The common phrase may also occur with full semantic force given to the word *amor.* In the *Poema de Yuçuf* we read how Potiphar and his wife Zalija bought Joseph as a slave when his brothers sold him:

Complólo el rey por su peso de alchohor,
llevólo a su mujer Zalija con amor;
tomáronlo por filho legítimo e mayor,
amáronlo entrambos de muy buen amor.

(stanza 64, BAE, vol. 57).

The construction 'amar de buen amor' is quite normal in Arabic, where the verbal noun may be used to express intensity, as in *nāma nawman* 'he slept a sleeping', *i.e* a long time or deeply. Since *habbāhu hubban* + an adjective would translate *amar de buen amor* perfectly into Arabic, the construction in the *Yuçuf* may well be an Arabism in this *aljamiado* text. This is of some interest since the adjective *buen* probably carries full meaning too, in that Zalija and her husband loved Joseph well, as a son, and this contrasts sharply with Zalija's later lust for him in stanzas 73-84, which is naturally *loco amor* or *fol' amor* (see below, p. 108), compared with the *buen amor* she originally bore him.

A similar intensified use of the same phrase occurs in Berceo's *Duelo que fizo la Virgen...*, stanza 64:

> Nunca repoyó omne, justo nin pecador,
> que non li dio consejo el complido sennor;
> a que de comer ovo copdicia o sabor,
> cevólo a su guisa muy de buen amor.

Here the meaning is clearly stronger than simply *de grado,* since Berceo is talking of Christ's love for mankind. We should therefore not exclude this phrase from our consideration, since in two widely differing contexts it is used to mean more than simply 'willingly'. [20]

These examples in Castilian are not sufficient to explain either the title or the use of the term within the text of the *Libro.* As we noted earlier, several critics believe that *buen amor* means, at least in part, the Love of God. It is odd that no examples of the term in this sense have been noted, since there are two well-known medieval writers who use it exactly in this sense. The first example is in Berceo's *Sacrificio de la Misa,* stanza 61. There are two extant manuscripts of this work, one in the Biblioteca Nacional (*BN*), and the other in Silos (*I*). The *BN* copy lacks most of stanza 61, and when Tomás Antonio Sánchez edited the work in his *Colección de poesías castellanas anteriores al siglo XV,* vol. II (Madrid, 1780), he observed (p. 189, n. 1): 'Estos versos que faltan en el Cod. de la Real Biblioteca se han suplido por el del M. Ibarreta', which is now Silos Ms. 93. In this manuscript we read, as a comment on the mixing of the water and the wine in the Mass:

> El vino significa a Dios nuestro Sennor,
> la agua significa al pueblo peccador;
> como estas dos cosas tornan en un sabor,
> assín torna el ome con Dios en buen amor.   (61).

---

[20] The hemistich *de muy buen amor* occurs constantly with one syllable short in the *mester de clerecía.* See J. Corominas, *DCELC,* III, p. 468 for the vacilation between *muy* and *mucho.*

8

Sánchez, perhaps misled by the hemistich immediately above, printed
the second hemistich of 61d as 'con Dios en *un* amor', with the result
that this important item of information was hidden away in the Silos
ms. Berceo clearly uses the term here to mean the love of God for
man and of man for God, the mutual love of Creator and creature.
This is the first recorded Castilian use of the term in a religious sense,
in a context that leaves no room for doubt, and which shows that when
Juan Ruiz speaks of «el buen amor que es el de Dios» in his prose prologue, he was not using the term in a meaning that it had not had
before.

Not very long after Juan Ruiz's second version of the *Libro* (1343),
Pero López de Ayala began his *Rimado de Palacio* c. 1367 and completed it before his death in 1407. This moralistic work bemoans the
decay in religious, social and moral values in the kingdom and in the
Church, preaching higher standards in all things. The first reference
to *buen amor* in this book is somewhat similar to Berceo's use of the
term. Ayala is complaining of the low standards that obtain amongst
the clergy of his times, and is horrified at the way in which some of
them handle the Host:

> Unos prestes lo tratan que verlos es pavor,
> e tómanlo en las manos syn ningúnt buen amor,
> syn estar confessados e aun ques peor,
> que tienen cada noche consigo otro dolor.   (220).

The term here has a clearly religious meaning, not as strong as in
Berceo, but certainly meaning 'love, respect for the Deity'. Later in
his book Ayala comes to his *Consejo para toda persona,* in which he
stresses the importance of a conscience at rest, inner peace and charity:

> Por mucho que ayunes e fagas oración
> y oigas muchas misas e muy luengo sermón,
> e des muchas limosnas e a pobres ración,
> si pas en ti no ovieres, estarás en ocasión.
>
> Ca si non perdonas al que te fallesçió,
> e te dura rencor contra él que a ti erró,
> la pas e caridat en ti ya fallesçió,
> e quien sin ella ayuna, atanto se perdió.   (536-537)

He continues to preach this need for inner peace and charity, and in
stanza 540 says:

> Si en sí pas oviera Judas aquel traydor,
> nunca él pensara de vender al Sennor;
> non puede el diablo ser nunca morador
> en casa que ay pas, concordia e buen amor.

Here the meaning is clear: *buen amor* is used with *paz, concordia,* and in other stanzas (537c, 541d, 542a) associated with these is *caridad.* Ayala is using *buen amor* here to mean charity or brotherly love. There are examples of *mal amor* in an opposite sense: «Al que podié prender faziél' mal amor» (*Alex.* 2231c), where the meaning is clear enough, since in the very next line Alexander does catch someone and send him «por al sieglo mayor»!

There are many expressions that involve the word *amor* in this social sense (Cf. Berceo, *Signos,* 59b, *Alex.* 1132c, *Alex.* 575a «fágote grant amor», 984a «faznos gran caridat».) These social meanings are almost certainly the basis for the expression *de (muy) buen amor,* 'willingly', almost 'with good grace'. *Amor* can also mean 'love, sake' as in «faré tanta de gracia por el vuestro amor» (Berceo, *Milagros* 257b), which leads to the phrase *por amor de* 'because of, in order to' as in «Coytaron la galea por amor de huviar» (*Apolonio* 386a), «Movióse por amor de antes recabdar» (*Alex.* 2148a).

Ayala's third use of the term is to be found in the section where Ayala «fabla de ix cosas para conoscer el poder del rey». Of these nine points, one leads to a discussion of the position of a *privado.* On recommending norms of conduct, Ayala states:

> Otrosí le conseje el tal a su sennor
> que en pedir non sea duro despectador;
> pida con buena graçia e con buen amor,
> e de lo que le dieren sea gradesçedor.   (679)

This recommendation against the rapacity of rulers associates *buen amor* with *buena gracia,* almost as in the English 'with good grace'. Clearly the *buen amor* of 540d is here used as a social rather than a moral quality, but essentially the meaning remains the same.

Ayala thus uses the term *buen amor* three times, giving a wider meaning than Berceo to the term. He uses it once in reference to the Deity, and twice in reference to brotherly love, charity, the love that should unite Christian with Christian, as an extension of that which unites Christian with God. These uses of *buen amor* in Ayala's book are most significant, since they add, with Berceo's sole example, the final meanings of the term as it has been variously understood by the critics of the *Libro*. At the same time they add meanings that have previously not been considered, namely brotherly love and charity. *Amor* by itself also occurs in this sense in the *Alex.* 1848*b* «se entre nos e ellos non ouier amor...» where Alexander is speaking of the need to treat the Persians well after his victory.

The term *buen amor* also occurs in the fifteenth century with the meaning of Courtly Love. There are probably many more such instances, but the following three suffice. They all appear in the *Cancionero de Palacio,* ed. F. Vendrell de Millás (Barcelona, 1945).

> Senyora, quando pensedes
> el buen amor que tenedes,
> sé que vos penediredes
> de que m'ayades perdido.

(Pedro de Santa Fe, no. 336, st. 2).

Santa Fe belongs to the first half of the fifteenth century. He was a *bachiller* in 1418, and frequented the courts of Aragón and Navarre. He uses the term to mean, one presumes, courtly love, as well as 'el amor bueno que tenedes'. Santa Fe uses the term again in the first stanza of poem 339:

> Buen amor, pues me mostrades
> de partir do no quería,
> yo partir no m'en poría
> mas apartar si sepades.

Here the term is used presumably to personify courtly love or as an endearment addressed to his lady. Sarnés is another poet of the same period, an Aragonese who also wrote in Catalan. His poem, no. 351, begins as follows:

> Sienta quien sentido tiene
> que partir de buen amor
> es dolor
> tal que sentir no se conviene
> sino a buen servidor.

Here Sarnés is clearly using the term to mean his love, whether personified or as a direct reference to his lady. In either case, the whole tone of the poem is that of courtly love. The term was thus alive in this sense both before and after Juan Ruiz's book.

To sum up, we have the following occurrences of the term *buen amor* in Castilian:

1. The Love of God: Berceo, c. 1250, Ayala, c. 1380.
2. Charity, brotherly love: Ayala; Natural affection as for a son, *Yuçuf*.
3. Courtly Love: *PFG* c. 1250, *Cancionero de Palacio*, poets 1420-50.
4. An endearment: fifteenth and sixteenth centuries.
5. The phrase *de buen amor*, thirteenth and fourteenth centuries, related to (2) above.

We should now consider the use of the term *bon' amor* in Provençal, since many critics (Menéndez Pidal, F. Lecoy, H. J. Chaytor and F. Márquez Villanueva primarily) believe that this is the origin of the term *buen amor* in Castilian, and that it means courtly love in both languages. It is already apparent that *buen amor* has at least three meanings in Castilian. The term does not occur, as far as I know, in mediaeval Galician poetry, though the expression *bem querer* is very frequent and seems to be the equivalent, though it is largely a verbal form, and appears to mean only courtly love. Since *bon' amor* and its equivalent *fin' amor* are so frequent in Provençal poetry, and since the Galicians imitated the Provençal style so closely, it is odd that these terms should not have been used. However, we should not exclude the possibility that an example may one day be found, although this would add nothing to our understanding of the term *buen amor* in Juan Ruiz's book if it meant simply courtly love. In his excellent study (see note 2), Gybbon-Monypenny gives a wide range of Provençal, Catalan, Old French and Italian uses of the term *buen amor*, showing that the Provençal terms are documented earliest. However, I propose to study only two poets, Bernart de Ventadorn, *fl.* 1140-1180 and Guiraut Riquier, who frequented the court of Alfonso X of Spain. All the quotations for Bernart's poetry are taken from Carl Appel's masterly edition, *Bernart von Ventadorn, Seine Liede* (Halle, 1915), giving the poem number and the line number following a comma. Of the two terms *fin' amor* is the commoner, but does occur as a variant of *bon' amor*, which would indicate that they were synonymous for courtly love:

> Tant l'am per fin' amor
> bon'
> que maintas vetz en plor.

(44, 69-70; see Appel, p. 260).

103

Other examples of *fin' amor* abound: «sí·m te fin' amors conhd' e gai », 7,11; «c'aitan fin' amors m'eschaya», 7,53; «si·m te conhd' e gai/fin' amors», 18,5-6; «li port amor tan fin' e natural», 41,31; «qu'ergolhs dechai e fin' amors capdolha», 42,21. There are many more such examples. The term also occurs in Old Spanish, *Razón feita d'amor:* «e quis cantar de fin amor» (ed. R. Menéndez Pidal, *RHi* XIII (1905), 602-18, line 55).

Bon' amor is also very frequent and will be quoted more fully from Bernart's works:

> Anc no vitz ome tan antic
> si a bon' amor ni pura
> e per sidons si' amatz
> non sia gais...
>
> (24, 41-44).

The next example shows that *bon' amor* could also be an endearment as in Spanish:

> Ai, bon' amors encobida,
> cors be faihz, delgatz e plas...
>
> (30, 50-51).

In an attributed poem we find the idea that when nature rejoices so should the poet's heart «qui bon' amor saup chauzir» (p. 282, line 8). Poem no. 22 uses an interesting expression which again indicates the meaning of *bona* in *bon' amor:*

> Ai Deus, can bona for' amors
> de dos amics, s'esser pogues
> que ja us d'aquestz enveyos
> lor amistat no conogues!
>
> (22, 9-12)

Here *bona* expresses the delightful, pleasing quality of the love, and what the *enveyos* have caused them to lose is later called «tal joi de fin' amor certana» (line 46).

There is one final point from a poem that Appel has shown to be by Aimeric de Belenoi, not Bernart. This is an answer to a disillusioned lover's misogynistic poem, and it ends:

> La lor amors es bona e non greva,
> car si failli primierament na Eva,
> la Maire Dieu nos en fetz patz e treva.
>
> (p. 295, lines 17-19)

In the mid-twelfth century the term *bon' amor* was thus used to mean courtly love, almost interchangeably with *fin' amor*. Apart from its use as an endearment, there are no other uses of the term. However, in the later poet, Guiraut Riquier, we find far more interesting material. He is important since he was almost continuously at the court of Alfonso el Sabio from 1262 onwards, where he enjoyed the monarch's favour and dedicated a large number of poems to him. Riquier was well known in Spain, and it is quite within the bounds of probability that Juan Ruiz knew of him and of his works. The first passages quoted are from his 947-line commentary on Guiraut de Calanso's *Canso del menor ters d'amor*. (All quotations are from *Die Werke der Troubadors... vierter Band*, ed. C. A. F. Mahn (Berlin/Paris, 1853). The lines quoted are on pages 213-214):

> L'entendemen per ver
> d'estas. III. partz d'amor
> que per lo trobador
> Gr. de Calanso,
> que dictet la chanso,
> foron terses nomnadas
> vos dirai, car uzadas
> son en non egalmen
> al mieu entendemen:
> l'un' es celestials,
> e l'autra naturals
> l'autra carnals, so'm par.   (110-121).

> La celestial es
> amar Dieu e servir...   (124-125).

> E l'amors naturals
> es may amar el mun
> homes, segon que son,
> que autras creaturas...   (136-139).

> Et es l'amor carnal
> aquela veramens
> c'omes e femnas vens
> e tol sen e saber
> a totz...   (156-160).

We shall return to this division of love into the traditional *agape, philos* and *eros* (corresponding roughly to soul, mind and body, thought, emotion and flesh and many other triadic systems). Riquier uses *fin' amor* and *bon' amor* to mean courtly love. There are numerous examples in his poems. I quote from the Mahn edition, giving poem and line numbers. If a date follows these, it is the date given in the manuscript used for the edition, which appears to be fairly reliable.

> E donc qui vol esser vers conoyssens,
> a fin' amor sia obediens,
> quar fin' amors non es ses gran temensa.　　(X, 12-14; 1260).

> Quar amatz suy per lieys, sol que'm captenha
> vas lieys assi, con fin' amors essenha.　　(L, 15-16; 1288).

See also XLVIII, 4 (1288) «chantar de fin' amor», 34 «fin amador», 55 «totz los fis enamoratz». There are numerous other examples: XXIII, 37 (1275) «assatz sembla que'l porti fin' amor», and XXVIII, 2 (1276), XXIX, 27 (1276), LXXXVI, 25, etc.

Riquier also uses *fin' amor* in a religious sense:

> Non pot esser vera patz ses amor,
> quar d'amor ven lialtatz, conoyssensa,
> e drechura, patz e perdos d'ofensa;
> mas fin' amor el mon gaire no cor.　　(LI, 41-44; 1290).

Compare this with «...Crist que pres naissensa/e mort per selhs que'l son fin amador», *id*, 23-4.

Bon' amor in Riquier's poems occurs mainly with the sense of charity, as in Pero López de Ayala. Often it implies not only charity and brotherly love (*amor natural*), but also the love and fealty of a vassal for his lord, as in «Narbona·m plai, quar porta bon' amor/e bona fe a son honrat senhor» (XIV, 51-52; 1266). It is interesting to note how *bon' amor* and *bona fe* are linked here. When Riquier, like Ayala, laments the moral decline of his age, he too uses the words *bon' amor*:

> Quar dreyt ni fes
> ni sens ni leyaltatz
> ni bon' amors
> no son entre las gens
> ni caritatz
> no y renha ni merces...　　(XVII, 1-6; 1270).

This passage closely resembles Ayala's stanza 540.

> ...a sel, de que no·m mor
> voler del sieu enans
> (car la razo es grans
> e mi ab bon' amor)
> al bon valen senhor
> N'Amalric de Narbona
> Gr. Riquier s'adona.
>
> (LXXVI, 20-26).

> E sopley mo senhor
> humilmen merceyan,
> que no·m torne a dan
> so que li vuelh per be
> dir e per bona fe.
> Qu'estiers a mon semblan
> per nulh fag pauc ni gran
> nulha re no·l diria,
> tant tem sa senhoria
> e dezir sa honor
> e li port bon' amor
> ab lialtat deguda.
>
> (LXXVII, 127-138; 1272).

This last quotation is from a long *letra* addressed to his liege-lord. In all these examples, *bon' amor* clearly refers to what Riquier called *amor natural*. There are however two interesting points. The adjective *bona* could clearly be used with *amor* to mean simply 'good, pleasing', or 'beneficial' as in «No·m sai d'amor si m'es mala o bona,/o·m val o·m notz, o·m manten o m'azira» (VII, 1-2; 1259), and «si aissi·m notz amors, en als m'es bona» (*id.*, 17). This should be compared with the passage quoted below from Riquier's *exposizio* of Calanso's poem. The two examples just given refer *bona* to sexual love, while in the quotation below it refers to *amor natural*:

> Al segon ters cove
> franquez' e merces,
> que par a me que·l mes
> per natural amor;
> car de Nostre Senhor
> n'avem comandamen,
> e natura cossen
> e vol e·ns fay amar
> mays home ses doptar

107

que autra creatura,
els parens per drechura
els pus propis pus,
com vos ai dig desus
lai al comensamen,
e creatz veramen
sert, qu' *est' amor es bona*
e play a Dieu, que·ns dona
tot quant avem de be.

(Lines 861-878).

Clearly this example fits perfectly into the general concept expressed by *buen amor* in Ayala's *Rimado,* stanzas 540 and 679. It is basically charity, brotherly love, enjoined by the commandment «Love ye one another». It is also used for social duty and obedience, as well as for friendship: «aquest mieu senhor / al qual port bon' amor» (LXXXIII, 39-42; 1282).

Finally *loco amor,* which Juan Ruiz contrasts with *buen amor,* also occurs in Riquier. He asked N'Enveyos in a *tenzo* if he would choose to have all the learning of the *clercx,* or win *joy d'amors* from every woman he ever desired. N'Enveyos replies that he prefers learning, for David, Solomon, Sampson and many others «per fol' amor fon lor valor delida» (LXXXVII, 31). Riquier agrees, saying he did not mean lechery, «c'ab fol' amor deu totz hom mescabar» (*id.,* 35).

One further use of the term *bona amor* in Ramón Llull's works is most significant. This use was already pointed out by Gybbon-Monypenny («*Lo que buen amor...*», p. 22) as being a clear example of the use of the term in a religious sense:

Jesus prenga·us de nos dolor,
Car tuit estam quaix en error,
e exilats de bona amor.

(*Los cent noms de Deu,* vs. 22-24).

Ah bona amor! E per qual tort
Que us haja fait a mala mort
M'ha acusat la mala amor
Qui em fa estar així pecador...?
Ah bona amor! Porets me dar
Contricció de ton mal far
Per ço que fuja mala amors...?

(*Medecina de pecat,* section I
(*D'Amor*), vs. 1-4 and 9-11).

It thus appears that in a religious, moral or social sense (all as Christian values) *buen amor* and *bona amor* have as their opposite *mala amor,* whilst in a sexual sense, that is as courtly love, *buen amor* is already part of *mala amor* (i.e. the Augustinian *amor mundi*), dismissed as *loco amor* or *fol' amor* by the moralists. From the religio-moralistic point of view, *buen amor* can only be *amor celestial* or *amor natural* as exclusively used by Riquier, whereas any sexual or even non-religious love (i.e. *amor mundi*) is dismissed as *mala amor.* The specifically sexual *buen amor* = courtly love is termed, with no distinction as to degrees of refinement, *loco amor, fol' amor.*

All the concepts that we have so far found in Castilian also appear in Provençal / Catalan texts. There is nothing in Juan Ruiz's use of the term that does not appear in both of these literatures, except of course the use of the title *Libro de buen amor,* and the intentional juxtaposition of the term's mutually exclusive meanings. It only remains to examine those passages in which Juan Ruiz uses the term and to attempt to determine which of its several meanings is or are intended.

* * *

The first occurrences of the expression *buen amor* are in the prose prologue to the book, following stanza 10. This, as is shown by Janet Chapman in her study in this volume, is a sermon preached on the text: «Intellectum tibi dabo, et instruam te in via hac, qua gradieris: firmabo super te oculos meos». (Vulgate, psalm 31: 10). Juan Ruiz relates this text to the mediaeval philosophical commonplace of the three faculties of the soul: understanding, will and memory (which latter also included consciousness, *cf.* Berceo, *Vida de Santo Domingo de Silos,* stanza 491). The author discusses each of these three faculties in turn: «E desque está informada e instruyda el alma, que se ha de salvar en el cuerpo linpio, e piensa e ama e desea omne el buen amor de Dios e sus mandamientos... E otrosí desecha e aborresçe el alma el pecado del amor loco d'este mundo.» Thus, with understanding, the will directs love towards God, not towards the *amor loco (fol' amor)* of this world. He goes on to say that once the soul has achieved «el *buen* entendimiento e *buena* voluntad, con *buena* rrembrança escoge e ama el *buen amor,* que es el de Dios...» it guides the body to

109

«fazer *buenas* obras», for «los *buenos* que mueren *bien* obrando» will be saved. The adjective *bueno* is stressed constantly in this passage, probably because *buen amor* could mean, and probably meant primarily, courtly love. This stress on *bueno* continues in what immediately follows: «E por ende devemos tener sin dubda que * obras siempre están en la *buena* memoria que con *buen* entendimiento e *buena* voluntad escoje el alma e ama el * amor de Dios por se salvar por ellas.» In both the places indicated by an asterisk (*) one would expect the adjective *bueno* in accordance with the preceding passage.

Without these good faculties, the body and the soul are ruined by «el pecado del amor loco deste mundo» and for this reason the Arcipreste says «fiz esta chica escriptura en memoria de bien e compuse este nuevo libro en que son escriptas algunas maneras e maestrías e sotilezas engañosas del loco amor del mundo que usan algunos para pecar.» [21] He then goes on to say that those who perceive these «malas maestrías» and «engañosas maneras que usan para pecar e engañar las mujeres, acordarán la memoria e no despreciarán su fama... e desecharán e aborresçerán las maneras e maestrías malas del loco amor, que faze perder las almas e caer en saña de Dios, apocando la vida e dando mala fama e deshonrra e muchos daños a los cuerpos.»

The Arcipreste is thus using *buen amor* to mean the first two of the three levels of love as described by Guiraut Riquier: *amor celestial,* as in Berceo, Llull and Ayala, and probably also as *amor natural,* the brotherly love enjoined by Christ, as in Riquier and Ayala. He is explicitly rejecting as *amor loco* the third kind of love, *amor carnal,* which in its courtly guise was known as *buen amor.* He does however tell his readers that if they so wish they will find material on this third kind of love: «Enpero, por que es umanal cosa el pecar, si algunos (lo que no los conssejo) quisieren usar del loco amor, aquí fallarán algunas maneras para ello.» His book will thus serve those who wish to practise the first two kinds of love (*celestial* and *natural*) as well as those more inclined to the third kind (*carnal* or *fol' amor*), since he can truthfully claim «Intellectum tibi dabo, etc.». He next indicates that we should

---

[21] The *chica escriptura* could be the prologue itself, while the *nuevo libro* probably refers to the second edition of the *Libro,* where the moralizing tone is stressed much more. On this last point, see G. B. Gybbon-Monypenny, «The Two Versions of the *Libro de buen amor:* the Extent of the Author's Revisions», *BHS,* XXXIX (1962), pp. 205-221. The expression *loco amor* occurs in proverbs in a slightly different sense, as in «Amor loco, yo por vos y vos por otro» —see Covarrubias, *Tesoro de la lengua castellana,* ed. M. de Riquer (Barcelona, 1943), p. 113(b), and variants in Maestro Gonzalo Correas, *Vocabulario de refranes...* (Madrid, 1924), p. 46.

«bien entender e bien juzgar la mi entençión por qué lo fiz e la senten-
çia de lo que y dize, e non al son feo de las palabras. E segund derecho las palabras sirven a la intençión e non la intençión a las palabras.»
This is a clear warning: so far he has only used *buen amor* in the
sense of the love of God or charity, giving *buen* the same value that it
has in *buenas obras, buen entendimiento, buena voluntad, buena memoria,* etc. For the third type of love he has so far only used the expression *loco amor,* restricting its sense to worldliness and the pursuit
and seduction of women. It is in this sense, however, that *buen amor*
is most used in the body of the book. By the device of *iteratio, bueno*
is stressed constantly in the prologue, to ensure that the first association made by the reader for the term *buen amor* is religious, not the
sexual meaning given to it by the poets. For these reasons he inserts
his warning about the «son feo de las palabras». The prologue-ser-
mon was seemingly added to the second version of the book with precisely this aim of making the religious meaning come to mind first
of all.

Buen amor is thus used in the book with two general meanings:
(i) the love of God, and consequently charity, brotherly love and (ii) the
courtly love of the poets, *loco amor.* There is an important distinction
here. The first kind of *buen amor* is good in the same sense as *buenas
obras,* but in the second it is simply a label for courtly love. We can
have *buen amor* of the first kind, with its opposite of *mal amor* as
illustrated by «fazer mal amor a» in *Alex.* 2231*c* above. On the other
hand, in the sense of courtly love we have simply a label, for if we
change *buen* to *mal* then all connexions are lost with courtly love. In
fact one could logically speak of *buen buen amor* and *mal buen amor*
in this sense. (For a derogatory use of *bonne amour* in Old French see
Gybbon-Monypenny, «*Lo que buen amor...*», p. 19). The distinction
is rather like that between 'a green house' and 'a greenhouse', since
we can have a white greenhouse just as easily as we can have a green
greenhouse. In terms of stress *buen amor* in meaning (i) is [,bwen
a'mor], while in meaning (ii) it is [bwena'mor], i.e. in the latter case
buen does not carry with it the full lexical force of *bueno* as in *buenas obras.*

Apart from the two occurrences in the sermon-prologue, where the
meaning is unambiguously religious, we have twelve other occurrences
of the term in the body of the book. Each will be quoted and discussed in turn.

III. In his prayer for help in writing his book, the Arcipreste calls on God (Stanza 13):

> Tú, Señor Dios mío, quel omne crieste,
> enforma e ayuda a mí el tu acipreste,
> que pueda fazer un libro de buen amor aqueste,
> que los cuerpos alegre e a las almas preste.

Menéndez Pidal indicated this passage in his study of the title of the book, and we can accept his view that this is a clear reference to the title of the book itself (see note 3). So far courtly love has not been mentioned explicitly, though the hemistich 'que los cuerpos alegre' (13*d*) begins to suggest *amor carnal*. There is an important point here. In the first version of 1330, stanza 13 was probably the third stanza. This would therefore be the first time the term *buen amor* occurred, and thus in the first version it would be much more ambiguous than in the second, with its preceding sermon making *buen amor* clearly *amor celestial*. Thus in the second version of 1343, Juan Ruiz made quite sure that the religio-moralistic sense was the first to be considered. However, in stanza 14, he forces the association with *amor carnal* (probably the only association in the 1330 version):

> Sy queredes, señores, oyr un buen solaz,
> escuchad el rromanze, sosegad vos en paz:
> non vos diré mentira en quanto en él yaz,
> ca por todo el mundo se usa e se faz.

This last line almost certainly refers to *buen amor* (*carnal*), but if this seems peculiar, then «segund buen dinero yaze en vil correo, / ansí en feo libro está saber non feo» (16*cd*). He gives many such similes before he reaches the fourth occurrence in stanza 18:

> So la espina yaze la rrosa, noble flor,
> so fea letra yaze saber de grand dotor;
> como so la mala capa yaze buen bevedor,
> assí so mal tratado yaze el buen amor.

(This is the reading of ms. *G*, since *S* appears to be corrupt here. In either version the meaning is basically the same.) There are two main levels, (i) a simple modesty topos from the author and (ii) the point that the name *buen amor* has become, through its association with courtly love, a «mala capa» for *amor celestial,* and this «mala capa» could make the book seem a «mal tratado». The meaning of courtly love for *buen amor* was clearly common enough for it to spring to mind, as well as the 'lexical' meaning of *amor celestial / natural*. Probably for this very reason the author inserted the sermon in his second edition. Also, occurrences III and IV refer to the book itself, and we should remember that the Archpriest was using a term that would be far more familiar to his public than it is to us.

Since «de buen seso non puede omne reír / abré algunas bulrras aquí a enxerir», says the author (45*cd*). He then tells the story of the 'Ribaldo de Roma' (46-63), [22] and points out its moral: «non ha mala palabra si non es a mal tenida» (64*b*), and joking on the sexual meaning of *buen amor,* says «entiende bien mi dicho (*G* libro), e avrás dueña garrida» (64*d*). [23]

He follows with a repeated warning about understanding his book aright:

> La bulrra que oyeres, non la tengas en vil,
> la manera del libro, entiéndela sotil;
> [saber el mal dezir bien encobierto, doñiguil,]
> tu non fallarás uno de trobadores mill.   (65).

Line 65*c* is taken from Ms. *G* since *S* does not make sense. It is rather complex (see Corominas's edition, pp. 86 and 88, for another interpretation), but the meaning appears to be «you'll not find one troubadour in a thousand who knows how to express evil well, charmingly disguising it». The meaning seems to be dual: that poets who write of courtly love cannot hide its real nature for all their noble language and references to *buen amor, fin amor,* etc., and secondly the opposite of a modesty topos, a sort of justification for the claims he makes for his book. These ideas are continued in the next stanza, which contains the fifth occurrence:

> Ffallarás muchas garças, non fallarás un uevo;
> rremendar bien non sabe todo alfayate nuevo;
> a trobar con locura non creas que me muevo,
> lo que buen amor dize, con rrazón te lo pruevo.   (66).

[22] For one view of the significance of this story, see A. D. Deyermond, «The Greeks, the Romans, the Astrologers and the Meaning of the *Libro de buen amor*», *RomN*, V, no. 1 (Autumn, 1963, 88-91). See also the study by Ian Michael in this volume.

[23] The proposed correction by S. Reckert, namely «avrás buena guarida» has not met with general approval. See S. Reckert «Avrás dueña garrida», *RFE*, XXXVII (1953), 227-237, and further details in the same critic's «Otra vez 'avrás buena guarida'», *RFE*, XLVII (1964), 445-448.

«It's easy to find egrets, but you won't find their eggs. Every new tailor doesn't know how to patch well —don't think I'm going to versify irresponsibly— I will prove by what I tell you what *buen amor* really means.» We are told that though it will be easy to take the simple surface meaning (*amor carnal*), we should also remember the serious higher meaning, the *sententia* of *amor celestial*. Also he will show *buen amor* (*carnal*) for what it really is.

VI.   Las del buen amor son rrazones encubiertas;
           trabaja do fallares las sus señales çiertas;
           si la rrazón entiendes o en el sesso açiertas,
           non dirás mal del libro que agora rrefiertas.   (68).

Buen amor is used here primarily as the title of the book. However, Juan Ruiz is also playing on the other meanings: since the book is so complex (as is *buen amor* itself), work hard on those passages where you find sure signs of it (as the love of God or as charity). If you understand the words (*razón*) and their meaning (*sesso*) aright, then you will not speak ill of the book you are now condemning (as being about *loco amor*).

Stanzas 71-76 explain *amor carnal*. It is quite normal to feel it, as great sages have said, and since our author is like any other sinner, he too has had «de las mugeres a vezes grand amor» (76*b*). This is only part of the *vanitas vanitatum,* for «salvo amor de Dios, todas son liviandat» (105*d*). However, he goes on to say that (courtly) love ennobles man (155-159), which is what the poets also claim, but immediately uses the image of the beautiful apple that smells sweet even when it is rotten (163). Unfortunately, since he was born to love (152-153) he cannot be free of it and so seeks «solaz bueno del amor con amada» (167*c*) —surely a reminiscence of the two meanings of *buen* in *buen amor*. The lady he is wooing rejects him, using the same reasoning that he adduced himself in his prologue sermon (173). There follows the long debate with don Amor, an attack on his disillusioning ways, the sins he causes, etc. (181-575). During his reply don Amor advises his victim to get an old go-between to help him, and one type in particular:

VII.   De aquestas viejas todas, ésta es la mejor;
            rruegal' que te non mienta, muestral' buen amor,
            que mucha mala bestia vende buen corredor,
            e mucha mala rropa cubre buen cobertor.   (443).

What is this *buen amor* that the author must show the old woman?
Almost certainly the meaning is once more intentionally ambiguous,
meaning both 'show her *amor natural,* charity, kindness' that is, be
kind to her, and 'show her the ways of courtly love', for as stanzas
437ff show, Urraca does not really understand the sophistications of
courtly love, only her own rather more earthy (and one could also
say, less hypocritical) view of it. She is after all not a cultivated noble,
only a highly efficient and cunning go-between. The delicacies of
amor purus and *amor mixtus* are not for her. Note too how the
word *bueno* is again stressed: a good dealer sells many a bad beast,
and a good topcoat hides a lot of bad clothes. The suggestion is that
buen amor «cubre mucha mala ropa», that it is really *amor loco* in
disguise, a misleadingly approving *significante* for a bad *significado.*

Despite being asked to treat the old woman kindly, Juan Ruiz
calls her forty-one very unendearing names in stanzas 924-927. These
names make it clear that she does not practise *buen* (=courtly) *amor.*
Her reply gives us the eighth occurrence:

VIII.   «Nunca digas nombre malo nin de fealdat;
           llamat me buen amor e faré yo lealtat,
           ca de buena palabra paga se la vezindat,
           el buen dezir non cuesta más que la nesçedat.»   (932).

Once more the adjective *bueno* is used in *iteratio,* and the expression
buen amor is used as an endearment, though clearly an inappropriate
one! The author comments:

IX.   Por amor de la vieja e por dezir rrazón,
           buen amor dixe al libro e a ella toda saçón;
           desque bien la guardé, ella me dio mucho don;
           non ay pecado sin pena nin bien syn gualardón.   (933).

This stanza continues the use of the term as an endearment, but at the
same time it is used as the title of the book. Clearly the rejection of
the «nombre malo» shows a preference for the «buen cobertor» (443*d*)
of *buen amor* —with the unsavoury meanings it hides. It is as
appropriate a name for courtly love as it is for a superannuated whore
who was called forty-one very unendearing names previously.

Later, the Arcipreste feels the need for another lady-love:

X.   Desque me vy señero e syn fulana solo
           enbié por mi vieja; ella dixo: «¿Adó lo?»
           Vino a mí rreyendo, diz: «Omíllome, don Polo,
           «fe aquí buen amor qual buen amiga buscólo.»   (1331).

9

BRIAN DUTTON

The use of *buen* in 1331*d* should be compared with its use in *iteratio* in the sermon-prologue, where the kind of *buen amor* is made clear by the association with *buenas obras,* etc. Here it is used ironically: the *buen amiga* is an aged whore turned go-between, so the *buen amor* she speaks of is not *bueno* in the first sense. By placing the two *buen*'s side by side, Juan Ruiz is making it quite clear that *buen amor* is grotesquely ambiguous. What Urraca offers is not *buen amor* but a *buen amorío*. The 'good love' that she has found happens to be a nun —specifically rejected by the courtly code (see Andreas Cape-llanus, *De Amore Libri Tres* (Castellón, 1930) I, viii, pp. 128-129). The lady should also be a Christian, and yet Urraca's subsequent ef-forts are directed towards the procuring of a Mooress.[24] These gross errors make it quite clear that Urraca rides rough-shod through the intricacies of courtly love, which must have seemed to her, and to the unsophisticated in general, an agreeable dalliance at best, and at worst a justification through the name *buen amor* for sensuality, a condoning of lechery resulting in a gross parody of the no less sens-ual but sophisticated courtly love of the nobles.

When Urraca speaks to the nun, doña Garoça (even her name seems ironic, for it is the Arabic *'arūsa,* 'bride'), she encourages her to accept the Arcipreste as her 'buen amigo':

XI.   Tened buena esperança, dexad vano temor,
           amad al buen amigo, quered su buen amor,
           sy más ya non, fabla[*ld*]e como a chat[*o*] pastor,
           dezilde «¡Dios vos salve!» [*e dexad*] el pavor.   (1452).

                                                   (Variants from *T*)

Note yet again the *iteratio* of *bueno,* and how «buena esperança» is presented as the opposite of «vano temor». As the «buen amiga» of 1331*d* sought out a «buen amor», so here since the man is her «buen amigo», doña Garoça should accept his «buen amor». The old woman

---

[24] Alfonso Alvarez de Villasandino (a poet whose life period follows that of the Arcipreste) has a poem on this theme in the *Cancionero de Baena,* no. 31*a.* He pleads that he who falls in love with a mooress should be for-given, presumably as much for breaking the courtly code as for the religious difference: «Quien de lynda se enamora / atender deve perdón / en caso que sea mora... Maguer sea cosa grave, / con todo mi coraçón / la rresçibo por señora... Por aver tal gasajado / yo pornía en condiçión / la mi alma peca-dora...» This was also forbidden by law —see Cejador, *Libro de buen amor,* note to stanza 1508. Crude sensuality was likewise rejected by the courtly code, at least in theory: «Nimia voluptatis abundantia impedit amorem... istorum talis amor est, qualis canis impudici.» (*De Amore,* I, v. 7.)

116

does not understand the sophistications of courtly love. For her *buen amor* is *bueno* because everybody likes it, *bueno* marks its agreeableness, and also implies a favourable moral judgement. It is in this sense that the «moças e viejas» shout in May «bonos son los amores» (*Alex.* 1953c). Doña Garoça understands *bueno* differently —for her *buen amor* is *amor natural* or even *celestial,* charity, brotherly love:

> Rresçibiome la dueña por su buen servidor,
> ssyenpre le fui mandado e leal amador;
> mucho de bien me fizo con Dios en lynpio amor,
> en quanto ella fue byva, Dios fue mi guïador.   (1503).

> La su vida muy lynpia en Dios se deleytava,
> en locura del mundo nunca se trabajava.   (1504cd).

> Para tales amores son las rreligiosas,
> para rogar a Dios con obras piadosas;
> que para amor del mundo mucho son peligrosas,
> e son las escuseras, perezosas, mentirosas.   (1505).

In other words, nuns are good for *buen amor* (*celestial, natural*) but not for *buen amor* (*carnal,* «locura del mundo», «amor del mundo»). Note too how the Arcipreste uses «con Dios en limpio amor», avoiding *buen amor* because he does not wish to be ambiguous in this case. No such ambiguity, because of the context, was possible in Berceo's hemistich «con Dios en buen amor» (see above p. 99). The apparent inconsistency of the *letuarios* in stanzas 1334-1338, in that though made by nuns they were reputed aphrodisiacs, is only apparent. Sweetmeats made by nuns have always been famous in Spain (made, in Miró's words, by «dedos místicos»), and when Urraca describes them, listing aphrodisíacs, she is painting an enticing picture for her client, and Juan Ruiz creates a huge joke for the reader.

When doña Garoça died, Juan Ruiz wrote a lost lament on her which he mentions as follows:

XII.   Con el mucho quebranto ffiz aquesta endecha,
> con pesar e tristeza non fue tan sotil fecha;
> emiende (entienda *GT*) la todo omne e quien buen amor
> que yerro e mal fecho emienda non desecha.   [pecha,

>   (1507).

The sense is a little obscure. The first two lines are clear enough, but when he calls on «todo omne e quien buen amor pecha» to emend («understand», *GT*) his *endecha* since error and a thing ill-done do not reject emendation, a problem arises. It is however clear that anyone who «buen amor pecha» can emend the poem, and this is intentionally ambiguous. Juan Ruiz is saying that his poem can be improved by any man who is (i) a true courtly lover and therefore knows the style or (ii) shows gratitude for an act of charity by returning it or (iii) corrects any aberrations in the poem that might offend against *amor celestial*. There are thus three levels of meaning, *amor carnal* (courtly love), *amor natural* (charity) and *amor celestial* «que es el de Dios». The expression «pechar buen amor» resembles closely the «portar bon' amor» in Riquier (see above pp. 106-108), an interpretation supported by J. Corominas (*ed. cit.*, p. 562) «tributa buen amor a otro».

When Urraca finally dies, the poet writes her epitaph:

XIII.   El que aquí llegare, ¡sí Dios le bendiga!
          e ¡síl' dé Dios buen amor e plazer de amiga!
          que por mí pecador un pater noster diga;
          si dezir non lo quisiere, a muerta non maldiga.   (1578)

The epitaph sums up clearly the grotesque meaning that *buen amor* had for the old bawd. In return for a Paternoster, she asks God to grant the offerer *buen amor,* at first sight *amor celestial,* but the second hemistich shatters this idea; 'e plazer de amiga', making the *buen amor* now quite clearly *amor carnal*. Juan Ruiz here highlights very cleverly the way in which *buen amor* as the name for the various kinds of love, *celestial, natural* and *carnal,* is dangerous and even grotesque.

The last time that the term is used in the book is also the most complex, a *tour de force* of punning, showing the strange effects of the interplay between the various meanings of the expression *buen amor*.

XIV.   Pues es de buen amor, enprestadlo de grado,
         non desmintades su nombre *nin* dedes rrefertado,
         non le dedes por dineros vendido nin alquilado,
         ca non ha grado nin *graçias nin buen amor conplado.*

(1630, ms.*S*)

          Pues de buen amor, enprestad lo de grado,
          nol' negedes su nonbre *nil'* dedes rrehertado,
          nol dedes por dinero vendido nin alquilado
          ca non ha grado nin *graçia buen amor el conplado.*

(ms.*T*)

(The reading of this stanza that seems most plausible to me on metrical, syntactical and semantic grounds would be that of *S*, replacing the italicized words with the italicized words in *T*. In line *b, nil'* (for *ni lo*) provides the missing object for the transitive verb *dedes*. In line *d, T* offers a syntactically simpler meaning, 'For bought *buen amor* has neither pleasure nor grace', the reading accepted by Corominas and also by Chiarini, who has 'el buen amor conprado' in his edition (Milan-Naples, 1964). *S* would require a more complex syntax 'for [the book] has neither pleasure nor grace nor *buen amor* [if] bought'. There are of course other readings, such as reading *ha* as *hay*, though these complicate the syntax even further. Either reading, *T* or *S*, is reasonable, though *T* offers more subtlety in making *buen amor* the subject of the sentence, in that it includes every meaning of the term, whereas the *S* reading excludes the meaning «the book», since this is the subject.) The first line states that since the book is about *buen amor* (Charity) it should be lent willingly —a pun on the synonomy of *de buen amor* and *de grado,* hence we should not «belie its name or give it grudgingly» (the book or charity) nor use it to get money, by sale or hire, for «bought *buen amor* has neither pleasure nor grace». The first meaning suggested is of course charity, *amor natural,* since this meaning is basic in the phrase «de buen amor». Since the book is about *buen amor,* we should not be mercenary about it, for bought *buen amor* «non ha grado, nin gracia» —whether as the book, as love of God, as charity or as *amor carnal. Buen amor* can only be bought in the sense Urraca used, namely as a *buen amorío,* but this can no longer be in any sense good, whether religious, moral or aesthetic, so we cannot have any kind of «buen amor el complado». Throughout the book the Arcipreste has been playing point and counterpoint on the term *buen amor,* taking this one *significante* and contrasting its several and often mutually exclusive *significados.* This last occurrence of the term amounts to a superb *concepto,* brilliantly combining several levels of meaning and, significantly, since this is the last occurrence, implying each and every one of the meanings the term *buen amor* could have.

It is quite possible that the several meanings of *buen amor* were normally not confused in his public's minds, since generally the context would make them quite distinct, one rarely suggesting the other. This is clearly illustrated by the contrast between the context in Berceo and the *PFG,* both roughly contemporary. For some reason Juan Ruiz was struck by this peculiar feature and in his book intentionally

119

brought together the several meanings in ambiguous contexts, thus revealing the glaring inappropriateness of the term *buen amor* for the love sung of by the poets, which he shows to be *amor loco,* the *fol' amor* of Riquier. The term is incongruous, and hence in a Bergsonian sense, funny, as a name for courtly love, sexual love, and by calling his book *El Libro de buen amor,* and talking of *buen amor* in all its meanings and in all sorts of ambiguous contexts, the moral danger lurking behind the apparently approving name *buen amor* is made clear, and the grotesque consequences of its literal interpretation by such people as Urraca, who were incapable of the delicate sophistry of *fin' amor,* shown to be ludicrous. It is of importance that the prose prologue was added to the second version and that it stresses constantly the first meaning of the term (*amor celestial*), making perfectly clear what must have been a very ambiguous beginning to the book in the first edition, where the first occurrence (III, stanza 13) would be by no means as clear. It is outside the scope of this paper to consider to what extent the nature of *buen amor* differs in the two versions. It would seem however that the first version is much more concerned with *amor carnal,* while the second contains proportionately more redeeming religio-moralistic passages.

The theme of the ambiguity of *buen amor* is of course only one of the many threads that run through the book, and at times one suspects that the author's zest carried him away so much, as in the Doña Endrina episode, that he often forgets for the moment his moral purpose, and then has to force himself to return to it —and this moral purpose is a constant point in the added passages of the second version. Nonetheless, the theme of *buen amor* is uniquely important, since this is the main theme of the book, and as such gave it its title. [25]

[25] I would like to express my warm thanks to my friend and colleague Dr. Robert White Linker, Professor of Romance Philology at the University of Georgia, for a great amount of help, so freely (and entertainingly) given during the composition of this study.

Since writing this study, several new examples of *buen amor* have come to light.

    1) *Castigos y ejemplos de Catón,* a *clerecía* poem of c. 1300

120   Hijo mío mucho amado, no seas sospechoso,
      no seas desdeñado ni seas temeroso,
      ça el que es tal siempre es rencoroso,
      ten con Dios buen amor y huye de ser celoso.

(See A. Rodríguez Moñino, *Los pliegos poéticos...del Marqués de Morbecq* (Madrid, 1962), pp. 61-63 and 191-213). This is a further example of the term used in a religio-moralistic sense.

2) *Libro del caballero Zifar*

The Señora del Lago says to the Caballero Atrevido, whom she later marries: «en señal de buen amor verdadero, fágovos señor de aquesta çibdat e de quanto he.» Variants: 'muy grande amor e verdadero', 'grande y verdadero amor'. (ed. C. P. Wagner, (Ann Arbor), p. 228). This is clearly a reference to human sexual love.

3) Juan Manuel, *Conde Lucanor:*

«Amor creçe amor; si amor es buen amor es amor; amor más de amor no es amor; amor de grand amor faz desamor.»

(Ed. Juliá, Madrid, 1933, p. 344).

This is used in a non-sexual sense.

Tratado de Santa María...
'...el que ama de buena amor...' (*BAE* 51, p. 440, col. a.)
This example occurs in a specifically religious context.

4) Lope de Stúñiga (mid-15th. century)

¿Quál bien puede ser igual
al mal que de mí bien sé,
por beneficio del qual
mi gran buen amor *es tal*
qual nunca jamás ya fue?

Lines 71-75 of 'O si mis llagas mortales...', text from C. Aubrun, *Le Chansonnier Espagnol d'Herberay des Essarts* (Bordeaux, 1951), p. 210 with emendations from the Módena songbook (Biblioteca Estense, 57: a.R.8.9, folio 53ᵛ.) This example clearly refers to courtly love.

5) Moxica (mid-15th. century)

La divina trinidat
... ...
estado vos den mayor,
paz, cordura, buen amor
con toda la christiandat.

Lines 377 and 382-4 of 'Dios vos salve rey humano'. Paris BN, Cancionero *H*, f. 50ᵛ.
This is another 'charity' reference.

University of Georgia

121

G. B. GYBBON-MONYPENNY

'Dixe la por te dar ensienpro':
Juan Ruiz's Adaptation of the 'Pamphilus'

The episode of Doña Endrina (stanzas 576-891) has features which clearly separate it from the other episodes that make up Juan Ruiz's erotic «autobiography»: it is much longer (nearly 400 stanzas in the original text, before the mss. were mutilated); it is the only episode in which the lover meets with no disappointment of his aims; it is the only episode which is followed by a clear statement of the author's purpose in relating it (sts. 892-909); and it is the only one of the «auto-biographical» episodes which is in reality a paraphrase of a single existing literary model. These last two facts in particular offer the critic a standing challenge: to compare closely the original and the adaptation in order to discover Juan Ruiz's methods of adaptation and to test the validity of his claims about his purpose in the light of what he actually does with the material. This challenge has been only parti-ally met. Lecoy, it is true, gives tables of correspondence between the episode and the *Pamphilus* and indicates the divergences between the two texts.[1] He also gives useful illustrations of Juan Ruiz's meth-ods as a translator and adapter by comparing selected passages (*Re-cherches...*, pp. 323-327). But he seems committed from the start to the belief that Juan Ruiz does little more than translate (see pp. 308 and 327) and he avoids the question of explaining how the result can be so different.

Other critics have tended either to generalise or to select particular features for comment. Those who have not discovered didactic or moralising aims in the *Libro* as a whole have merely concerned them-selves with the relative literary merits of the two versions of the story. While Morawski and after him Lecoy treat Juan Ruiz's version as

---

[1] Félix Lecoy, *Recherches sur le «Libro de buen amor»* (Paris, 1938), pp. 309-317.

little more than a youthful scholar's exercise,[2] other critics have generally followed the line taken by Menéndez y Pelayo, who dismissed the *Pamphilus* as «una fría abstracción erótica» from which Juan Ruiz had miraculously evolved a masterpiece.[3] Even Ulrich Leo, though he discovers considerable merits in the *Pamphilus*, stresses the poetic superiority of Juan Ruiz's version.[4]

Those who see a didactic purpose in the *Libro* naturally seek to explain the episode of Doña Endrina as part of that purpose. Spitzer and, following him, María Rosa Lida argued that it is wrong to treat the episode as unrelated to or different from the other episodes: it shares their function as illustrations of the facets of *loco amor*.[5] T. R. Hart's attempt to discover a symbolic value in the episode (the behaviour of protagonist and *tercera* illustrating *cupiditas* as a perversion of the values of *caritas*) forms part of his allegorical interpretation of the whole *Libro,* an interpretation rejected by Lida on the grounds that Juan Ruiz's didacticism is of a severely practical nature, devoid of mysticism.[6]

Two critics who made some effort to interpret the differences between the two versions and who decided that the changes made by Juan Ruiz were for didactic purposes were F. Lázaro and Jorge Guzmán.[7] Where, however, Lázaro thinks that the effect of the changes was to increase the social realism of the episode and so bring home more effectively its didactic message, Guzmán sees the main point as the building up of the role of Trotaconventos in order to illustrate more effectively the snares which such *falsas viejas* (909c) set for young women.

In looking for the differences between the two texts and attemp-

---

[2] Joseph de Morawski, *Pamphile et Galatée par Jehan Brasdefer* (Paris, 1917), p. 54; Lecoy, *Recherches...*, p. 327.

[3] M. Menéndez y Pelayo, *Historia de la poesía castellana en la Edad Media* (Madrid, 1910), vol. I, Ch. V, p. 286. See also, in particular, G. Cirot, «L'épisode de Doña Endrina dans le *Libro de buen amor*», *BH*, XLV (1943), 139-156.

[4] Ulrich Leo, *Zur dichterischen Originalität des Arcipreste de Hita* (Frankfurt, 1958), Chs. VIII-IX.

[5] Leo Spitzer, «Zur Auffassung der Kunst des Arcipreste de Hita», *ZRP*, LXIV (1934), pp. 265-266 (in the Spanish version, «En torno al arte del Arcipreste de Hita», in *Lingüística e historia literaria* (Madrid, Gredos, 1955), pp. 151-153); María Rosa Lida, «Notas para la interpretación, influencia, fuentes y texto del *Libro de buen amor*», *RFH*, II (1940), p. 106.

[6] T. R. Hart, *La alegoría en el «Libro de buen amor»* (Madrid, 1959), Ch. V; rev. by Lida in *RPh*, XIV (1961-2), 340-343.

[7] F. Lázaro Carreter, «Los amores de don Melón y doña Endrina», *Arbor*, No. 62, XVIII (1951), 210-236; Jorge Guzmán, *Una constante didáctico-moral del «Libro de buen amor»* (México, 1963 —State Univ. of Iowa Studies in Language and Literature, No. XIV), Ch. II.

ting to see the significance of those differences for the understanding of Juan Ruiz's purpose, Lázaro and Guzmán were on the right lines. But in neither case did the analysis go far enough and I do not think that either has made out a convincing case on the evidence adduced. [8] I feel justified, therefore, in trying to cover the same ground rather more thoroughly in the hope that by presenting a clearer and more complete picture of the differences between the two versions I may make it easier to arrive at an understanding of what Juan Ruiz was attempting in his adaptation. [9]

The basic plot, common to both versions, divides naturally into a series of scenes: I. The protagonist declares in a soliloquy that he is in love with a young woman; she is socially his superior and therefore not easily to be won. II. The protagonist appeals for advice to Venus, who counsels persistence and cunning, deceit where necessary and the help of a go-between. III. The protagonist meets the young woman in a public place; the meeting leaves him hopeful, but worried about how to proceed further in view of the danger of the affair becoming public. IV. The lover calls in an old bawd, who already knows the young woman and promises to help. V. The bawd has a first interview with the young woman; this establishes that the latter is interested in the protagonist but is cautious about getting involved with him. VI. The bawd reports to the lover that the young woman is about to be married to another. This produces a storm of lamentation, which the bawd calms by telling the lover that she can arrange matters provided that he is more liberal in his treatment of herself. VII. In a second meeting with the young woman the bawd extracts an

---

[8] More differences of detail between the *Pamphilus* and the Endrina episode are given by María Rosa Lida de Malkiel than by either Lázaro or Guzmán, in *La originalidad artística de la Celestina* (Buenos Aires, 1962), pp. 377-378, 439-440, 542-547, 557-565; this is, however, only incidental to her analysis of the relations between these texts and the *Celestina* and she does not seek to give a complete picture of Juan Ruiz's departures from the text of the *Pamphilus* or to draw inferences from them. Thomas Garbáty, «The *Pamphilus* Tradition in Ruiz and Chaucer», *PQ*, XLVI (1967), pp. 464-465, summarizes briefly the plot differences between the *Pamphilus* and Juan Ruiz's version and alludes to Juan Ruiz's addition of comments of «religious didacticism». I shall unavoidably cover some of the same ground as these two critics.

[9] For the *Pamphilus* I use the edition by E. L'Evesque in G. Cohen, *La comédie latine en France au XIIe siècle* (Paris, 1931), Vol. II, pp. 167-224. One difficulty that arises in a study of this nature is that there is no way of knowing how far the version of the *Pamphilus* known to Juan Ruiz may have differed from the text as we know it, nor how far he may have made use of commentaries by other scholars. In the absence of any evidence on that score one can only resort to a standard edition and assume that Juan Ruiz would have known substantially the same text.

admission that the girl is in love with the protagonist, counters her fears about his reliability, her parents' opposition, etc., and persuades her to visit her house in search of distraction. VIII. The lover appears at the bawd's house, gains admission and is then left alone with the girl while the bawd pursues a fictitious errand. He forces the girl to submit to him. When the bawd returns, she counters the girl's recriminations with excuses and with the advice that the best thing is to marry the young man.

Naturally, Juan Ruiz takes over much more than just the bare bones of the plot: in the main, he follows each scene of the *Pamphilus* step by step and, as Lecoy amply demonstrates, takes over much of the language and imagery as well (*Recherches...*, pp. 323-327). It is unnecessary to illustrate this fact here: it is the differences between the two texts that concern us. Some of these differences can be said to arise logically, if not inevitably, from the fact that a story originally conceived in isolation as a dramatic dialogue has been incorporated into a larger work in narrative form. The plot needs an introduction in order to justify its presence in the *Libro;* the dialogue needs linking passages of narrative and explanation; the characters require names and a setting that match the other episodes of the *Libro.* All these modifications are to be found; they are not in themselves significant as indications of the author's purpose. In addition, the fact that Juan Ruiz chose to make this episode follow the discussion with the god of Love has minor consequences: some opening stanzas are added in which the protagonist reflects upon Don Amor's advice and his own past failures in love and determines to seek a fresh love. In the *Pamphilus* we know only that Pamphilus is in love with Galatea. But in line 181 he tells her that he has been in love with her for more than three years; the fact that Endrina is presented in 580*d* as a freshly sought out victim («busqué e fallé dueña de qual so deseoso») makes rather anomalous the echo of line 181 of the *Pamphilus* in st. 661 («tiempo es ya pasado de los años más de dos»). Again, Juan Ruiz cannot very well incorporate Venus's advice on courtship so soon after the ending of Don Amor's lesson without some comment; so Venus herself is made to allude to the advice already given by her «husband» (st. 608) and we are reminded of the source of that lesson by a reference to Ovid in st. 612. [10] Ob-

---

[10] In 574*cd*, as ms. *G* gives it, we are given advance warning of this second lesson in love by Amor himself: «Pánfilo mi criado, que se está bien de vagar, / con mi muger doña Venus te verná a castigar.» These lines have been replaced in *S* (the second version of 1343) by the following: «Pésales por mi tardança, a mi pesa del vagar, / castiga te castigando e sabrás a otros

126

viously more significant is the epilogue (sts. 892-909), in which Juan Ruiz explains that he himself is not Don Melón (909b) and claims that the story has a moral purpose, namely to forewarn «las dueñas» against the snares laid for them by false wooers and treacherous old bawds.

The fact that Juan Ruiz chose to narrate this story in the first person and to leave us with the impression, for something like half the episode, that the protagonist is the same as the «arcipreste» of the other episodes makes it logical that he should set it in the same *milieu*. In fact there are few actual references to places; the impression that Juan Ruiz has strongly «Castilianized» the story owes little to concrete details. Doña Endrina is from Calatayud (582c); the mythical cousin used as an opening gambit lives in Toledo (657a); the lover is said to be from Hita (845a). The first meeting between the lovers takes place in a plaza (653a, 659b) where there is a *portal* (658b, 669a; the modern *soportal?*). Doña Endrina breaks off the first encounter with Don Melón on the excuse that her mother will be returning from Mass (686b), perhaps a slightly more localized touch than the original «sed modo de templo venient utrique parentes» (*Pamphilus,* line 241). The final meeting takes place in Trotaconventos's shop (st. 871), whose doors had been provided by the Abbot of San Pablo (875c) and whose contents had been described by Trotaconventos in st. 862. That is really all.

Some external modifications to the characters are similarly to be expected, if only in their names. Whereas Jehan Brasdefer, whose version of the *Pamphilus* stands alone as an individual work, retains the lovers' classical names (though the Old Woman becomes Houdée), Juan Ruiz calls the lovers Melón and Endrina and gives the Old Woman a generic nickname which describes her function: Trotaconventos. [11] A fourth character, Endrina's mother Doña Rama, is intro-

---

castigar.» In my article on the two versions of the *Libro*, BHS, XXXIX (1962), 205-221, I suggested (pp. 213-214) that this change represented an «editorial» tidying up consequent upon the insertion of st. 575.

Juan Ruiz's description of Amor as the husband of Venus is a curious detail that might provide a clue as to his sources of information on the mythology of love. In such standard authorities as the *Roman de la Rose* (lines 1588-89) or the *Ovide Moralisé* (Bk. I, lines 652-680) Venus and Cupid-Amour are mother and son, the classical myths being known via the *Metamorphoses.* The only work in which I have seen Amour described as Venus's husband is Nicole de Margival's *Dit de la Panthère d'Amours;* see H. A. Todd's edition (Paris, SATF, 1883), lines 1,012-14. It is, perhaps, no more than coincidence that in this work too the poet-lover is advised by both god and goddess in turn as to how to approach his beloved (see lines 189ff, 986ff).

[11] The generic nature of the name «Trotaconventos» is attested by Don Amor's allusion to «estas trotaconventos» in 441d, by Venus's taking up of this

duced very briefly, while in the epilogue there is what could be understood as an allusion to her father in the periphrastic «la fija del endrino» (909a), though he does not figure in the story.

Elsewhere in the *Libro* proper names tend to have a simple and obvious symbolism: Almuerzo (st. 1191), Ayuno (st. 1181), Carnal (st. 1070 etc.), Cuaresma (st. 1067 etc.), Furón (st. 1619), Garoza (st. 1346 etc.), Jueves Lardero (st. 1068), Pepión (658b). [12] It is not unreasonable, therefore, to assume that the names have some symbolic value in this episode too. «Trocaconventos» seems self-explanatory; «Rama» is presumably no more than the branch from which the fruit hangs; it is «Melón» and «Endrina» which are more enigmatic. Several interpretations have been offered. Lázaro explains «Endrina» as the «ciruelita agria y áspera» who answers back sharply («Los amores...», p. 227); Leo regards «Endrina» as the prize to be gobbled up by the lover (he reminds us that the reference in 665a to «otras endrinas» makes it something of a class name), while «Melón» is comically grotesque, «calvo y bobo» (*Originalität...*, Ch. IX); Anthony Zahareas describes «Endrina» as a «pun of sensuality» (i.e., fruit ripe for plucking); [13] Lida comes nearer to finding a symbolism that is genuinely functional within the framework of the episode: «Endrina» is the fruit whose delicate bloom (her reputation) is easily spoiled by handling, while «Melón» is the fruit whose smooth exterior gives no hint of its interior condition; Lida quotes the proverb, «el melón y el casamiento, ha de ser acertamiento». [14] Corominas offers an explanation of «Melón» that would make the symbolism of the names yet more logical: he claims that for Juan Ruiz «melón» meant «badger», being derived from Hispano-Latin MELONEM, and declares that the badger is well known for its fondness for such fruit as the sloe plum and for its raids on gardens. [15]

---

comment in 645d («qual don Amor te dixo, tal sea la trotera») and by the generic nature of the statement in 697a: «Busqué trotaconventos qual me mandó el Amor.»

[12] The «Don Polo» of 1331c, a nickname with which Trotaconventos apparently taunts the Archpriest after failing to establish relations between him and the second widow, remains obscure. The «Apodas» of 1329d may not be a proper name at all: see the edns. of G. Chiarini (Milan-Naples, 1964) and J. Corominas (Madrid, 1967), Notes to 1329d.

[13] A. N. Zahareas, *The Art of Juan Ruiz, Archpriest of Hita* (Madrid, 1965), p. 157.

[14] María Rosa Lida de Malkiel, «Nuevas notas para la interpretación del *Libro de buen amor*», NRFH, XIII (1959), pp. 56-58.

[15] Corominas, edn., Note to 727c (pp. 278 and 280). While it is logical that the lover should be symbolized by a predator, Corominas' total rejection of any link between Melón's name and the fruit seems too sweeping; it is surely

There is also some modification of the social attributes of the characters. In the *Pamphilus,* the go-between is described merely as «...anus subtiles et ingeniosa / Artibus et Veneris apta ministra satis» (lines 281-282). She depicts herself as having come down in the world, at least financially: «Divitias habui multas dum floruit aetas; / Copia decreuit, pluribus indigeo» (lines 323-324). But she is evidently a professional bawd or matchmaker, from her claims to know the arts of Venus (lines 425-426) and her concern over payment for her services (lines 302-305, 523ff). Trotaconventos has a definite profession, that of pedlar of trinkets (sts. 699-700); as Juan Ruiz explains, this gives her access to many houses without arousing suspicion concerning her activities. In st. 705 she refers to her activities as a matchmaker. In sts. 717-718 she claims that if she is properly paid she will obtain for the lover not only Endrina but «otras mocetas de cuello alvillo» through her arts. In st. 826 she alludes to the pestering of a client on whose behalf she is selling a ring. In st. 862 she claims to have a rich supply of fruits in her shop. She is thus given a considerable range of professional activities. Juan Ruiz omits the detail of the Old Woman having known better days; Lázaro suggests that this is because Trotaconventos is only a type, an exemplar, and that her past is therefore of no interest. [16]

There are no great differences between the descriptions of the lover in the two texts. In the *Pamphilus* the Old Woman describes him as outstanding among the young men of the town (lines 339*ff*), of good family (line 349) and wealthy (361). However this description is for Galatea's benefit: Pamphilus has already told Venus that he is not rich and is compelled to work to maintain himself (lines 49-52) and Venus has advised him to conceal his poverty (line 116). In the *Libro,* the lover begins by being identified with the «arcipreste»; but in 598c he tells Venus that Endrina is of nobler descent than he, in sts. 635-636 Venus tells him to conceal his poverty, in st. 658 he tells Endrina of his parents' plan to marry him off and in sts. 727-732 Trotaconventos refers to him as «Don Melón de la Huerta» and describes him in terms

reasonable to expect that a fourteenth-century public would make the association and Juan Ruiz would surely enjoy the ambiguity of the pun.

[16] Lázaro, «Amores...», p. 223. See also Lida, *Originalidad artística...,* p. 558, Note 29. Lida also raises the question of whether Trotaconventos practised magic; she concludes that though Juan Ruiz hints at her magic powers, he does not depict her using them (*Originalidad artística...,* pp. 559-560 and p. 560, Note 31).

which match very closely those used by the Old Woman concerning Pamphilus.

The most striking single change in the external attributes of the characters is in the status of the girl. Galatea is a marriageable girl (*puella*), very much under her parents' care; she is rich (lines 49-50), which constitutes an obstacle for Pamphilus, especially as Galatea says that she cannot get married without the agreement of her friends (lines 401-402); she also complains that her mother is very vigilant (lines 595-596). Endrina is similarly young, wealthy and of good family (sts. 596, 598), similarly under her mother's eye (sts. 686, 824*ff*); but she is a widow (sts. 582, 759-760). Critics have suggested various reasons for the change: Lecoy (*Recherches...*, p. 318) and Spitzer (in his review of Lecoy, *RFH* I (1939), p. 274) thought it due to Juan Ruiz's Castilian sense of propriety; in Lecoy's words, «cette transformation diminue quelque peu l'odieux de l'aventure et du rôle de la vieille...». Lázaro thought that the aim was simply to complete the gallery of feminine types pursued by the protagonist in the *Libro* («Los amores...», p. 219); it must be pointed out that the lady is a widow in two later episodes, sts. 1318-20 and 1320-31. A view that seems to show greater awareness of medieval attitudes is that of Hart: he points out that it was the duty of the medieval widow to remain faithful to the memory of her husband and the symbol of faithful widowhood was the dove; hence Trotaconventos's ironical comparison of Endrina to «la tortolilla» in 757*b*. The seduction of a widow was if anything more reprehensible than that of a marriageable girl (*Alegoría...*, pp. 95-98). Juan Ruiz apparently makes a similar allusion to loyal widowhood in st. 1329:

> Ffabló la tortolilla en el rregno de Rrodas:
> diz «¿Non avedes pavor, vos, las mugeres todas
> de mudar vuestro amor por aver nuevas bodas?»

Probably the most striking difference between the two versions of the story is that of style; an immediate awareness of this difference is at the base of most of the literary comparisons drawn by the critics. One might, therefore, expect to find that an analysis of the two styles would reveal much about Juan Ruiz's aims in adapting the story. Doubtless a detailed stylistic analysis, carrying further the type of comparative study initiated by Lecoy (*Recherches...*, pp. 323-327) would be rewarding. [17] But I think that it would tell us more about Juan

---

[17] See also F. Weisser, «Sprachliche Kunstmittel des Erzpriesters von Hita», *Volkstum und Kultur der Romanen*, VII (1934), 164-243 and 281-348.

Ruiz's craftsmanship as a whole than it would about his intentions with regard to the *Pamphilus*. I doubt whether it could be shown that particular motives or a particular attitude to his theme had induced Juan Ruiz to write a particular passage in precisely the way he did. The rhetorical devices used could be identified, classified and counted and the statistics compared with those of the original. But we can rarely know the medieval writer or reader's precise reactions to particular words, phrases, combinations and so forth. Any judgement of the effects aimed at by a medieval writer is bound to be in some degree subjective and is always in danger of being anachronistic. As an example I would refer to two contrasting opinions of Don Melón's lamentation (sts. 783-791): for Ulrich Leo (*Zur dichterischen Originalität...*, Ch. VI) it is a serious and effective *amplificatio* of a stock literary theme, a genuine love poem; for Zahareas (*The Art of Juan Ruiz...*, pp. 126-128) it is a piece of burlesque, a deliberately comic *reductio ad absurdum* of a worn-out genre. I do not see how the most detailed analysis could prove or disprove either of these two views. [18]

A similar difficulty applies to the language put into the mouths of the three characters, if we attempt to consider it as indicative of character or attitude. The revelation of character through individual speech-habits is surely a modern concept of the function of dialogue in a narrative. Figures in medieval fiction are normally generic and exemplary and their behaviour will tend to be presented as that of the type they represent. To take an example: the modern reader is struck by the brusquely colloquial language put into the mouth of Doña Endrina as her first reaction to the Archpriest's declaration of love: «...Vuestros dichos non los preçio dos piñones» (664*d*), «...Buscat a quien engañedes con vuestras falsas espinas» (665*d*), or as her first answer to Trotaconventos: «...Callad ese predicar / que ya esse parlero me coydó engañar» (740*ab*). It would be dangerous to assume that such language was intended to reveal that Endrina was of a brusque, graceless disposition or that she was not of the highest social class; all

---

In addition to giving ample examples of the various stylistic devices used by Juan Ruiz generally, Weisser studies in detail sts. 871-877 (pp. 319-323) and compares a number of passages of the *Pamphilus* with their equivalents in the *Libro* (pp. 338-348).

[18] Corominas, in a note to 785*a* (p. 302 of his edition), supports Leo's view, calling it a «pasaje vívido, apasionado y aun impresionante»; he claims that what he calls the «fuerte trabazón estilística y retórica» of Juan Ruiz's version corresponds to the intensified use of leonine hexameters in the original, though much superior as a poetic method. The fact remains that none of this proves whether Juan Ruiz intended the lament to be taken seriously or as a parody of the genre.

that we can say of it is that it appears to show that the author had an ear for the popular phraseology of his day and used it to enliven his dialogue.

It is for reasons such as this that I prefer to confine my investigation to differences of content between the two texts and to leave aside the question of style.

The differences that I have described up to now are on the whole, as I suggested earlier, such as arise inevitably out of Juan Ruiz's chosen method of adaptation. With the exception of the choice of names for the characters and the choice of civil status for the heroine, they do not give us any hint of what Juan Ruiz was intending. But there are further differences of incident or of the content of what characters say which, because they are not necessary, seem to be deliberate. It is here that we may reasonably look for significance; even if the author is not consciously manipulating the plot to a deliberate end, such alterations may well prove to be indicative of an underlying viewpoint. I propose to examine these differences as they arise scene by scene. For the sake of brevity I shall refer to the *Pamphilus* as *P* and to the *Libro de buen amor* as *Libro*.

I. *The opening soliloquy* (P 1-24, Libro 576-582b): The differences here are structural: to link the episode to what has gone before, Juan Ruiz has introduced some reflexions on Amor's advice (sts. 576-579) and an account of the discovery of the new beloved (sts. 580-582b). Pamphilus's opening soliloquy has not disappeared, as María Rosa Lida apears to think (*Originalidad artística...*, p. 378), but has been transferred intact to form part of the address to Doña Venus (sts. 588-595).

II. *The interview with Venus* (P 25-42, Libro 583c-648): Apart from the inclusion of the opening soliloquy, Juan Ruiz has modified the lover's appeal very little, though there is some rearrangement of the order of elements. I note the following differences of detail: the «certis telis» of *P* 41 become a «saeta enarbolada» (*Libro* 597a); st. 599, which describes how Endrina is much sought after in marriage but spurns all offers, is presumably a development of *P* 50 («Et decus et dotes copia saepe rogat»): *Libro* 600cd («I must win her by work and cunning») appears to be a mistranslation of *P* 52, «Sed quod habere queo, quero labore meo» («I work to earn all I require»), though it becomes relevant as a comment on the methods the lover is to use; *P* 59-60 where the lover says that he has repeatedly tried to forget his love only to find that it burns the more fiercely, seems to have become *Libro* 602, in which the lover declares that he has told Endrina of his love many times, only to be rebuffed; [19] again, *Libro* 605*bcd* appears to mistranslate slightly *P* 65-66, where the lover begs for *either* deliverance from torment *or* success in his wooing.

In Venus's reply, Juan Ruiz has inserted two stanzas (608-609) in which Don Amor's earlier advice is referred to and the Archpriest's bad temper is suggested as the reason for Amor's having cut short his lesson. Sts. 614-622 are a considerable expansion of the *exempla* given by Venus to illustrate the virtue of persistence (*P* 77-80), of *Ars* (*P* 83-92) and of *Officium* (*P* 93-94), but none of them seems to add anything of significance. Juan Ruiz introduces a couple of variations into the lover's approach (627*c* «non olvides los sospiros, en esto sey engañoso»; 629*b*, «un poquillo como a miedo non dexes de jugar») that add to the element of deceit in courtship. For the abstract *senectus* against which Pamphilus is warned (*P* 137-138) he substitutes the *madre vieja* of sts. 643-644, thus anticipating the introduction of Doña Rama into the story and at the same time strengthening the argument for employing a *tercera* (st. 645). St. 646, in which Venus warns against frightening or offending the girl by being too hasty with physical advances, seems to be a substitute for *P* 139-140, in which Venus tells Pamphilus that he need have no fear. None of these alterations indicates any serious difference in attitude, nor do they alter the general tenor of the lesson.

On his own once more, the lover reflects upon Venus's advice (*P* 143-150, *Libro* 649-651), expressing disappointment in each text that she has not alleviated his distress. The Archpriest makes the further point that he is now thrown back on his own resources: «ayuda otra non me queda sy non lengua e parlares» (649*d*). This seems to echo his dissatisfaction after the departure of Don Amor (sts. 575-577), when he protests that his previous courtships appear to have been conducted in accord with Amor's «castigos», though without success.

III. *The lovers' first meeting* (*P* 153-244, *Libro* 653-686): The description of the beloved's approach is expanded by Juan Ruiz from the

---

[19] If this change is deliberate and is not the result of misunderstanding the Latin, it is a disconcerting emphasis on an inconsistency in Juan Ruiz's narrative. St. 580 implies that Endrina is being sought out for the first time, as the putting into practice of Don Amor's advice, and st. 657 suggests an opening gambit by one who has never spoken to the lady before. Yet st. 602 and st. 740, in which Endrina scornfully refers to previous approaches by Melón (and which is a gratuitous addition to the dialogue by Juan Ruiz), clearly indicate that the couple had been sparring for some time, as they have in the *Pamphilus*. Such a lack of precision over details in the adaptation should, perhaps, warn us to beware of attaching too much significance to isolated differences of detail.

one line (*P* 153) to a whole stanza (653), introducing such conventional courtly images as that of the beloved's eyes sending forth arrows of love (653*d*). Pamphilus's declaration in the next line that the occasion is an excellent one for approaching her is transformed by Juan Ruiz into the opposite sentiment that the place is not suitable for love-talk (654*a*). This appears to pave the way for a change later: in the *Pamphilus* the lines «ludendo loquimur! loquitur sic saepe iuuentus! / verbula ficta iocis iurgia nulla movent» (173-174) are interpreted by the editor, very reasonably, as a humorous and tolerant comment by Galatea on Pamphilus's opening gambit. In the *Libro* they become part of the narrative: «Abaxé más la palabra, dixel' que en juego fablava, / por que toda la gente de la plaça nos mirava...» (659*ab*). Endrina remains silent until her scathing outburst of 664*d*: «vuestros dichos non los preçio dos piñones...», while the Archpriest is worried from the start about the public nature of the encounter. This leads to another change: Pamphilus's plea, «Sed tamen auscultet me gracia uestra benigne» (195), is converted into a suggestion by the Archpriest (668*b*) that they should withdraw to the comparative privacy of «aquel portal» and in the next stanza Doña Endrina's movements are described as she complies with the suggestion: «bien loçana e orgullosa, bien mansa e sosegada, / los ojos baxó por tierra en el poyo asentada.» The most significant change in this first meeting however, is in the reaction of the girl to the lover's request to be allowed to kiss her when opportunity offers. Galatea comments that it is a dangerous step to take, but agrees on condition that Pamphilus tries to go no further (*P* 237-240); Endrina refuses all but «la fabla de mano» (686*a*). Both girls take their departures at once and promise that there will be further opportunities for talk. But whereas Galatea makes a superfluous and presumably coquettish plea: «Et memor alterius quisque sit interea» (*P* 244), Endrina makes no such plea to be remembered. As a result *P* 249, «Illius hic frustra quod sim memor illa rogauit», finds no echo in the corresponding passage in the *Libro* (687ff). In fact, Pamphilus's eight lines of rejoicing are reduced to three in the *Libro* (687*bcd*). [20]

In this first meeting, then, Juan Ruiz modifies appreciably the attitudes and behaviour of the lovers: the Archpriest is evidently concerned about conducting his courtship in public and his delight at the success of the first meeting is restrained compared with the joy dis-

---

[20] Lida (*Originalidad artística...*, p. 378) suggests that this reduction is due to the influence of the courtly tradition which has a predilection for lamentations but little interest in happy states of mind.

played by Pamphilus; this may in both cases be due to the influence of the courtly tradition (the courtly lover's concern for secrecy is reflected in the first love episode, in sts. 90-91, and again in Don Amor's advice, in sts. 562 and 567-571); but it may also be intended to reflect a more cautious and calculating approach by the lover. Endrina is shown to be markedly more suspicious and cautious in her reactions to this approach and the effect is created of a considerably more prudent person.

IV. *The lover's first interview with the go-between* (P 281-338, *Libro* 697-722): The description of the go-between's professional activities has already been mentioned (p. 129). It should further be pointed out that this description is largely applied to the profession as a whole rather than to an individual (as in 699b, «*estas* echan el laço, *estas* cavan las foyas...»). Trotaconventos herself adds to these generalisations about her calling in a brief interruption of the Archpriest's speech (sts. 703d-705), an interruption which does not occur in the *Pamphilus*. The activities of which she boasts are of a largely mischievous nature, as she cheerfully declares in a metaphor: «Muchos panderos vendemos que non suenan las sonajas» (705d). It is perhaps his description of their activities (700ab, «Como lo han uso... andar de casa en casa...») that led Juan Ruiz to change the story slightly: whereas Pamphilus goes to see the Old Woman (P 283, «...ad eam vestigia uertam»), Trotaconventos comes to the Archpriest's house (*Libro* 701a).

Pamphilus, after the briefest of introductory remarks, goes straight on to describe his love for «uicinam meam quam noscis Galatheam» (P 289); the Old Woman's first reaction (P 299) is to warn him that he has a rival, but she adds that the rival's tight-fistedness has prevented her from helping him. Don Melón, after the interruption referred to above, goes on to declare that he loves a lady who seems to return his love (*Libro* 706b), but that for fear of trouble he has hitherto concealed the fact. Trotaconventos again interrupts to promise skilled assistance and to ask who the lady is (st. 709). On learning who it is she claims to know her and comments that as a widow she will be easier to work upon (sts. 711-710), [21] only then taking up the point that there is a rival in the field. In both texts the go-between goes on to stress the effectiveness of the timely gift and to claim that success with the girl depends on her cooperation; but Trotaconventos makes the

---

[21] Sts. 710 and 711 are clearly in the wrong order in the Salamanca ms., after which Ducamin numbered them. Ms. *G* gives them in the order 711, 710.

additional claim that other «moçetas de cuello alvillo» will be procured for the lover (st. 718). The meeting ends rather differently in each version. Pamphilus promises all the Old Woman asks provided that she delivers Galatea to him (*P* 313-320); the Old Woman replies that she is ashamed to ask for things but has fallen on hard times and she asks for the freedom of Pamphilus's house (*P* 321-328); Pamphilus promises this and begs her to be careful in her approach to Galatea (*P* 329-340). In the *Libro* the lover promises gifts rather more briefly and then hastens to proffer three stanzas of advice (719-722); there is no echo at all of *P* 321-328.

What emerges in this passage is Juan Ruiz's concern to generalise about the activities of *terceras*. Coupled with this is a more cheerfully cynical attitude taken by Trotaconventos towards her profession (e. g., in sts. 705 and 718) and the absence of that note of self-pity shown by the Old Woman of the *Pamphilus*.

V. *The go-between's first interview with the girl* (*P* 339-440, *Libro* 723-765): The Old Woman's approach to Galatea consists of a soliloquy in which she praises Pamphilus as the outstanding young man of the town; then, catching sight of Galatea at her door (*P* 353), she tells her that she retracts nothing of what Galatea may have overheard. The editor, E. L'Evesque, assumes that the Old Woman has known all along that Galatea was in her doorway and could hear all her words. While there is nothing in the text to guarantee the correctness of this interpretation, it seems a very reasonable one. Trotaconventos, on the other hand, goes to Endrina's house crying her wares as a pedlar and is invited in. She leads the conversation in the required direction by commenting that Endrina should get out more; the town is full of attractive young men, with Don Melón de la Huerta outstanding among them. In both texts the go-between then continues to sing the praises of the lover, leading up to an invitation to the girl to say what she thinks about him (*P* 356-380, *Libro* 728-736). Both promise to respect the girl's confidence; but the Old Woman's advice to Galatea to lay aside «stultum pudorem» is not echoed by Trotaconventos.

The reaction of the girl differs considerably: Galatea says (*P* 381-384) that it is not «rusticitas» or «stultus pudor» that is holding her back, but she wonders whether Pamphilus has paid the Old Woman to put these ideas to her. Endrina first asks who the young man is that Trotaconventos is talking about, apparently ignoring the mention of Don Melón in 727c, and on being told his name again reacts with sharp displeasure, declaring her intention not to be taken in by the pair of them (st. 740); [22] she generalises about the sorrows of women who allow themselves to be deceived (st. 741) and declares that she has other worries to cope with (st. 742).

The discussion now follows a very different course in each text. The Old Woman (P 385-400) insists that it is her own idea that Galatea should marry Pamphilus, she having no thought of profit, and stresses that it would be a very good match as both are well-born, rich and good-looking. Galatea (P 401-404) replies that the first approach, by the Old Woman or by Pamphilus, should be to her «amicis». The Old Woman says (P 405-412) that of course the parents' consent is desirable, but meanwhile Galatea should meet Pamphilus and experience the delights of being in love. Galatea replies (P 413-420) that a girl can soon lose her reputation that way and that, though her inclinations are to do as the Old Woman suggests, fear of scandal holds her back. The Old Woman promises (P 421-426) to keep their meetings secret from the gossips and says that there will be nothing to fear. Galatea now closes the meeting with a series of hasty points (P 427-440): she asks for advice on what to say to Pamphilus; she expresses doubt as to whether she ought to confide her secret desires to the Old Woman, but decides to test her good faith; she admits that in her earlier meeting with Pamphilus a close *rapport* was established, but asks the Old Woman to keep it a secret; finally she asks her not to tell Pamphilus immediately of her feelings for him and urges her to test him «multo temptamine» to see whether he admits to the same degree of love for her.

In the *Libro,* Trotaconventos seizes upon Endrina's complaint about her other worries (st. 742) and argues that she needs a man like Don Melón to protect her from all these things. She then tells the fable of the bustard and the swallow as an example of failure to listen to good advice, which leads to being despoiled by the rapacious (sts. 743-755). She ends by commenting upon Endrina's lonely state as a widow,

---

[22] Michael S. Pincus, «Doña Endrina Revisited», *RomN* VII (1965-66), 71-72, thinks that Endrina asks the suitor's name in st. 737, because, knowing Trotaconventos of old, she is not listening properly to her. But to read such «psychological» subtleties into a medieval text seems ill-advised. In fact, 727c is obviously taken straight from P 343-344 and the repetition of the name in 738d echoes the repetition of it in P 357. Having discarded the device of the Old Woman's overheard soliloquy, Juan Ruiz seems to have felt the need to account for the second mention of Melón's name and to have had recourse to the same stylistic device used in sts. 709-711, where Trotaconventos asks the Archpriest who the lady is and, on being told, reveals that she already knows her.

comparing her ironically to the faithful «tortolilla» (757b) and stressing the wretchedness of a house with no man in it. Endrina replies (sts. 759-760) that she cannot marry again before the year of mourning is up. Trotaconventos retorts that the year is already up and, seizing on the reference to mourning, points out how unbecoming are black clothes and a downcast mien (sts. 761-763). Endrina begs Trotaconventos not to press her so hard; she says that she has been plagued with offers of marriage (sts. 764-765c)... At this point there is a *lacuna* in the mss. of six stanzas: when the text resumes we are launched into the fable of the wolf whose good omen proves false (sts. 766-779). The *moraleja*, of which two stanzas survive (780-781), is that man should be content with his lot and not go looking for riches elsewhere. Another *lacuna* follows, this time of 32 stanzas, and the text resumes at the point where the go-between is telling the lover that the girl is to marry someone else. We do not know, therefore, who tells the story of the wolf, but the *moraleja* suggests that it is Endrina. Nor do we know how the meeting ends; whether, for instance, Endrina suggests that Don Melón's feelings should be tested, or whether Trotaconventos's warning to Melón that Endrina is about to marry another (implicit from Melón's reactions in sts. 783ff) is her own device to extract more payment from him. [23]

The changes made in this section are the most sweeping in the whole story and it is abundantly clear that Juan Ruiz was aiming at considerably more than a mere paraphrase.

The difference in the way in which Trotaconventos first approaches Endrina is, perhaps, due to the desire to illustrate the general statement about the habits of *viejas*, «andar de casa en casa» (700b), and the advantage of their calling as *buhonas*. It also allows the author to introduce a touch of dramatic irony by having Endrina say to the bawd «entrad, non rreçeledes» (723d), reminding us unintentionally that it is she who has cause to fear.

The differences in the subsequent discussion have a clear starting point in the fact that Endrina is a widow with a widow's difficulties and obligations. But the whole question of Endrina's widowhood is brought up by Trotaconventos because of the way Endrina reacts to her first approach. Whereas Galatea admits from the start that she

---

[23] Cejador, in his edition (Madrid, 1914), Note to st. 782, suggests this latter explanation. But Lida (*Originalidad artística...*, p. 546, Note 22), while regarding this as an improvement on the original, does not think that it is justified on the evidence of the texts.

is half in love with Pamphilus and is concerned mainly about Pamphilus's sincerity and about the observance of the conventions, Endrina is sharply hostile and suspicious; she knows very well that young women are often the victims of deceit (st. 741). As a result, Trotaconventos switches her attack to play upon Endrina's weakness —her loneliness as a widow and her fears of being exploited by sharks. When this puts into Endrina's mind the duties of widowhood, Trotaconventos quickly stresses its irritations —the obligation to wear mourning and the absence of a man about the house. As Lida points out (*Originalidad artística...*, p. 562) this scene brings out Trotaconventos's gift for improvisation. It also brings out Endrina's prudence and her awareness of the potential dangers in the situation. She is far less willing to be persuaded than Galatea and therefore Trotaconventos has to exercise far more cunning than the Old Woman.

VI. *The go-between's second talk with the lover* (P 441-548, *Libro* 782-823): Only the last stanza of Trotaconventos's report to Don Melón has survived, so we do not know whether any changes were made there. The lover's ensuing lamentation has been studied by Lecoy (*Recherches...*, p. 326) and Leo (*Zur dichterischen Originalität...*, Ch. VI) as an example of Juan Ruiz's technique of *amplificatio*. The differences of content are greater than either critic indicates. Stanzas 783-784 are an interpolation by Juan Ruiz in which Melón curses Trotaconventos for bringing such bad news and *viejas* in general for the deceits they practise upon the world. Pamphilus (P 451-462) exclaims that his mind and body will not function because of his grief, that all his hopes have gone, that he can perceive no haven and that Galatea alone has the power to save him. Melón describes the weakness of his limbs (st. 785) but then goes on to apostrophize his heart, his eyes and his tongue, blaming them for getting him into this trouble. He next curses women in general (st. 790), accusing them of falseness, a sentiment nowhere expressed by Pamphilus. This is more than mere *amplificatio*: a different attitude is expressed by each lover. Pamphilus is shocked and grief-stricken and concerned only with his own case; Melón is angry as well and generalizes upon the theme, blaming not only his own susceptibility but also treacherous *terceras* and fickle women.

The subsequent exchanges follow very much the same course in each text, though there are some differences of detail. The note of cautious hope expressed by Pamphilus when rallied by the Old Woman (P 495-498) is converted by Juan Ruiz into further words of encouragement by Trotaconventos (sts. 802-803*b*); her description of her talks with Endrina (sts. 807-812) gives more concrete details of her visible reactions than does the corresponding description in *P* 505-517 and adds one or two extra touches: in 808*c* she describes her trick for getting Endrina to talk about Melón: «Fago que non me acuerdo, ella va começallo»; in 809*d* she emphasizes the secrecy of their conversations: «Quando alguno vyene otra rrazón mudamos»; in 811*d* she adds the slyly titillating comment: «Paresçe que con vusco non se estaría dormiendo»; finally, in 812*cd* she stresses her power over the girl and her willingness to exercise it if properly paid: «Sy por vos non menguare abaxarse ha la rrama, / y verná doña Endrina sy la vieja la llama.»

In this scene, then, there are two main developments: Melón is made to express bitter generalisations about *terceras* and fickle women; Trotaconventos's manipulation of the situation and the feelings of the pair of lovers is made more explicit and more subtle.

VII. *The go-between's second meeting with the girl* (*P* 549-650, *Libro* 824-867): Juan Ruiz interpolates a brief scene in which Trotaconventos gets Endrina's mother out of the way by a trick so that she can talk to Endrina undisturbed. [24] The ensuing dialogue is very similar in the two versions. [25] I have noted the following differences: firstly, when Endrina admits her love but expresses fear of her mother's interference (sts. 844-845*b*, corresponding to *P* 591-596), Trotaconventos prefaces her reply with a curse upon the head of Doña Rama (845*cd*); then in both texts the girl asks for advice, adding the rider that deceitful advice is shameful; in *P* the Old Woman replies that fear of wagging tongues will not stop her advising Galatea properly and she will meet any challenge on that score; she concludes that Pamphilus is worthy of Galatea and the latter can go ahead without fear of the consequences (*P* 601-618); [26] in the *Libro* Trotaconventos says «vergüença que fagades yo he de çelar» (848*c*); then, after echoing

[24] This interpolated scene is prepared for in a sense by Trotaconventos's comment in 812*c*: «abaxarse ha la rrama». Lázaro («Los amores...», p. 225) suggests that Juan Ruiz was influenced by the traditional presence of the mother in the *ambiente* of peninsular lyric poetry, especially of the Galician-Portuguese *cantiga de amigo*, where she is frequently the main obstacle to the lovers.

[25] L'Evesque treats *P* 549-556 as a monologue to herself by the Old Woman. But I see no reason why these lines should not form part of the ensuing speech to Galatea, as they are of Trotaconventos's speech to Endrina.

[26] Corominas, in a note to 848*a* (p. 326 of his edition), points out that *P* 605-606 are normally attributed to the Old Woman, though L'Evesque prints them as part of Galatea's preceding speech.

the Old Woman's defiance of possible accusers (sts. 849-850b), she declares that Don Melón will help them scotch any evil rumours (850cd). In other words, where the Old Woman says that Galatea will have no cause to be ashamed, Trotaconventos says that any cause Endrina may have for shame will be covered up.

When the girl still hesitates, torn between love and fear, the go-between, after urging her to follow the dictates of her heart, invites her to her own house as a distraction from her worries (P 619-650, Libro 852-864). In P the scene immediately changes to the Old Woman's house, with no indication of any interval of time. Juan Ruiz inserts a passage (sts. 865-867) in which he describes how Endrina agrees to go because, like a hare, she has been driven to the stage of not knowing what she is doing and does not see the trap laid for her. This reminds us of Endrina's earlier plea that Trotaconventos should not press her so hard (st. 764); she is being persuaded against her better judgement. The time having been agreed upon, Trotaconventos goes off to warn Don Melón to take advantage of this opportunity, urging him to be a man (sts. 868-870).

VIII. *The dénouement* (P 651-780, Libro 871-891): Two interpolated stanzas describe the successive arrivals of Endrina and Melón at Trotaconventos's shop. The ensuing speech in which Trotaconventos feigns surprise at Melón's arrival is a magnificent adaptation of an already skilful original (P 651-660). But it also implies one change in the action: whereas in the *Pamphilus* it is Pamphilus who forces the door (P 655, «Arte seram retro paulatim uique reducit...»), Trotaconventos opens the door for Melón on the excuse that otherwise he will break it down (876a). Only the beginning of Melón's speech has survived (st. 877), but it contains one point not in P: Melón keeps up the fiction that he did not know that Endrina was there («¡Vieja, por esto teníades a mí la puerta çerrada!»).

The ensuing *lacuna* covers the rest of the lover's speech, the go-between's departure on a pretext, the rape, the lover's defence of his conduct, the go-between's return and the girl's first bitter reproaches to her (P 663-740). The numbering of the ms. indicates that 32 stanzas are missing, which suggests that the same ground could easily be covered. But the final scene is so different that one cannot tell at what precise point in the narrative the *lacuna* ends.

In P, when the Old Woman returns and asks what has happened (P 723-728), Galatea accuses her of dissembling and of deliberately engineering her downfall (P 720-740). The Old Woman denies responsibility for what has happened in her absence and asks Pamphilus for his account of it (*P* 741-750). Pamphilus claims that his fault was not serious and that it would be improper to tell about it (*P* 751-756). In bitter mockery, Galatea urges him to tell the Old Woman what she already knows; she herself has perceived the trap too late; what is to become of her now? (*P* 757-768). The Old Woman brings the scene to an end by declaring that it is no good crying over spilt milk; they should get together and find a solution; let them make up and get married —and remember the Old Woman who brought them together (*P* 769-780).

The ms. of the *Libro* resumes with Trotaconventos asking Endrina why she stayed in the house with Melón when she found herself alone with him. Her best hope now is to avoid publicising her disgrace, which would ruin her prospects of marriage. She adds cynically that all men behave like Melón (sts. 878-881). Endrina, in her turn, curses *viejas* in general and laments that Trotaconventos's previous helpfulness has turned to nothing; if the birds and the fishes perceived the traps laid for them they would never be caught; once a woman has been caught in such a trap she is abandoned by family and seducer alike and becomes a wanderer, lost in body and soul (sts. 882-885). Trotaconventos «ovo ya conçiençia»: she replies that the wise man does not waste time on grief but seeks a solution for his troubles; let her, who is being blamed for the wrong that has occurred, be the instrument by which things are put right and she proposes they should get married. A final stanza tells us that this marriage took place (sts. 886-891). [27]

---

[27] Corominas argues, in a note to 891*a* (p. 344 of his edition), that «casados» does not here mean «married»: Endrina merely becomes Melón's mistress. In support of this argument he refers to 795*b*, 1316*a*, 1508*b*, 1576*c* «y otros pasajes del *Libro*», points to the use of «marido» and «mujer» in modern Latin America in the sense of «lover» and «mistress» and argues that as «casar», «casado» and even «bodas» were equivocal «velado», «velarse» were used for the sacrament. If the couple got married, he adds, this would be a «historia de amor logrado, esencialmente irreprochable». Leaving aside this remarkable opinion, Corominas's interpretation ignores the evidence of the texts. In sts. 759-760, Endrina says:

> ...non me estaría bien
> casar ante del año; que a bivda non convien,
> fasta que pase el año de los lutos que tien,
> casarse, ca el luto con esta carga vien.
> Sy yo ante casase, sería enfamada, ...
> ...del segundo marido non sería tan onrrada, ...

Trotaconventos confirms that they are discussing marriage in 761*b*: «tomad aqueste marido por omne e por *velado*». That this is not a mere subterfuge but that the lover seriously wants to marry the girl is borne out by *Libro* 598-600,

The main differences in this final passage are, firstly, that Juan Ruiz displays more clearly the guile of both lover and go-between in setting the stage for the girl's downfall and, secondly, that afterwards both Endrina and Trotaconventos generalize: Endrina bitterly about the treachery of *viejas* and the disastrous result of not seeing the traps they set, Trotaconventos cynically about how all men are alike and «least said soonest mended».

The differences that I have pointed out are facts, verifiable in the texts (though I may prove to have been biassed in the selection and presentation of them); that they represent a conscious modification by Juan Ruiz of his source would, I imagine, also be beyond dispute. Where there is obviously room for disagreement is in the interpretation of these facts; in other words, in deciding what Juan Ruiz was trying to achieve by this modification of his model. The following comments are offered, therefore, in the awareness that they provide not a final answer but simply a personal view.

The plot common to both versions is built upon the interaction of the behaviour of the three protagonists. It is not, however, a psychological study in any modern sense; we are not shown behaviour as a means to understanding character, but simply as leading to a particular outcome. The downfall of the girl is brought about because (i) the lover, considering his chances of winning the girl to be poor from a social viewpoint, treats the affair as a campaign to be won by strategy, entrusts the wooing to a professional bawd and does not scruple to take advan-

corresponding to *P* 49-54, where the obstacle to marriage of Endrina's social superiority is stressed. The lover alludes to his family's plan to marry him («cassar me») elsewhere in st. 658, but he tells Endrina that he refuses because of his love for her. When told Endrina is to marry another, Melón laments: «Ffasta que su marido pueble el çementerio / non casaría con migo, ca sería adulterio»: (795*ab*). The source for this is *P* 473-474: «Nec uiuente suo michi nuberet illa marito; / crimen legitimos est uiolare thoros». Trotaconventos's advice in 890*c*: «vos sed muger suya e el vuestro marido», echoes *P* 778: «hec tua sit coniux; uir sit et iste tuus». It seems to me more logical to treat these terms, as they occur in both texts, as literal rather than as euphemisms. What Juan Ruiz calls «lo feo de la estoria» (891*d*) is the unscrupulous way in which Endrina is tricked into a compromising situation and violated. Leo's view (*Zur dichterischen Originalität...*, Ch. XI) that this is really an illicit affair in which the go-between fulfils her traditional role of bawd, with the marriage introduced at the end as a sop to readers' susceptibilities, was attacked by Lida in her review of Leo's book *RPh* XIV (1960-61, 228-237): she argues that marriage is Pamphilus's aim from the start, but that because of his social inferiority he can only hope to achieve this aim by compromising Galatea and so forcing her family's consent; for this purpose he needs the help of a go-between. The passages I have referred to indicate that this is also Juan Ruiz's view of the plot.

tage of the opportunity she engineers for him; (ii) the go-between skilfully and unscrupulously exploits the girl's weaknesses; (iii) the girl is
genuinely attracted to the lover and so allows herself, against her better judgement, to be tricked into a compromising situation.

Let us consider how Juan Ruiz has modified the behaviour of the
characters in relation to the mechanics of the plot. The development
from Pamphilus to Melón is comparatively slight. This is logical enough
in view of the fact that once the lover has handed over direction of
the affair to the go-between his role is subordinate and the outcome
depends less on him than on the battle of wits between the go-between and the girl. At the first meeting with the girl he displays an
anxiety about being observed in public with her that is not shown by
Pamphilus and his delight at his initial success is more restrained.
When told by Trotaconventos that Endrina is to marry someone else
he is more self-accusing in his grief than Pamphilus and in addition
he is bitter in his denunciation of women and go-betweens. At Trotaconventos's house he is more obviously in league with Trotaconventos
than Pamphilus with the Old Woman; she opens the door for him
and he feigns surprise at finding Endrina there. The gap in the mss.
prevents us from knowing whether he took a different line in self-de-
fence from Pamphilus after the event.

Endrina's widowhood may make her more worldly-wise than Galatea, but it does not make her more sensual, as Zahareas and Pincus
appear to believe, nor does it make her easier to lure into a fresh relationship with a man, in spite of what Trotaconventos claims in
sts. 710-711; on the contrary, Endrina displays considerably more
caution and a great deal more «sales-resistance» than Galatea.[28] She
reacts with sharp hostility to Melón's first approach and, though she
agrees to meet him again under socially acceptable conditions (sts. 680-
681), she firmly refuses the kiss that Galatea grants. She reacts with

---

[28] Zahareas, *Art of Juan Ruiz...*, pp. 152-158; Pincus, «Doña Endrina Revisited», p. 72. Zahareas's view is based largely on the assumption that Don
Amor's portrait of the Ideal Woman (sts. 431ff) and the view of women that
emerges from his lesson generally form part of the image of Doña Endrina.
The one factor which he leaves out of account is Endrina's actual behaviour.
Endrina's yielding to persuasion at only the second visit of Trotaconventos
may seem to indicate a somewhat inadequate will to resist. But it is, perhaps,
advisable not to take too literally the apparent time-sequence of the plot. I have
already referred (see Note 19) to the confusion created by Juan Ruiz over
whether Melón and Endrina have met frequently or not at all before the story
begins. Trotaconventos's description of Endrina's reactions to discussion of
Melón (sts. 807-812) creates a similar confusion over whether they have talked
together more often than on the occasion narrated in the plot, especially 808a,
«yo a las vegadas mucho canssada callo».

similar sharpness when she learns that it is Melón whom Trotaconventos represents and, though she appears to show signs of weakening
under Trotaconventos's pressure (sts. 764-765), she puts up considerable resistance and will not admit, as Galatea does, that she is attracted
to the lover.   She is well aware of the dangers involved in relations
with men (st. 741).   At the second meeting with the go-between, the
behaviour of the two girls is much the same : each admits her love
and asks for advice; each agrees to go to the go-between's house and
so falls into the trap.   But Juan Ruiz adds a plea on Endrina's behalf
that she has been so hunted that she no longer knows what she is
doing (sts. 865-866).   The gaps in the mss. prevent us from knowing
how Endrina behaved when left alone in the house with Melón, that
is, whether she let herself be seduced or was raped.   Her behaviour
at the end is limited to recriminations and here she differs from Galatea in that she generalizes about the traps laid for her kind.

Trotaconventos's behaviour differs from that of the Old Woman
largely in respect of the tactics which she adopts in the face of Endrina's resistance; she is given greater scope for deployment of her
professional skill and we are shown that skill to greater effect.   But
some difference of attitude is also revealed.   The Old Woman, in her
one comment on her status (P 321-328), is on the defensive about her
demands for payment, explaining that she has come down in the
world.   Trotaconventos, on the other hand, makes no such apologetic
explanation; rather, she speaks with cynical pride for her profession
as a whole, boasting of the mischief they do (sts. 704-705) and claiming
to be able to ensnare any girl (st. 718).

A case could be made for the view that the motive behind these
changes was simply that of artistic improvement: if a critic like Morawski could feel that in the *Pamphilus* the immediate *rapport* established between the lovers makes the subsequent intervention of the
go-between superfluous (*Pamphile et Galatée...*, p. 25), might not Juan
Ruiz have had a similar view? By making the girl more prudent and
more hostile in her reaction to their advances he made the task of lover
and go-between more difficult and the intervention of the latter more
necessary.   He also provided himself with greater opportunities for
showing the go-between exercising her talents —certainly the first interview between Trotaconventos and Endrina is considerably more effective than that between the Old Woman and Galatea.

But Juan Ruiz does not only alter the behaviour of his characters, he also deliberately inserts at various points in the story generalisations on the subject: st. 685 (Endrina on the dangers of kissing), sts. 699-700 (the Archpriest on the harm done by *viejas*), sts. 704-705 (Trotaconventos on the same theme), st. 741 (Endrina on the fate of women who listen to *viejas*), st. 784 (Melón's curses upon *viejas* in general), st. 790 (Melón's curses upon fickle women), sts. 865-866 (the author's comment on how a woman can lose her head if sufficiently driven), sts. 882-884 (Endrina's curse upon *viejas* and her comment on how women would not be caught if they saw the traps in time), 881*d* (Trotaconventos's comment that all men are like Melón). These generalisations are very much in the spirit of the epilogue (sts. 892-909), in which Juan Ruiz stresses that his aim has been to warn women against the snares of *loco amor* (904*b*), *fabla chica, dañosa* (907*a*), *falsa vieja* and *rriso de mal vezino* (909*c*).

This didactic spirit is also furthered by the changes in the behaviour of the characters. The lover, whose identity is partly merged with that of the author, serves as a vehicle for some of his general statements (sts. 699-700, 784, 790); but the extra touches of caution and guile in his conduct also make him more representative of the *mal vezino*. The go-between's greater cynicism and her greater display of virtuosity underline more clearly the *maestrias e sotilezas engañosas,* as Juan Ruiz calls them in his Prologue (Ducamin, p. 5), of *loco amor.* Endrina is certainly more prudent and more on her guard than Galatea. But, paradoxically, this reinforces Juan Ruiz's argument: it is not enough for a girl to have good intentions or even to be prudent; she must be forewarned and forearmed, she needs *entendimiento* (the key word of the Prologue). María Rosa Lida (*Originalidad artística...*, p. 440) regrets that Juan Ruiz, like the author of the *Pamphilus,* failed to get away from the psychologically inadequate *dénouement* («brutal herencia de la comedia grecorromana») in which the heroine is tricked and ravished, not seduced. But, surely, it is central to the didactic argument for which Juan Ruiz uses the plot that Endrina is trapped through a moment of unguarded weakness, not through yielding to her own desires.

Juan Ruiz's allusions to his model —574 *cd* (in ms. *G* only), 698*cd*, 891*cd*— suggest that he expects his readers to remember his source and so to appreciate what he has done in adapting it. Whether he was sincere in his didacticism, as María Rosa Lida has consistently maintained, or whether, as Menéndez Pidal and more recently Zahareas have believed,[29] he took an ironical view of the didactic tradition, his intention in adapting the *Pamphilus* seems to have been, partly at least, to demonstrate that this well-known plot could be made into an effective *exemplum*.[30]

University of Manchester

[29] R. Menéndez Pidal, *Poesía juglaresca y orígenes de las literaturas románicas* (Madrid, 6th edn, 1957), pp. 207-209; Zahareas, *Art of Juan Ruiz...*, passim.

[30] See also the comments by Roger Walker in his article in this volume, pp. 249-251.

11

RITA HAMILTON

The Digression on Confession in the 'Libro de buen amor'

Félix Lecoy, in his *Recherches sur le «Libro de buen amor»*, dealt exhaustively (or so it had seemed until recently) with Juan Ruiz's treatment of the sacrament of Penance (sts. 1128-61), which is a digression from his account of the *Pelea* between Don Carnal and Doña Cuaresma. [1] He made a summary of the forty-five stanzas in which it appears and added the derogatory statement: «Cette simple analyse suffit à montrer que ce développement non plus ne brille pas par la rigueur de la composition ni la richesse des points de vue», (p. 195). In spite of this, however, he went on to make a careful scrutiny of the whole section, to verify all Juan Ruiz's references and to examine his theological preoccupations. Finally, he suggested that here Juan Ruiz shows himself to be a responsible man of his time: «Notons pour terminer que la Confession est un sujet volontiers traité au Moyen Age par les moralistes, en dehors de toute préoccupation théologique. N'est-ce point en effet le sacrement auquel le fidèle a le plus souvent recours...?» (p. 194). In fact, Lecoy considered the digression worthy of serious critical attention. The approach of recent critics differs from his in various ways. A. N. Zahareas sums up his own views in this statement: «The parodic digression of the misapplication of Christian rites strengthens the humour of this mock-epic narrative by adding the hilarious incongruity of the digression with the frame story.» [2] On the other hand, María Rosa Lida, in *Two Spanish Masterpieces*, comments: «A priest preaches to Sir Carnal and confesses him (here the poet discourses very seriously on 'How a Sinner should confess and

[1] Félix Lecoy, *Recherches sur le «Libro de buen amor»* (Paris, 1938), pp. 194-199.
[2] Anthony N. Zahareas, *The Art of Juan Ruiz, Archpriest of Hita* (Madrid, 1965), p. 136.

Who has the Power to Absolve him')». [3] Another opinion is held by Professor Rafael Lapesa who, in his paper on «El tema de la muerte en el *Libro de buen amor*», referred to Don Carnal's Confession as «un episodio totalmente cómico». [4] These diferent interpretations suggested that a re-examination of the text might well be called for and the result of this re-appraisal is the subject matter of this article.

Juan Ruiz's discussion of the sacrament of Penance falls into two unevenly divided sections. The first gives a general definition of the form and matter of the sacrament in sixteen stanzas (1128-43), three of which are devoted to the narrator's protestations of his own inability to deal with the subject adequately; the second (1144-61) explores far more thoroughly one requirement, affecting particularly the minister of the sacrament, that of jurisdiction. This matter was so important that St. Thomas Aquinas, in his definition of the sacrament, included the warning that «besides the power of order, the priest must have jurisdiction over the penitent so as to be able to command him to perform the acts which belong to the sacrament». [5] Three centuries later, the Council of Trent was to reiterate this by stating that «absolution is a judicial act, and that as judicial power extends only to one's subjects, ordinary or subdelegated jurisdiction is necessary for valid absolution» (*Penance...*, p. 201). It is this important matter that Juan Ruiz discusses in the second part of his digression and he declares his interest in it by writing with a good deal more enthusiasm and conviction and considerably more authority than he had shown when he was giving his general definition of the sacrament.

Lecoy's adverse criticism of the digression called attention to its lack of form and to the poverty of its ideas. Juan Ruiz, he claims, is interested in two aspects only of the whole vast subject of the sacrament of Penance: «la nécessité de la confession auriculaire; interdiction aux prêtres de confesser les paroissiens d'une autre obédience que la leur» (*Recherches...*, p. 198). Lecoy reproaches him particularly for making no reference to the controversy that had raged over the privileges that had been given to the friars in the matter of confession, even though he introduces a friar as the confessor of Don Carnal. The

---

[3] María Rosa Lida de Malkiel, *Two Spanish Masterpieces: the Book of Good Love and the Celestina* (Urbana, Illinois, 1961), p. 43.

[4] Rafael Lapesa, «El tema de la muerte en el *Libro de buen amor*», paper delivered at the Second Congress of the International Association of Hispanists at Nijmegen, 1965, and printed in *Estudios dedicados a James Homer Herriott* (Wisconsin, 1966), 127-144.

[5] B. Poschmann, *Penance and the Anointing of the Sick*, translated and revised by F. Courtney (London, 1963), p. 176.

reproach is justified only if it refers to the lack of overt mention of the controversy for, implicitly, the presence of the friar throughout the scene is the key to our understanding of Juan Ruiz's treatment of the question of jurisdiction.

The controversy to which Lecoy referred had arisen because, in 1227, Pope Gregory IX had granted to the Dominicans the authority to hear confessions everywhere. The same privileges were later extended to the other mendicant friars and confirmed by successive Popes. [6] Secular priests continued to be bound by the strict regulations concerning the limitations of their power of absolution, concerning jurisdiction that is to say, and Juan Ruiz prepares to present all the ironies of such a situation by introducing a friar to be the confessor of Don Carnal. Friars had jurisdiction everywhere because it was given to them directly by the Pope; secular priests had jurisdiction in their own parishes but had the heavy responsibility of discovering for themselves the extent of that jurisdiction so as to avoid falling into sin by exceeding its many possible limitations.

The friar takes the initiative in discussing the sacrament of Penance by refusing to accept the list of his sins written out and sealed for secrecy by Don Carnal. Here Juan Ruiz uses the method he is accustomed to employ for didactic passages: that of the *enxiemplo*. From the story of the friar's rejection of a written and sealed list a lesson about the necessity for confession by word of mouth, auricular confession, is taught to all, both laymen and clerics. Later, the Archpriest will seem to be addressing only his fellow clerics but here he has all Christians in mind:

> Non se faze penitençia por carta nin por escripto,
> sinon por la boca misma del pecador contrito;
> non puede por escripto ser asuelto nin quito,
> menester es la palabra del conffesor bendito. (1130).

There is no means of telling whether this instruction was being given by the friar or by the narrator but the stanza that immediately follows leaves no room for doubt that the lesson has been taken over by Juan Ruiz himself, as the narrator: «Pues que de penitençia vos fago mençión, / repetir vos querría una buena lyçión» (1131*ab*); and when his personal intervention is over, the narrator turns again to the friar who has been standing by throughout to bring him forward with the words: «El frayle sobre dicho que ya vos he nombrado» so that he can re-

---

[6] Addis and Arnold's *Catholic Dictionary* (London, 1957), p. 634.

sume his role in the scene which the narrator's digression had interrupted.

The serious tone in which Juan Ruiz introduces the subject of Confession — «devedes creer firme mente, con pura devoçión, que por la penitençia avredes salvaçión» (1131cd) — and the long apology for his possible shortcomings as an instructor give the impression that he is about to make an intensive study of the sacrament. In point of fact, all he does is to summarise the definitions to be found in Gratian's twelfth-century *Decretum*. Lecoy, in pointing this out, suggested that Juan Ruiz merely reproduced what he had learnt in the course of his own theological studies (*Recherches...*, p. 196) and this may indeed be what is meant by «salvo un poquillo que oy disputar» (1133d). Edward J. Hanna, writing about the opinions of medieval doctors with regard to the sacrament of Penance, has this to say: «They are practically unanimous in holding that confession is obligatory; the only notable exception is Gratian who gives the arguments for and against the necessity of confession and leaves the question open».[7] Hanna is referring to the concluding sentences of the first *distinctio* of Gratian's *Tractatus de Poenitentia*: «Cui autem harum potius adhaerendum sit, lectoris judicio reservatur. Utraque enim fautores habet sapientes et religiosos viros». This calls forth a stern footnote from the post-Tridentine correctors: «Certissimum est, et pro certissimo habendum, peccati mortalis necessariam esse confessionem sacramentalem, eo modo ac tempore adhibitam, quo in concilio Tridentino post alia concilia est constitutum».[8] But this advice was not available to Juan Ruiz who seems to have felt free to make both sides of the argument equally convincing. Lecoy does not mention that Gratian, after stating the orthodox ruling, proceeds to marshal the opinion held by authorities supporting the opposite view, that is, that contrition alone, without confession, can obtain the forgiveness of sins, but it is precisely this that explains Juan Ruiz's procedure. He begins by saying that contrition, confession and satisfaction are all necessary for the valid reception of the sacrament unless a man is in danger of death, when contrition alone is sufficient. He then gives the argument in favour of the power of contrition alone to obtain forgiveness. He does this by selecting three examples from the Scriptures, Mary Magdalene,

---

[7] Edward J. Hanna, article on «Penance» in *The Catholic Encyclopaedia* (New York, 1907), p. 626.
[8] Migne, *Patrologia series latina*, vol. 187, col. 1562.

St. Peter and King Hezechiah, and these three examples give a concise statement of the argument against the necessity of confession.

It is not difficult to see that these are the two sides of the great debate that was carried on throughout the Middle Ages about the relative importance of the subjective factor (i.e. contrition) and the external signs (confession, absolution and satisfaction). In the next century, in 1478, Pope Sixtus IV censured the propositions of the Spanish theologian Pedro Martínez de Osma who, «ruling out the power of the keys, held that the guilt and punishment of mortal sins are forgiven by contrition alone» (Poschmann, *Penance...*, p. 195). This is recognisably what Juan Ruiz implies when he says: «Por contriçión e lágrimas la santa Madalena / fue quita e absuelta de culpa e de pena» (1141*cd*) and more emphatically about St. Peter: «sé yo que lloró lágrimas triste con amargura, / de satisfaçión otra non fallo escriptura» (1142*cd*). As for King Hezechiah, Juan Ruiz wittily contrasts the minimal external sign «ala pared tornado» (1143*b*) with the substantial reward of fifteen more years of life granted, evidently, because his contrition had obtained pardon for his sins:

> lloró mucho contrito, ala pared tornado;
> de Dios tan piadoso luego fue perdonado
> quinçe años de vida añadió al culpado.   (1143*bcd*).

Juan Ruiz, however, does not commit himself. Like Gratian he leaves the question open, allowing his three examples to make their point without further comment from him. Instead, he abruptly changes the direction of his interest and turns to the question of jurisdiction. Lecoy remarks: «En ce qui concerne le second point, on ne voit quelle raison a poussé Juan Ruiz à le traiter sinon son caprice» (*Recherches...*, p. 199). Another, more compulsive reason is suggested by the presence of the friar who, during all this time, has been waiting to give Don Carnal absolution. The question of jurisdiction resolved itself quite simply for the layman into the necessity of confessing his sins only to his parish priest. For the priest, on the other hand, there were more complicated considerations for, from much earlier times (the first record of a sin reserved to be dealt with by the bishop is in England in 1102; see Poschmann, *Penance...*, p. 146), there were exceptional cases where absolution could not be given by a simple priest but must be sought from a bishop or a higher prelate or, occasionally, only from the Pope himself. There were books in which these reserved cases were set out and explained. It was incumbent upon the

153

simple priest, therefore, to inform himself about them and not to fall into grave sin by giving absolution to a man over whom he had no jurisdiction. Juan Ruiz's method of commenting on this situation is one of the most striking illustrations of his own statement that «las del buen amor sson rrazones encubiertas» (68a). It is, in fact, his contribution to the controversy about the privileges enjoyed by the friars.

In the first place, he makes an accusation:

> Muchos clérigos synples que non son tan letrados
> oyen de penitençia a todos los errados,
> quier a sus parrochianos, quier a otros culpados,
> a todos los absuelven de todos sus pecados. (1144)

There are two faults noted here: absolving other parishioners than their own and absolving all sins indiscriminately. From this point to the end of the digression, Juan Ruiz discusses these abuses and suggests ways in which they can be avoided. His tone is so changed as to suggest that he is no longer addressing all Christians as before but now particularly his own fellow clerics. Lecoy notes that the parable of the two blind men, traditionally applied by dogmatic writers to the penitent, is adapted by Juan Ruiz to apply to the priest who exceeds the limits of his jurisdiction. As well as this, the rhetorical questions that follow: «¿qué poder ha en Roma el juez de Cartajena, / o qué juzgará en Françia el alcalde de Rrequena?» (1146ab) and particularly the closing popular, down-to-earth metaphor «non deve poner omne su foz en miese ajena» (1146c) show Juan Ruiz using a jocular, familiar style to present the case considered from the cleric's point of view rather than from that of the penitent.

This attitude is maintained in the following stanzas where the matter of reserved cases is dealt with «¿Por qué el sinple clérigo es desto tan osado?» (1149d) asks Juan Ruiz after stating that even an archbishop has limitations on his jurisdiction and must not deal with cases reserved for the Pope. There are, he says, many other cases which can be dealt with by bishops but are «mucho defendidos a clérigos menores» (1150d). At this point, he prepares to give his list of recommended reading for those whose would keep themselves from error in this matter: «Trastorne byen los libros, las glosas e los testos: / el estudio a los rrudos faze sabios maestros» (1151cd). This conjures up a picture of the religious at his studies and is certainly not directed to the public in general. The list of books of reference is a formidable one so that the picture is also one of almost unremitting toil. It is useful now to recall the words used by Juan Ruiz to introduce these clerics «muchos clérigos synples que non son tan letrados» and the irony of the situation becomes apparent. Long hours of concentrated study are required of simple secular priests «que non son tan letrados» to enable them to discover what their powers are while, standing there, exempt from any such preoccupations is a friar privileged to hear confessions everywhere and prepared to absolve even the hypocritically repentant Don Carnal.

Lecoy made a scholarly investigation of all the authorities mentioned in this context and he doubted whether Juan Ruiz had, in fact, read them all. What is certain, as Lecoy's own researches show, is that Juan Ruiz knew that they contained information relevant to the matter he was dealing with. It was the mass of material available for consultation that he was calling to mind and this is borne out by the fact that, after the ones mentioned by name, he makes a gesture towards

> Decretales más de çiento, en libros e en questiones
> con fuertes argumentos e con sotiles rrazones
> tyenen sobre estos casos diversas opiniones
> pues, por non dezir tanto, non me rrebtedes, varones.　　(1153).

And there he leaves the matter. He reduces his audience now to one and seems to meet him face to face:

> Vos, don clérigo synpre, guardat vos de error,
> de mi parrochiano non seades confesor,
> de poder que non avedes non seades judgador,
> non querades vos penar por ajeno pecador.　　(1154).

The note of personal reproach may simply be a skilful exploitation of the autobiographical method but what Juan Ruiz says here he has said before; this sounds like a restatement of the situation as a domestic problem. Moreover, from this point onwards, the advice given is helpful, understanding and reassuring. Detailed and scrupulously accurate information is given about the entirely different behaviour that is tolerated and indeed expected when the penitent is at the point of death. Any parish priest would be grateful for such clear and precise instruction. There is nothing parodic, comic or hilarious about this thoughtful reminder of the duties which the minister of the sacrament must be prepared to perform when any of the faithful is in danger of death:

mas en ora de muerte o de gran necesidat,
do el pecador non puede aver de otro sanidat,
a vuestros e ajenos oyd, absolved e quitad.

En tiempo de peligro, do la muerte arapa,
vos sodes para todo arçobispo e papa;

(1156b-1157b)

Juan Ruiz explores all the possibilities of the situation. If the
dying man's own parish priest is at hand and the penitent can speak
before he dies, then he should make his confession to him «para mejor
estar» (1158d). If the man recovers, he would again be bound by
«comun derecho» and would need to have his grave sins forgiven by
those competent to deal with them «Vaya a lavarse al rrío o a la fuente» (1159d) and he explains the metaphor:

Es el papa syn dubda la fuente perenal,
ca es de todo el mundo vicario general,
los rríos son los otros que han pontifical,
arçobispos e obispos, patriarca, cardenal.

(1160)

This is the end of Juan Ruiz's digression on the sacrament of Penance. His detailed description of all that a *clérigo synple* must know
about the use of his power of the keys and the limitations placed upon
it by the matter of jurisdiction makes its own point and needs no further comment from him. The significance of his choice of a friar to
be Don Carnal's confessor would have been clear to his readers. The
contrast is sharply marked between the secular priest's responsibilities
and the privileges of the friar. This must have been overlooked by
María Rosa Lida when she wrote: «A priest preaches to Sir Carnal
and confesses him.» Zahareas considered that Juan Ruiz was exem-
plifying «priests who know nothing about absolution yet are given the
right to hear confession. Since they are ignorant they cannot discrim-
inate...» (*The Art of Juan Ruiz*..., p. 134). This is not being fair
to Juan Ruiz who nowhere disputes the right of secular priests to give
absolution; nor, indeed, could he possibly have suggested that such
right should be withheld because of ignorance. He calls attention to
their lack of book-learning and there is, if anything, a certain compas-
sion discernible in his attitude. Many secular priests have not a great
deal of book-learning and yet they are expected to master numbers of
learned volumes, «las glosas e los testos» and to consult the «Decreta-

les más de çiento.» This does not mean that he is condoning their lack of learning. Merely by calling it to mind he is criticising adversely the state of affairs in which inadequately equipped priests are placed in the predicament of either sinning by exceeding the limits of their jurisdiction or of studying with concentration the books which contain the relevant information.

Juan Ruiz has called attention to the ambiguity of the Church's teaching on the sacrament of Penance, to the proliferation of «reserved cases» and to the existence of «diversas opiniones» (1153c) about them even in the Decretals. All this is informed criticism. By introducing a friar to be Don Carnal's confessor Juan Ruiz shows that he is aware of the rules of jurisdiction: a secular priest would have needed special permission to hear the confession of one who was not his parishioner. At the same time, there is no mistaking the scorn which Juan Ruiz shows for the friars by making one of them exercise the doubtful privilege of giving Don Carnal absolution.

As a piece of composition the digression on Confession deserves Félix Lecoy's pejorative description, for its form does little to enhance the reputation of Juan Ruiz, the poet; its content, however, suggests that in this passage, more than in any other section of the *Libro*, the voice of the narrator may possibly be that of Juan Ruiz, «Arcipreste de Hita».

King's College,
University of London

KEMLIN M. LAURENCE

The Battle between Don Carnal and Doña Cuaresma in the Light of Medieval Tradition

The allegorical battle that takes place between the forces of Don Carnal and of Doña Cuaresma is one of the most outstanding episodes in the *Libro de buen amor*. Strangely enough, it has been either ignored or treated in a very cursory fashion by many critics, but most of those who have dealt with this part of the poem share this opinion. Puymaigre is the only one to disagree: he dismisses the *Pelea* as a mere imitation of the thirteenth-century French *fabliau, la Bataille de Caresme et de Charnage*. He acknowledges the fact that Juan Ruiz does not follow his supposed model slavishly and admits that no more than the central idea is borrowed from the French poem, but he suggests at the same time that a more faithful adherence to the original might have yielded more successful results: «Peut-être aurait-il gagné quelquefois à copier plus servilement son modèle». [1]

However, it is precisely Juan Ruiz's innovations that most other critics have praised and critics such as Menéndez y Pelayo, Cejador and Northup consider that he improved upon his model. [2]

These critics, as well as many others, [3] have accepted unquestioningly a direct connection between the *Pelea* and the French *fabliau*. But Amador de los Ríos in the last century hesitated to be too categorical about this relationship: «Tuviera o no presente Juan Ruiz la *Bataille*

---

[1] Puymaigre, *Les Vieux Auteurs Castillans* (Paris, 1862), Vol. II, p. 101.

[2] *El Libro de buen amor*, Edición y notas de J. Cejador y Frauca (Madrid, 1913), Vol. II, p. 76; M. Menéndez y Pelayo, *Antología de poetas líricos castellanos* (Madrid, 1892), Vol. III, p. xcv; G. T. Northup, *An Introduction to Spanish Literature*, 3rd edn., revised by Nicholson B. Adams (Chicago, 1960), p. 105.

[3] E. g. Julio Puyol y Alonso, *El Arcipreste de Hita, estudio crítico* (Madrid, 1906). Chandler Rathfon Post, *Medieval Spanish Allegory* (Harvard Univ. Press, 1915), p. 145.

de Charnage e Carême, es lo cierto que dio a este episodio no escasa novedad». [4]

Lecoy was the first critic to give serious consideration to this question and arrived at the conclusion that Juan Ruiz did not draw inspiration for his *Pelea* directly from the French *fabliau:* «nous avouons ne pas croire à l'existence d'un lien direct entre le poème français et le poème espagnol». [5]. He shows that many of the supposed innovations introduced by Juan Ruiz have parallels in other versions of the combat, [6] although they are absent in the French *Bataille,* and suggests that the popularity of the theme, evidenced in the large number of surviving works on the subject, reveals the existence of «un substrat commun à toute l'Europe surtout à l'Europe méridionale» (Lecoy, *Recherches...,* p. 247). Juan Ruiz and before him the thirteenth-century French author, as well as the subsequent writers on this theme, all found their subject-matter in a tradition rooted in the realities of medieval religious and social life and current throughout medieval Europe.

Despite the convincing evidence adduced by Lecoy in support of this theory, it is not uncommon to find the *Bataille de Caresme et de Charnage* still being quoted as the undisputed source of Juan Ruiz's *Pelea.* [7] Many misleading statements concerning this episode have gone unchallenged and the object of this article is to restate Lecoy's theory and to present further evidence in its support by examining the Flesh-Lent tradition as exemplified in analogous European works. The investigation of these and other pertinent writings reveals, as I hope to show, that Juan Ruiz drew heavily upon traditional material even in the minor details of the *Pelea.* This is a very significant fact which should serve as a guide to our interpretation of the episode. If the fight between Flesh and Lent, including at times the come-back of Flesh after initial defeat, was as commonplace a theme in the Middle Ages as it appears to have been, we are not justified in interpreting the *Pelea,* ending as it does with the triumphant return of Carnal in the company of Amor, as a «rehabilitación de la carne pecadora, una desenfrenada expansión de la alegría del vivir contrapuesto al ascetismo cristiano» (Menéndez y

[4] José Amador de los Ríos, *Historia crítica de la literatura española* (Madrid, 1863), Vol. IV, p. 186, Note 1.
[5] Félix Lecoy, *Recherches sur le 'Libro de buen amor'* (Paris, 1938), p. 246.
[6] See Luigi Manzoni, *Libro di Carnevale dei secoli XV e XVI* (Bologna, 1881); and Grégoire Lozinski, *La Bataille de Caresme et de Charnage* (Paris, 1933).
[7] E.g. Northup & Adams, op. cit., p. 105; Angel Valbuena Prat, *Historia de la literatura española,* 7th edn. (Barcelona, 1963), vol. I, p. 145; Julio Caro Baroja, *El Carnaval, análisis histórico-cultural* (Madrid, 1965), p. 101.

Pelayo, *Antología...*, Vol. III, p. lxxxvii), peculiar to our author. Using the *Pelea* as evidence, Menéndez y Pelayo further makes the Archpriest the unconscious precursor of a «neo-pagan insurrection» (*Antología...*, Vol. III, p. lxxxviii); but the attitudes expressed or implied in the *Pelea* are far from unique for the period in which it was written. Elsewhere in medieval Europe preachers were constantly inveighing against the licentious behaviour of their flock at large at Eastertide, a fact which indicates that it is unjust to single out the Archpriest for attack on this point. John Bromyard, a fourteenth-century English preacher, was particularly vocal in his condemnation of the licence of Easter celebrations. In the following lines G. R. Owst summarizes Bromyard:

> The rigours of Lent now give place to the rejoicing of Eastertide; and the thoughts of men and women turn to the open, the merry greensward, May-Games and revelry, whither they will go with heads rose-garlanded for the feasts and shows. But for the preacher it is a season of gloom. All the good work of Lenten shrift and sermon threatens to be undone. For the Devil, like a king seeing his subjects rebel in Lent, collects his army to recapture them at Easter *cum augmento*. [8]

This comment helps us to understand the medieval background which was responsible for the flight of Doña Cuaresma and the triumphant return of Don Carnal in alliance with Don Amor. To interpret the *Pelea* as evidence of Juan Ruiz's personal sensuality and self-indulgence appears to be wholly unjustifiable. The theme of joy is undeniably present in this episode as Green has suggested, [9] but I hope to show that in favouring the feasting and gaiety of Easter rather than the austerities of Lent, Juan Ruiz is not unique and falls completely within the medieval tradition of the yearly contest between Flesh and Lent. In point of fact, as we shall see, his treatment of the subject can be shown to be relatively restrained in comparison with other versions of the battle.

In attemping to show Juan Ruiz's reliance upon traditional material, it is not my intention to detract in any way from his obvious artistry in handling the theme. The success of the piece is in no small measure due to the spirited style in which it is written and the imagination with which it is presented. Lecoy (*Recherches...*, pp. 247-249) comments on

---

[8] G. R. Owst, *Literature and Pulpit in Medieval England*, 2nd edn., (Oxford, 1961), p. 393.

[9] Otis H. Green, *Spain and the Western Tradition* (Madison, 1963), Vol. I, pp. 61-62.

the strong local colour of the *Pelea* and uses the subtlety of the Arch-priest's arrangement of his field as evidence of the poet's personal contribution to the topic. We have ample proof of his skilful mani-pulation of borrowed material in the Doña Endrina episode and in his Satire on the priests of Talavera. But this article is concerned not to show what Juan Ruiz added to the Carnal-Cuaresma tradition but to assess precisely what he owed to it.

Lecoy lists the principal differences between the *Bataille* and the *Pelea* under four headings: 1. The form of the Challenge. 2. The outcome of the Battle. 3. Carnal's confession and his escape to the infidels. 4. Carnal's revenge and his alliance with Amor.

In considering the form of the Challenge, Lecoy shows very clearly how much the French and Spanish works differ on this point —in the *Bataille,* the challenge is purely verbal whereas formal letters are ex-changed between Cuaresma and Carnal in the *Pelea.* Lecoy (*Recher-ches...,* pp. 249-250), underlines the significant fact that two very simi-lar letters, written in the same type of formulaic language, are to be found in the works of the Bolognese clerk Guido Faba, who includ-ed a letter from Quadragesima to Carnisprivium and a *responsiva con-traria* in his collection of model letters *Doctrina ad inveniendas, inci-piendas et formandas materias,* written around 1229. [10]

A century before Juan Ruiz therefore, there already existed in Italy exact parallels to the letters addressed by Cuaresma and Carnal to each other.

What Lecoy does *not* mention however, is the survival of another Italian letter, written in Latin, which is the equivalent of the missive directed by Carnal to his supporters. It is the *Littera quam scribit Carnisprivium suis subditis,* which is reproduced in Manzoni's work (*Libro di Carnevale...,* pp. 237-238). [11] It begins with the formal open-ing: «Carnisprivium Epicuri regis et reginae uoratricis filius omnibus subditis nostris coquis quataris et locatam bacanalia quam coquinalia tenentibus salutis t'sticiam (*sic*) non paruam mandat». Carnisprivium warns his subjects of Quadragesima's approach; she will be armed with

---

[10] These letters are to be found in Pado Savj-López and Matteo Bartoli, *Altitalienische Chrestomathie* (Strassburg, 1903), pp. 79-80.

[11] Carnisprivium, Carniprivium, Privicarnium (and in the Mozarabic Litur-gy Carnestollendas) are different forms of the name given to Quinquagesima Sunday because originally the Lenten abstinence from meat for the clergy be-gan on this day, or more precisely on the following Monday, although for the laity, it did not usually start until Ash Wednesday. See *Enciclopedia Cattolica* (Rome, 1949), Vol. III, Cols. 906-907.

«cepis aliis poriis scalugris radicibus et aliis machinis rabidis et acutis» and comes at the head of an army of «infinita animalia monstruosa videlicet anguilles pises cancros et alia figuras demonum habentia et orribilia»; the lady will preach famine under the name of fasts to weaken their bodies and hasten death. Wherefore he exhorts his men to be prepared to attack her with «carnes et quicquid in mensa erit.» The conclusion brings to mind Cuaresma's use of a shell as her seal and of Carnal's choice of Valdevacas as his «lugar amado» («Tornavacas» in ms. S). «Datum in contubernio amplo coquinae nostrae sub sigillo stridentium maxillarum oris et appetitus nostri die et anno incacationis eius millesimo ut hic». I have been unable to locate a similar letter by Lent to her subjects but it is more than likely that one existed.

Moreover, letters of challenge appear in the Italian sixteenth century *El Contrasto di Carnevale et de la Quaresima* (Manzoni, *Libro di Carnevale...*, p. 1), which indicates the persistence into the sixteenth century of a literary tradition which we see represented in the letters of Guido Faba in the thirteenth century and in the work of Juan Ruiz in the fourteenth.

The next point discussed by Lecoy is the outcome of the conflict, which is one of the most significant differences between the *Bataille* and the *Pelea*. In the former, Charnage is made to win, whereas in most versions and particularly the Italian ones, his defeat (sometimes only temporary as in the *Libro de buen amor*) is the usual result. Apart from the *Bataille,* there are two other works in which victory falls to Flesh, a sixteenth-century French work *le Merveilleux Conflit* and the Italian *Contrasto di Carnevale et de la Quaresima* of the same century. [12] Lecoy refers to these and claims that «la victoire de Carnage au cours du combat proprement dit, semble être une forme légèrement aberrante de la forme traditionelle première du thème : Juan Ruiz ne la connaît pas». (Lecoy, *Recherches...*, p. 250). With these words Lecoy dismisses this important difference between the two works which appears to me to be significant and to deserve some attention.

Lecoy (*Recherches...*, pp. 245-246) and Lozinski (*La Bataille...*, pp. 85-90) link the origins of the *Bataille-Pelea* to the medieval *débats*. In the *Bataille-Pelea* the champions of the opposing sides are not presented as debaters pleading their cause verbally as they are in the primitive debates but are personifications, one representing the asceticism of

---

[12] Anatole de Montaiglon and James de Rothschild, *Recueil de Poésies Françoises des XVe et XVIe Siècles*, vol. X (Paris, 1875), pp. 110-127. For the *Contrasto,* see Manzoni, *Libro di Carnevale...*, p. 1.

Lent, the other the licence of Carnival. The issue is decided by combat and the supporters of each side are drawn from those foods associated with the respective seasons. In the *Bataille* the author shows a preference for the less austere of the two opponents and gives the victory to him. He concludes with the comment that Carême will be permitted to return for six weeks in every year. It is the same type of result that we get in the *Merveilleux Conflit* and the *Contrasto*. It is clear that these works are much closer to the genre of the debates of which they are descendants. An issue is at stake and the authors permit it to be decided according to their interpretation of Lent as an unwelcome and unsuccessful attack on the enjoyment of the pleasures of the flesh. In the other works, i.e. those in which Lent is allowed to win and of which the *Pelea* is an example, the course of the battle appears to be determined not necessarily by the author's preference but by the realities of the Christian calendar; they are *pièces d'occasion* and even when, as happens in some works, the author displays a marked lack of sympathy for the figure of Lent, she is made to win the contest all the same.

It is necessary to emphasize this point because critics have tended to read into the transience of Cuaresma's victory, meanings which cannot be valid. Américo Castro, for example, sees in this transformation of Doña Cuaresma «victorious» into Doña Cuaresma «fugitive» an instance of the influence of Arabic culture upon Juan Ruiz.[13] Castro comments with accuracy upon the fluidity and dynamism of the entire episode: «Life here is drive and cyclic movement, not a succession of fixed and closed units of content» (*The Structure*, pp. 414-415), and suggests elsewhere (p. 402), that the struggle betwen the opposing forces of Lent and Flesh as presented in the *Libro* cannot be compared with the medieval disputes between Body and Soul. It is perfectly true that the entire episode is characterized by a dynamism and sense of change and movement that are totally lacking in the disputes to which Castro refers. We move from the gaiety of Carnival through the austerity of Lent and then enter once more into the joyous celebrations associated with Eastertide which heralds the return of Carnal and of Amor. But I do not believe it necessary to seek an explanation of our poet's attitudes in «the spirit of the Islamic God, who dignifies the flight toward mystic sublimity without disdaining to speak of the less seemly aspects of the body's function» (Castro, *The Structure*,

---

[13] Américo Castro, *The Structure of Spanish History*, trans. Edmund L. King (Princeton, 1954), pp. 415 and 424.

p. 449). The answer is to be found in Christian practice itself and we may trace the inspiration specifically to an observance which formed part of the yearly liturgical cycle of the Church. [14] According to this observance, Flesh and Lent met in yearly conflict on Shrove Tuesday, Flesh was vanquished and Lent allowed a brief reign until Easter. [15] It is to this that we must ascribe the apparent ambivalence of our author's attitudes which results in the shifting course along which the episode runs.

The next point concerns Carnal's confession and his escape to the infidels. In those works in which victory falls to Flesh, there is no mention of Confession. But elsewhere, as we shall see later on, we get ample evidence of a traditional association between defeated Carnival and the Sacrament of Penance. In the *Libro de buen amor* he is made to confess his sins —and this gives Juan Ruiz an opportunity to indulge in a lengthy digression on the subject of Penance (stanzas 1131-60); the friar gives him absolution and imposes upon him a penance described by Lecoy as a «curious method of religious edification» (Lecoy, *Recherches...*, p. 195, note 1). The discourse on Penance appears to be a serious treatment of a much-debated topic in the Middle Ages and María Rosa Lida interprets it as proof of a moralizing purpose. [16] Manzoni holds a similar view and is convinced of a didactic purpose in Juan Ruiz:

> Là [in the *Libro de buen amor*] il trionfo di Quaresima su Carnevale è accompagnato da tutte quelle considerazioni ascetiche colle quali lo avrebbe accompagnato un buon predicatore, e l'intendimento dell' autore non potrebbe essere messo in dubbio. (Manzoni, *Libro di Carnevale...*, pp. x-xi.)

[14] Victor Frankl places the Archpriest's use of allegory within the Christian tradition; «no hace falta recurrir a un Islam orteguianizado», *El Antijovio de Gonzalo Jiménez de Quesada y las concepciones de realidad y verdad en la época de la Contrarreforma y del Manierismo* (Madrid, 1963), p. 186.

[15] One of Eustache Deschamps' *Ballades* (No. 350, «Contre le Carême») makes Charnage enlist the aid of May and Easter in his contest against Carême:

> ...en Mars est sa saisons
> Une foiz l'an; contre lui nous tenons
> Vigreusement. May le metra en caige,
> Pasques aussi; nous trois le destruirons.

Oeuvres Complètes, ed. le Marquis de Queux de Saint-Hilaire (Paris, SATF, 1882), vol. III, p. 76.

[16] María Rosa Lida de Malkiel, «Nuevas notas para la interpretación del *Libro de buen amor*», *NRFH* XIII (1959), p. 30. See also the article on «The Digression on Confession» by Rita Hamilton in this volume.

But there are other opinions. Zahareas regards it as pure parody. [17]
Otis Green also emphasizes the element of parody, particularly in the
form of penance imposed on Carnal: «The edification is not altogether
serious —its curiousness consisting precisely in its having been turned
inside out for the purposes of medieval laughter» (*Spain and the Western Tradition*, p. 61).

While parody is obviously an important element in the episode, to
see parody in its every detail is to look at it with modern eyes and consequently to commit an error of anachronism. What we consider to
be a «curious form of religious edification», to use Lecoy's words,
was perhaps less curious to the medieval mind. To prescribe a specific
diet for every day of the week as a counteragent to a particular sin
appears to be a rather farcical notion to us today, but the medieval
mind was fascinated by numbers and took delight in these correspon-
dences between sins and virtues; [18] the medieval confessor was in fact
more or less a regulator of diet since fasting and abstinence were considered such important forms of penance. [19] Missals and breviaries of
the period often contain dietary advice:

> vous y trouverez... une série de conseils hygiéniques relatifs à
> chaque saison, à chaque mois, formulés dans des quatrains
> naïfs, si naïfs même parfois, que la pruderie du *siècle des lu-
> mières* nous en interdit la traduction... Une légère pointe de
> gastronomie et de science culinaire se mêle à ces préceptes, ou
> plutôt à conseils tout maternels. [20]

Comments on the efficacy of fasting and abstinence as weapons
against sin are to be found in the writings of the fathers of the Church, [21]
who also taught the inflaming qualities of flesh-meats and the spiritual
benefits to be derived from a non-meat diet. [22] I believe that what we

[17] Anthony N. Zahareas, *The Art of Juan Ruiz, Archpriest of Hita* (Madrid, 1965), p. 136.
[18] E. g. Hugues de Saint-Victor, *De quinque Septenis* in Migne, *Patrologia
Latina* (Paris, 1879), Vol. CLXXV, Cols. 405-414. The *quinque septenis* here
referred to are: (1) The Seven Vices; (2) The Seven Petitions in the Lord's
Prayer; (3) The Seven gifts of the Holy Ghost; (4) The Seven Virtues;
(5) The Seven Beatitudes. Using the Petitions of the Lord's Prayer as a basis,
Saint-Victor indicates the virtue associated with each petition and the opposing vice against which it operates.
[19] See Herbert Thurston, *Lent and Holy Week* (London 1904), p. 86. Penance also included prohibitions about hair-cutting, washing and clothing.
[20] Guillaume Durand, *Rational ou Manuel des Divins Offices*, trans. by
Charles Barthélemy (Paris, 1854), Vol. V, p. 349, note 20.
[21] See Durand, *Rational*, vol. III, Book VI, chaps. VI and VII, pp. 183-201.
[22] Lecoy quotes part of a French poem which deals with this theme, *Recherches...*, p. 195, note 1.

assume today to have been written with a purely parodic intention was meant to be treated, and was treated, with less flippancy in medieval times, and while Carnal's penance might have been intended to arouse mirth, it also had its more serious aspects and was not introduced in order to throw the disquisition on Confession into incongruous relief.

It is a similar error of anachronism that leads Zahareas to suppose that Carnal's confession might be ascribed to the fact that he is wounded (Zahareas, *The Art of Juan Ruiz*, p. 135). This too is traditional material. The practice of making a general confession on the eve of the Lenten fast may be traced to early Christian times and is responsible for the fact that the day preceding Ash Wednesday is called Shrove Tuesday in English. A twelfth-century English homily gives evidence of this pious custom:

> Our soul is sorely wounded; for every sin is the soul's wound; and the priest is a physician of souls; and therefore ought we to come to our priest ere we begin to fast, and of him receive shrift, which we ought to keep all this Lenten time in fasting, in alms deeds, and in good prayers, vigils, unwashen garments, and smart castigations, and in such other good deeds, according as each man prefers to repent of his foul sins. [23]

Ash Wednesday was particularly a time of repentance for public sinners and although public penance had almost disappeared by the fourteenth century, it is not at all surprising that the traditional victory of Lent over Flesh should end in the Confession of the latter. The confession, banishment, testament and death of Carnival all form part of Shrovetide folklore. It is also possible that the imprisonment of Carnal may reflect the ancient custom of incarcerating penitents «in a monastery or some other place of confinement, at least until the end of Lent» (Thurston, *Lent...*, p. 85), and his escape on Palm Sunday brings to mind the tradition of freeing prisoners on Palm Sunday which was also known as Dominica de Indulgentia. [24]

Evidence of the shriving of Carnal after his defeat also appears in other works. Sometimes it is only mentioned, as in an Eclogue by Encina, [25] but we also possess in Italian two actual confessions of Carne-

---

[23] *Old English Homilies of the Twelfth Century*, Second Series, edited and translated by R. Morris (London, 1873), p. 56.

[24] Thurston (*Lent...*, p. 237) tells of a seventeenth-century traveller Fynes Moryson who gives a contemporary account of the release of a boy from prison by the Pope's order. He had been imprisoned for killing a boy of his own age on Palm Sunday.

[25] Juan del Encina, *Teatro completo*, edn. of the Real Academia Española (Madrid, 1893), p. 79.

vale in which the burlesque element predominates. Carnival customs have traditionally relied heavily upon parody and burlesque and an examination of the Italian forms in particular reveals that, if anything, the more frivolous aspects of the tradition have been attenuated in the Archpriest's work. It lies outside the scope of this article to elaborate upon the digression on Confession but it would be interesting to discover precisely why Juan Ruiz chose to introduce such an apparently serious and detailed debate when parody is more normal.

A brief look at the Italian Confessions mentioned above will indicate the difference between these and the treatment given in the *Pelea*. [26] The first one opens with an invocation to the cock:

> Io mi confesso al martire glorioso,
> a san Gallo, che pati tanto male,
> per dare a noi la pace con riposo,
> per merito gli fu cavato l'ale;
> allo honorato patre San Goloso,
> alla sposa sua madonna gallina,
> che martire con lui fu in la cucina. [27]

Throughout the entire poem Carnival commends himself to all the gastronomic delights in which he has indulged so freely. The second Confession is written in a similar vein:

> me confesso a miser san capone
> quanto le grasso, le piu bon.
> E me confesso a madona sancta ocha
> quando le mior, la me par piu poca
> e al nostro devoto padre m. san faxan
> se gen ho anch uno.

[26] See Manzoni, *Libro di Carnevale...*, pp. 121-125; 235-236.

[27] The cock figures largely in Carnival folklore and throughout Europe throwing at cocks and cock-fighting were popular Shrove Tuesday sports. This custom is referred to by Caro Baroja (*El Carnaval...*, p. 82), who gives various reasons for this attack on the cock in particular; one of them is that the cock was considered to be a lascivious bird and symbolic of lust «que deve ser reprimida en todo tiempo, y especial en quaresma» (Alexo Venegas, 1565). Another explanation put forward by Covarrubias (see *Tesoro de la Lengua Castellana* - gallo) is that since hens are the usual Shrovetide fare, killing cocks in sport preserves them from the fate of being left «solos y biudos». Cf. *Libro de buen amor*, Stanza 1098:

> Essa noche los gallos con grand miedo estovieron,
> velaron con espanto nin punto non dormieron:
> non avia maravilla que sus mugeres perdieron,
> por ende se alboroçaron del roido que oyeron,

This one is clearly a parody of the *Confiteor* and includes the

mia colpa
mia colpa mia grandissima torta,

terminating with the blasphemous invocation:

In nomine caponis
et pisonis grassis
et raphiolis speciatis
et bene informaiatis. amen.

A similar note of irreverence is struck in the *Contrasto* when Carnevale, having successfully terminated his battle with Quaresima, utters
his «morning prayer»:

Santissima gallina incoronata,
che per figliuolo havesti un caponcello,
alla lasagna fusti maritata
in compagnia del dolce fegatello
et la salciccia fu martirizata
et pesta bene et messa in un budello
et per farle patir pena et gran duolo
la fu impiccata et messa al fumarolo.

(Manzoni, *Libro di Carnevale...*, pp. 51-52.)

Yet another «prayer» is to be found in the *Rappresentazione et Festa
di Carnasciale et della Quaresima* (Manzoni, *Libro di Carnevale...*,
pp. 117-118.)

The traditional association of Carnival and Confession survives in
folk customs of today. In certain communities in Italy Carnival is
made to confess, not his own sins but those of the community: «L'uso
di una publica denuncia di vizi e magnane della communità pur sotto
forma *scherzosa o parodistica* è assai diffuso.»[28] There is evidence
of the survival of similar traditions in Spain, although in this case a

---

[28] *Enciclopedia Cattolica*, Vol. III, Col. 904. Very often this public confession by Carnival was followed by his being «put to death». Survivals of
this are to be seen in the Carnival customs of the West Indian islands of St.
Lucia and Martinique, where, according to one variant of the tradition, an
effigy representing Carnival is carried in procession on Ash Wednesday and
subsequently «put to death», the effigy being burnt and then consigned to the
sea. Despite the traditional black-and-white clothes of the «mourners», the
spirit of the occasion is entirely carnivalesque and is characterized by burlesque songs and merrymaking. See Daniel J. Crowley, «Festivals of the Calendar
in St. Lucia» in *Caribbean Quarterly*, Vol. 4, No. 2, p. 113, and F. C. Simmons,
«Terre Bois Bois» in *Caribbean Quarterly*, Vol. 6, No. 4, pp. 282-285.

burlesque will replaces confession (Caro Baroja, *El Carnaval...*, p. 118). The modern mind finds it difficult to accept the apparent irreverence with which the sacred was parodied in medieval times. Carnival traditions are a supreme example of this, and Juan Ruiz is by no means the most extreme exponent of the literary genre to which these traditions gave rise.

Carnal's revenge and his alliance with Don Amor have been generally considered to be clever strokes of originality whereby Juan Ruiz is able to link the episode with the theme of Love. Lecoy refers to the suggestion of a similar ending in Guido Faba's *responsiva contraria* and quotes the following excerpt from it: «Donte parola che tu fino sabbato sancto, e no plu, deibe demorare... saipando k'ello die preclaro de la Pasca noi veremo incoronati cum gilli e fiore, e faremmo l'auxelli supra le ramelle cantare versi di fino amore» (Lecoy, *Recherches...*, p. 251). From the very start of the *Pelea* it is made clear that Doña Cuaresma does not intend to put up any resistance after Holy Saturday. Her letter to her followers greets them «fasta la pascua mayor» (stanza 1069*d*), while she imposes a specific time-limit upon herself in her challenge to Don Carnal: «fasta el sábado santo dar vos he lyd sin falla» (stanza 1076*c*). Her terms are obviously dictated by the Calendar of the Church and she already knows before Ash Wednesday how limited her reign is to be. Carnal will return at Easter with Spring and with Love. Post has suggested the French *fabliau Des Chanoinesses et des Bernardines* as a possible source for the alliance between Carnal and Amor (Post, *Medieval Spanish Allegory*, p. 145), but there is no need to seek a precise literary source for this innovation. As we have already seen, Guido Faba's letter offered a precedent within the specific context of the Flesh-Lent conflict and in any case, the association of Love, Flesh and Easter springs quite naturally out of the customs and traditions of a society which observed with great assiduity the rigours of the Lenten season and, as is to be expected, welcomed the physical and moral relief of Easter. [29] Medieval preachers were very conscious of the dangers of Eastertide temptations and issued

---

[29] It is difficult for the modern man to comprehend the austerity of Lenten observance in the Middle Ages. Marriage was not permitted during this season (this explains the popularity of Quasimodo Sunday as a day for weddings —see *Libro*, stanza 1315) and continence was prescribed to those already married. All public games, sports and amusements were strictly forbidden and wars and lawsuits were suspended. All of this was designed to enable the faithful to devote themselves entirely to pious activities during the holy season of Lent. See A. Baillet, *Les Vies des Saints* (Paris, 1739), vol. IX, pp. 115-124.

frequent warnings concerning them as we see in the following extract from an English homily:

> Good men and wymmen, now is passed the holy tyme of Ester, and iche man and wyman is shryven and houseled (received communion), so that thei have forsaken the devell and all is werkes and been turned to God and to is servyce.

The devil is greatly displeased by this general show of piety and makes a special effort to recapture the shriven faithful; he is assisted in his task by food and weather:

> ffor now he seis that the tyme is fayre and warme, and metes and drynkes amenden and been more delicious than thei were, and many beth now fayre clothed and wymmen nycely arrayed: all this him thenketh that is conabull (convenient) to him, and thus with many colours he disseyvith the pepull (quoted by Owst, *Literature and Pulpit...*, p. 400).

Medieval social and religious customs are revealed in many other details of the *Pelea* as well. [30] Lecoy comments upon the fact that Juan Ruiz replaces the more usual medieval Court of Love with a procession. [31] He ascribes this, not to the influence of the Classical poets where processions of Love may also be found, but to the poet's intention to parody a liturgical procession, and suggests that he probably had in mind «la procession la plus ancienne du rite chrétien, la procession des Rameaux: l'Amour rentrant dans ses Etats, c'est le Christ arrivant à Jérusalem aux acclamations d'une foule enthousiaste» (Lecoy, *Recherches...*, p. 261). That Juan Ruiz intented to parody a

---

[30] Even such a minor point as the mention of a general spring-cleaning on Ash Wednesday might have had some basis in reality. Cejador, in his edition of the *Libro* (vol. II, p. 110), mentions the custom of washing kitchen utensils on Ash Wednesday to get rid of the grease, etc., but a more thorough cleaning is suggested by Stanza 1176. If we examine Brueghel's painting of the Carnival-Lent Battle *Der Streit des Karnevals mit dem Fasten* (1559), we observe that one of Lent's supporters appears to be engaged in the task of window-cleaning. This task must have been particularly associated with the opening of Lent to have been incorporated by the artist into the picture. Although the OED gives no early documentation of the term, one is tempted to wonder whether the English spring-cleaning is related to a medieval «Lent-cleaning», a physical manifestation of the spiritual cleansing with which Lent was ushered in.

[31] This parodied procession in which Amor and Carnal appear to be substituted for the risen Christ, strikes the modern reader as pure blasphemy. A somewhat different view would have been taken by the medieval man with his taste for humorous blasphemy of this kind. See C. S. Lewis, *The Allegory of Love* (London, 1959), p. 20.

liturgical procession is correct; but his parody is based, not on the
Palm Sunday but the medieval Easter Sunday procession, an account
of which is to be found in the *Rationale* of Durandus, Book VI,
Caput LXXXVIII:

> In hac processione, praecedunt luminaris... Crux enim
> praecedit, ut carnem nostram crucifigamus cum vitiis et con-
> cupiscentiis, et post cruces vexilla, quae sunt victoriae Jesu
> Christi insignia. Sequuntur sacerdotes dealbati, exultantes in
> laudes resurrectionis.

The singing of the hymn *Te Deum laudamus* (transformed in the *Libro*
into *Te Amorem laudamus*) on Easter Sunday is described in Durandus Book VI, Caput LXXXVII, while the verses 'exultemus et laete-
mur', 'venite exultemus', 'benedictus qui venit', and 'mane nobiscum'
all appear either in the Divine Office or the Masses of Easter week.
This explanation of the procession as a parody of the festivities of
Easter gives greater unity to the entire episode; it makes the parody
more pertinent and helps to account for the inclusion of the *Pelea*
which leads up to it. [32]

The cold reception given to Don Amor in various Spanish cities
during the Lenten months also appears to have traditional analogues.
In the *Canzone d'un Fiorentino al Carnevale,* Carnevale is forced to
flee from the city of Florence because the asceticism of its inhabitants
makes life intolerable for him. He makes his way to Rome where
he hopes to be made more welcome (Manzoni, *Libro di Carnevale...*,
pp. 53-78).

The foregoing makes it clear that much of the material of the
Pelea is drawn from a highly developed medieval tradition based on
the Calendar of the Church. This Flesh-Lent-Easter tradition was characterized by its emphasis on gaiety and lack of enthusiasm for the

---

[32] It is interesting to note that Le Grand d'Aussy gives the following
description of an Easter custom, and although Love does not figure in it,
it appears to have some features in common with the Easter procession in the
Libro de buen amor: «L'un des jours de la semaine de Pâques, les étudiants
des écoles, les clercs des églises, les jeunes gens de la ville, s'assembloient
dans la place publique au bruit des sonnettes et de tambours. Les uns por-
toient des étendards burlesques; les autres étoient armés de lances ou de
bâtons. De la place, ils se rendoient, avec le tapage horrible dont on imagine qu'étoit capable une pareille cohue, à la porte extérieure de l'église principale du lieu. Là ils chantoient Laudes.» P. J. B. Le Grand d'Aussy, *Histoire de la Vie Privée des François, depuis l'origine de la Nation jusqu'à nos
jours*, 2nd edn. (Paris, 1815), p. 48. This custom possibly represents a degene-
ration of the original procession of which Durandus writes.

asceticism and rigours of Lent. These attitudes are symbolically reflected in the representation of Carnival as a gay, youthful, lovable character while Lent is an old, wrinkled hag of particularly unprepossessing appearance and temperament. The only sympathetic portrayal of Lent is to be found in a Croatian work *Poklad i korizma*[33] by Marko Marulic' (1450-1524), a summary of which is given by Lozinski, *La Bataille...*, pp. 118-119). It is an entirely edifying work which urges us to rejoice at the death of the Flesh and the victory of Lent, because her victory has rescued us from the power of the Devil. But apart from this instance, even in those battles which end in the defeat of Flesh, there is little sympathy for his opponent.

Naturally, those in which she loses paint her in damnable colours. In the *Bataille,* Charnage is:

> Riches... de terre et d'avoir
> Et de bons amis esforciez;
> Moult es amez et essauciez
> Par tout le monde, et honorez
> De dus et de rois coronez,
> Et d'autre gent par mainte terre.　　　　　(11. 26-31).

Carême, on the other hand, is:

> 　　　　　le felon,
> Qui moult est fel et anieus:
> Ce sevent bien li familleus
> Qui ont esté en son país.
> De povres gens est moult haïs.　　　　　(11. 34-39).

In the *Merveilleux Conflit,* Charnage is «un maistre gars, un vaillant champion» but Carême is «Triste, hydeux et maigre personnage». Similarly, in the *Contrasto,* Carnasciale is:

> Fresco et colorito,
> allegro, badiale et compagnone
> da ogni gente amato et reverito (Canto Secondo Stanza L)

but Quaresima is:

> pallida, magra et tutta accidiosa...
> nessun trovava che ben le volesse. (Canto Secondo Stanza XLIX)

This hostile attitude towards Lent is understandable in works whose authors are prepared to give victory to Flesh. What is surprising, how-

---

[33] See *Pjesme Marka Marulic'a*, ed. I. K. Sakcinski (Zagreb, 1869).

ever, is the lack of sympathy with which Lent is portrayed even when she is allowed to be the victor. This is particularly evident in Italian versions. In the *Transito e Testamento di Carnevale* (Manzoni, *Libro di Carnevale...*, pp. 135-153), the protagonist Carnevale «padre diletto» dies in order to make way for his opponent, but in the final stanza Death is moved to take pity on him and promises to restore him to life. The poem ends on a note of hope:

> ...vale,
> ma torna presto o padre Carnevale.

In the *Frottola di Carnevale* Quaresima is described as «una vecchia con bruta ciera» (Manzoni, *Libro di Carnevale...*, pp. 79-85), and in the *Rappresentazione et Festa di Carnasciale et della Quaresima,* she wins the fight but is assisted by an odd assortment of rogues and ruffians with symbolic names, Mangia-Spada, Malizia, Quercio, etc., while Carnasciale enlists the help of the young and noble. Eustache Deschamps in his ballad *Contre le Carême* expresses extremely strong feelings on the subject of Lent:

> Maudit soit-il, et benoit soit Charnage.
> Caresme met les povres gens au bas,
> Jeuner les fait et estre mal servis,
> Et les contraint par grief labours de bras...

The presentation of Lent as an unlovable old woman and of Carnival as an amiable and handsome young man was therefore traditional and Henri Merimée sums up these attitudes when he recounts Carnival customs in which the two symbolic figures appear. [34] Lent is summoned by Carnival to a rendezvous but she is so horrible to look at, that the very sight of her causes her opponent to drop dead.

The preceding pages give us some idea of the material from which Juan Ruiz drew the inspiration for his *Pelea:* the choice of this particular theme may reveal something of the personality of our author to us, but despite the liveliness of the piece, his handling of this theme is, if anything, rather restrained, and upon close analysis the episode does not provide us with proof of Juan Ruiz's «buen diente y mejor estómago» which Sánchez-Albornoz sees revealed in it. [35] This same critic refers to the «sabroso paladeo» with which the combatants are

[34] Henri Mérimée, *Spectacles et Comédiens à Valencia, 1580-1630* (Toulouse-Paris, 1913), pp. 92-93.
[35] Claudio Sánchez-Albornoz, *España, un enigma histórico* (Buenos Aires, 1956), vol. I. p. 496.

evoked, while Otis Green refers to the «*cooked* dishes of meat and game» (*Spain and the Western Tradition*, p. 61). These are misleading comments because an examination of the text fails to yield the gastronomic treat which we are led to expect from the above-quoted critics. This is not the case in the French *Bataille* which contains a collection of dishes accompanied by their appropriate seasonings and sauces. [36] In the *Pelea,* as Aguado points out, the combatants are generally live animals with relatively few exceptions. [37] These exceptions are smoked and dried meat or fish, cecina, tocino, jamón, while a few cuts (uncooked) appear. [38] An unprejudiced examination of the text reveals that the brilliance and vitality of the piece derive from a good-humoured clash between live animals and not from the gourmet daydreams of a gluttonous priest.

To sum up, the *Pelea* reveals an enormous sense of fun and enjoyment of life on the part of its author but to regard it as Juan Ruiz's hymn of praise to rebellious flesh is to fail to appreciate the tradition from which the episode sprang; both the initial victory of Lent and her subsequent flight are to be attributed to the Christian calendar and not to the caprice of the poet. Gybbon-Monypenny suggests that the piece was probably composed separately and «later on fitted into the frame-work of the *Libro* without too much regard for either the logic or the chronology of the narrative». [39] It is true that while it main-

---

[36] Corroboration of the existence of these dishes may be found in the fourteenth-century French recipe book *Enseignements* referred to by Lozinski.

[37] José M. Aguado, *Glosario sobre Juan Ruiz* (Madrid, 1929), p. 195.

[38] The only debatable item is the *fresuelos fritos* of the *G* MS., which reads *quesuelos friscos* in the *S* MS. While cheese was at this period considered a «mets gras» and as such would quite rightly have supported Carnal, I prefer the *G* reading (See *Libro de buen amor* edited by G. Chiarini, Milan-Naples, 1964, pp. 207-208). Aguado (*Glosario...*, pp. 398-9) describes *fresuelo* < freir? as the «único guiso que lidia en la batalla» and explains that in Asturias *frixuelos* is the name given to «unas tortas de harina amasadas con huevos y fritos en manteca». Corominas (DCELC-filló) suggests a different derivation, *foliola,* which is responsible for the Galician *fillò, fillòs;* other dialectal variants are *fiyuela* (León), *filloaga* (Zamora), described as «morcilla hecha con sangre de cerdo, arroz, canela y azúcar», i. e. a type of black-pudding. Another form of the same word is *frisuelo* for which Corominas finds documentation in the meaning under discussion only in the 1817 Academy Dictionary, but which clearly appears to coincide with our *fresuelo.* Caro Baroja (*El Carnaval...*, pp. 94-95) refers to the custom of eating *filloas* in Galicia at Carnival-time. These he describes as «tortillas de leche, sangre de cerdo y harina»; he also maintains that throughout Spain some form of black-pudding is characteristic of Carnival fare. It seems most likely that this is what *fresuelo* here represents. See also V. García de Diego, *Etimologías españolas* (Valencia, 1964), pp. 487-488.

[39] G. B. Gybbon-Monypenny, «The two versions of the *Libro de buen amor*», *BHS* XXXIX (1962), p. 217.

tains a precise chronology within itself, the episode seems to have been inserted at random at this particular point of the poem, but what is significant is that this traditional conflict between Flesh and Lent is made to achieve thematic unity within the structure of the poem, by the alliance between Carnal and Amor at Eastertide— Juan Ruiz's contribution to the tradition is the parody of the Easter procession which gives him the opportunity to indulge in a biting piece of anti-clerical satire. The whole *Pelea* leads up to this and serves as prologue to it. Gybbon-Monypenny also believes that Juan Ruiz did not necessarily intend the episode to have any «profound significance in relation to the *Libro* as a whole», [40] which is possibly true; its *raison d'être* lies in the fact that it serves as an introduction to the satirical piece that follows, which is in the direct tradition of the anti-clerical goliardic satire of the period.

University of the West Indies

[40] Gybbon-Monypenny, «The two versions...», p. 217.

IAN MICHAEL

The Function of the Popular Tale in the 'Libro de buen amor'

The *Libro de buen amor* contains thirty-five popular tales,[1] which occupy more than one fifth of the total work. References to many of them have been included in Stith Thompson's monumental *Motif-Index of Folk-Literature,* which incorporates the results of the work of R. S. Boggs and J. E. Keller.[2] A glance at these general indices will serve to demonstrate Juan Ruiz's place in the vast medieval tradition of the popular tale, although they do not provide even a minimal coverage of his possible sources. Nevertheless, these classifications by theme of versions of popular tales are at least as useful as glossaries to the linguist; they provide a starting-point for discovering other versions of the particular tale with which the researcher is confronted, which otherwise he might think unique.

Otto Tacke and Félix Lecoy both expended much energy in tracking down the possible sources for Juan Ruiz's tales,[3] but they do not ap-

---

[1] I follow Kenneth Jackson in preferring this term to «folk-tale», «fable», etc., which may have restrictive or unsatisfactory connotations, and I use «popular» in the sense of «enjoyed by some or all classes of medieval society», not in any «folk» sense; for a discussion of this difficulty, see Kenneth H. Jackson, *The International Popular Tale and Early Welsh Tradition,* The Gregynog Lectures, 1961 (Cardiff, University of Wales Press, 1961), pp. 2-4. Jackson also provides an excellent account of the main theories propounded in folklore research up to the present time, pp. 37-51.

[2] Stith Thompson, *Motif-Index of Folk-Literature,* second edition (revised) (Copenhagen, 1955-58), 6 vols.; in the study of each tale, my references to this work will consist of the word *Motif* preceding Thompson's classification number, followed by his category-title in parentheses; R. S. Boggs, *Index of Spanish Folktales classified according to Antti Aarne's «Types of the Folktale...»* (Helsinki, Folklore Fellows Communications no. 90, 1930); J. E. Keller, *Motif-Index of Mediaeval Spanish Exempla* (Knoxville, Tennessee, 1949). I shall also refer to *The Types of the Folktale: A Classification and Bibliography* by Antti Aarne, translated and enlarged by Stith Thompson (second revision) (Helsinki, FF Communications no. 184, 1961); my references to this work in the study of each tale will consist of the word *Type* preceding Aarne's classification number, followed by his category-title in parentheses.

[3] Otto Tacke, «Die Fabeln des Erzpriesters von Hita im Rahmen der

pear to have borne in mind Joseph Bédier's warning about the uncertainty of relying solely on extant written versions:

> ... le caractère essentiel des contes populaires est de se transmettre, non pas seulement de livre en livre, mais de bouche en bouche. Les livres sont donc un *véhicule* puissant, mais non unique. [4]

Kenneth Jackson also makes this point:

> ... when we are dealing with literatures in which oral telling is known or believed with good reason to have played a very large part we ought not to assume that some particular version known to us —call it B— of any given story is *directly* derived from version A unless there is some definite and irrefutable piece of evidence other than identity of plot to prove that version B does actually come from version A and not from some third version now lost. (*The International Popular Tale...*, p. 49).

Francis Lee Utley attempts to make a sharp distinction between «oral» and «literary» tales:

> The oral tale is usually modern, and if properly collected it bears the stamp of collector, place, date, tale-teller, and provides the exact unaltered text. The literary tale has none of these clear signs of oral transmission. This leads us to a startling paradox —that most or all medieval «folk tales» are literary, since that is the only way in which they could have been preserved. [5]

But it is patent that a literary tale may have been recounted by a reader to his friends and thus have gradually taken on the characteristics of an oral tale, or that an oral tale may have been taken up by an author who then eliminated the signs of oral transmission.

An example of the perils that may be incurred by failing to allow of the possibility of oral transmission, or at least of lost intermediary written versions, is provided by Lecoy's study of the source of the

---

mittelalterlichen Fabelliteratur», *RF* XXXI (1912), 550-704; Félix Lecoy, *Recherches sur le Libro de buen amor de Juan Ruiz...* (Paris, 1938). Lecoy has pointed out Tacke's errors and revised many of his conclusions. See also Dorothy Hite Claybourne and Chauncey Edgar Finch, «The Fables of Aesop in *Libro de buen amor* of Juan Ruiz», *Classical Journal*, LXII (1966-67), 306-308, who suggest that Juan Ruiz had a reading knowledge of Greek.

[4] *Les Fabliaux. Etudes de littérature populaire et d'histoire littéraire du moyen âge* (Paris, 1893), p. 54.

[5] «Folklore, Myth and Ritual» (pp. 103-104), in *Critical Approaches to Medieval Literature*, ed. Dorothy Bethurum (New York, 1960), pp. 83-109.

tale known as *Vulpes* (or The fox who played dead); after examining the Greek and Arabic versions and comparing them with the versions in the *Conde Lucanor* and the *Libro de buen amor,* he concludes: 1) that the Greek version, although older, must represent a tradition «plus travaillée» than the Arabic version; 2) that the Spanish authors are nearer the Greek version than the Arabic; 3) that, of the two Spanish versions, Juan Ruiz's is much nearer the sources than Don Juan Manuel's (*Recherches...*, p. 140). These conclusions might seem acceptable if Lecoy had not gone on to say:

> Les deux derniers points nous permettent en outre de suppo-
> ser une version arabe plus proche de la version grecque que
> l'actuelle seule conservée. (*Recherches...*, p. 140).

This is surprising, since, if we assume that Juan Ruiz knew no Greek, points 2 and 3 would rather lead one to suppose that there had existed intervening Occidental versions (in Latin or French) between the Greek version and Juan Ruiz's but Lecoy had already decided for unstated reasons that

> Le roman, dans son ensemble, est certainement d'origine orien-
> tale; les conditions dans lesquelles la forme occidentale s'est
> constituée sont mal connues, mal connus également les chemins
> par lesquels certains traits de la forme orientale sont venus à la
> connaissance d'écrivains européens. (*Recherches...*, p. 138).

Whether Lecoy's suppositions are well founded or not is of little real importance, but they do serve to show that certainty in these matters is at a premium. The hunt for sources may offer the further disadvantage of concentrating interest of a folkloric kind on to the origin and propagation of individual tales while paying little attention to a particular author's artistic use of them.

A number of scholars have followed the comparative approach and have undertaken comparisons of Juan Ruiz's treatment of particular tales with other versions of them,[6] but it is clear that any conclusions drawn from such comparisons can only be tentative if the direct sources

---

[6] They include: F. Lecoy, *Recherches...*, pp. 114-171; Ramón Menéndez Pidal, «Nota sobre una fábula de don Juan Manuel y de Juan Ruiz», in *Hommage à Ernest Martinenche* (Paris, 1938), pp. 183-186, reprinted in *Poesía árabe y poesía europea* (Col. Austral), pp. 118-123; L. G. Moffatt, «Pitas Payas», in *South Atlantic Studies for Sturgis E. Leavitt* (Washington, 1953), pp. 29-38; Irma Césped, «Los *fabliaux* y dos cuentos de Juan Ruiz», *BFC*, IX (1956-57), 35-65.

13

of each version are not known for certain: details that might be thought typical of Juan Ruiz may have already existed in his source; Juan Ruiz and the other authors with comparable versions may have known the tale in more than one form. If the latter were sometimes the case, it is likely that they will have chosen the source version most suited to the tone of their particular work and to their diverse temperaments. Don Ramón Menéndez Pidal made this valuable point in his study of Juan Ruiz's and Don Juan Manuel's distinct versions of The fox and the crow:

> Aun el más original autor debe un 80 por 100 a la tradición cultural en que se educó; pero ya es parte de su originalidad la mera selección que practica sobre el caudal de recuerdos que la tradición entrega a todos en común (*Poesía árabe...*, pp. 122-123).

Jackson, moreover, warns of the dangers of limited comparisons:

> ... it is a disastrous mistake to confine one's comparative study to one or two other versions, very likely quite aberrant and untypical, which one happens to know —more particularly if they seem to suit one's theory (*The International Popular Tale...*, p. 47).

A further problem of the popular tale is that of the moral element. After his version of the tale of *Vulpes,* or The fox who played dead, Don Juan Manuel sums up the moral in a pair of his atrocious «viessos»:

> Sufre las cosas en quanto devieres,
> estraña las otras en quanto podieres.

In these lines and in the preceding detailed moral lesson in prose put into the mouth of Patronio when he is giving the solution to the Conde Lucanor's problem, it is clear that the point of *Vulpes* for the Infante was that one should put up with minor inconveniences but resist any imposition that threatens one's existence. The Archpriest in his version of the tale first puts the moral in the mouth of the fox itself after it has run off:

> Dixo: «Todas las coytas puede ome sofrir,
> mas el coraçón sacar e muerte rresçibir
> non lo puede ninguno nin deve consentyr;
> lo que emendar non se puede, non presta arrepentyr.» (1420).

The moral in the first three lines is similar to Don Juan Manuel's, but the last line shows a new interpretation and in the following stanza the now changed moral is transferred to the mouth of Doña Garoça:

> Deve catar el omne con seso e con medida
> lo que fazer quisiere, que aya d'él salyda. (1421*ab*).

By the next stanza Doña Garoça is particularizing the new moral to the situation of a woman, finally scorned by her lover, losing «toda su onrra, la fama e la vida» (1422*d*). Thus in a few lines Juan Ruiz skilfully adjusts the more obvious moral lesson to be derived from *Vulpes* to the moral required at that moment in the episode of Doña Garoça.

These distinct moral points extracted from the tale by the two authors serve to indicate that the popular tale, although it often has an implicit moral lesson, need not possess a lesson at all and, indeed, may frequently be capable of imparting quite different lessons. Bédier maintained that the French *fabliaux* «...ne sont point des dits moraux; mais, ce n'est pas dire qu'ils doivent nécessairement être immoraux» (*Les Fabliaux...*, p. 9) and he concluded: «...l'intention morale n'est jamais qu'accessoire» (*Les Fabliaux...*, p. 272). Bédier claimed that the dynamism of the popular tale lay elsewhere, in

> ...la *singularité* de la situation, qui le rend plaisant, tragique, facile à retenir; d'autre part, dans la *généralité* des sentiments, qui lui permet de s'accommoder aux moeurs les plus diverses»

> (*Les Fabliaux...*, p. 222).

Jackson appears to hold a similar view: «It [*scil.* the popular tale] must be interesting and must have a 'point' which can be successfully put across...» (*The International Popular Tale...*, p. 5 [Jackson is apparently speaking of a narrative point, not a moral point]); «...man has always loved stories and story-telling for their own sake as entertainment and always will love them for that reason» (*The International Popular Tale...*, p. 43). The fact that a moral point is not necessarily implicit in the tale is demonstrated by Juan Ruiz's version of The lazy men (457-467). The closing moral is put in the mouth of Don Amor:

> «Por ende mi amigo, en tu coraçón non yaga
> nin tacha nin vyleza de que dueña se despaga.» (467*cd*).

181

In the Archpriest's version the lady is unable to decide which of the two sluggards is the lazier and despises them both. In the version in Grimms' *Kinder- und Hausmärchen* called «Die drei Faulen», the three lazy men are the sons of a king and the laziest is rewarded with the kingdom.[7] Sometimes, therefore, what is essentially the same tale is capable of vastly different moral interpretations. In his study of the *fabliaux* Per Nykrog departs from Bédier's view that the moral lesson is only an accessory element:

> ... il n'est pas impossible que cette moralité —qui souvent a tout l'air d'être imposée à l'auteur comme une sorte d'obligation— soit inhérente au genre, et constitue un vestige d'une phase primitive de son évolution...[8]

But Nykrog is discussing «moralités tirées des événements racontés» (*Les Fabliaux*, p. 248) and does not convincingly rebut Bédier's opinion that the moral lessons are not an *essential* or organic part of the tales.[9]

For most medieval collections of tales, the comparative approach offers the great advantage of concentrating interest on the features peculiar to a particular author and, if undertaken under proper conditions, can help to illuminate the individual author's method and style. The function of the tales in these cases will not be hard to uncover: they generally have the traditional two-fold task of entertaining and teaching. Unlike the *Conde Lucanor* and the other medieval Spanish books of *exempla*, the *Libro de buen amor* is by no means a mere collection of tales gathered into a loose framework. With Juan Ruiz popular tales are accessory only; they are always subordinated to

---

[7] See Johannes Bolte and Georg Polívka, *Anmerkungen zu den Kinder- und Hausmärchen der Brüder Grimm* (Leipzig, 1918), III, p. 211.

[8] Per Nykrog, *Les Fabliaux* (Copenhagen, 1957), p. 249.

[9] Anthony N. Zahareas, *The Art of Juan Ruiz, Archpriest of Hita* (Madrid, 1965), uses a partial quotation from Nykrog (*Les Fabliaux*, p. 103) to support his contention that «these amusing, coarse tales *almost always* preach a moral or demonstrate a lesson» (p. 80, my italics); but Nykrog admits that the number of *fabliaux* that have an expressed moral lesson is lower than Zahareas would have us suppose: «Un tiers seulement des fabliaux n'a pas de moralité exprimée, un autre tiers a des leçons exprimées avec des formules assez diverses, et le dernier tiers se partage entre les contes qui sont formellement caracterisés comme des 'exemples' et ceux qui se terminent sur un proverbe.» (*Les Fabliaux*, p. 101). Furthermore, it is impossible to see what kind of moral lesson can be drawn from some of the *fabliaux* whose titles alone Bédier considered so obscene that he would refer to them only by numbers. Examples of highly original lessons (or non-lessons) drawn from traditional tales can be found in James Thurber, *Fables for Our Time* (New York, 1952), and *Further Fables for Our Time* (New York, 1956).

his main purpose. It would be of interest, therefore, to study the points in the *Libro* at which the tales occur, the way in which Juan Ruiz adjusts them to his narrative, and their relevance to his main theme; in short, to discover whether or not they have a consistent function in the poem.

The first important point is that the tales are not spread evenly throughout the *Libro* but occur at certain specific points. This was noticed by Lecoy:

> Elles [*scil*. les fables] se rencontrent, non pas reparties à travers tout l'ouvrage, mais groupées en deux ou trois développements particuliers... (*Recherches*..., p. 113 [he actually notes five points]).

If the Seven Deadly Sins section is counted separately from the Archpriest's Debate with Don Amor, there are in fact ten points at which tales occur and two of these episodes contain no less than ten tales each:

I. Introduction (44-70): Tale 1 (one tale).
II. First love affair (77-104): Tales 2 and 3 (two tales).
III. Reflections on Destiny (123-165): Tale 4 (one tale).
IV. Third love affair (166-180): Tale 5 (one tale).
V. Archpriest's Debate with Don Amor, Part I (181-216): Tales 6 and 7 (two tales).
VI. Seven Deadly Sins (217-371): Tales 8, 9, 10, 11, 12, 13, 14, 15, 16 and 17 (ten tales).
VII. Archpriest's Debate with Don Amor, Part II (372-575): Tales 18, 19, 20 and 21 (four tales).
VIII. Doña Endrina (576-891): Tales 22, 23 and 24 (three tales).
IX. Doña Garoça (1332-1507): Tales 25, 26, 27, 28, 29, 30, 31, 32, 33 and 34 (ten tales).
X. Song of the Clerics of Talavera (1690-1709): Tale 35 (one tale).

I now propose to examine the tales in their context in order to see whether any general conclusions may be drawn about their over-all function in the poem.

I. INTRODUCTION (44-70)

Tale 1: *Dispute between the Greeks and the Romans* (46-63).

Motif H 607.1 (Riddles: Symbolic Interpretations); *Type* 924A (Novelle: Clever Acts and Words); Lecoy, *Recherches...*, pp. 164-168.

Scholars have lavished more attention on this tale than on any of the others [10] because it occurs in a section the explicit purpose of which «is to clarify the manner in which we must read and understand the narrative» (Zahareas, *The Art...*, p. 26). The various interpretations of the tale have, however, diverged considerably. Leo Spitzer held the view that, despite the mutual misunderstanding of the Greeks and the Romans, God's purpose is achieved («En torno...», p. 124). María Rosa Lida de Malkiel interpreted the tale as follows:

> ... ambas interpretaciones son igualmente legítimas, aunque no igualmente valiosas; lo que escoge el lector que tiene la ventura de ser docto y virtuoso no es igual a lo que elige el necio y pecador: es «lo mejor» (67*d*). ...La admisión de diversas interpretaciones de valor diferente no es incompatible con la creencia en la realidad firme de lo interpretado. («Nuevas notas...», p. 31).

A. D. Deyermond considers that this argument of M. R. Lida

> ... does not get us much further: the difficulties raised by the outcome of the disputation remain, since the meaning chosen by the Greek has not... been shown to be either accurate or profitable.
>
> («The Greeks...», p. 91).

In his lengthy study of the tale (*The Art...*, pp. 43-60), Anthony Zahareas takes a similar view: «Both err, yet the wise loses while the fool wins» (p. 44). Although there is ample scope for argument here, it seems to me that the real interest of the tale lies in the incongruity

---

[10] See Leo Spitzer, «En torno al arte del Arcipreste de Hita», *Lingüística e historia literaria* (Madrid, 1955), pp. 105-109; M. R. Lida de Malkiel, «Nuevas notas para la interpretación del *Libro de buen amor*», NRFH, XIII (1959), 17-82, especially pp. 30-32, and *Two Spanish Masterpieces: The «Book of Good Love» and «The Celestina»* (Urbana, Illinois, 1961), p. 32; T. R. Hart, *La alegoría en el «Libro de buen amor»* (Madrid, 1959), pp. 25-28; A. D. Deyermond, «The Greeks, the Romans, the Astrologers and the Meaning of the *Libro de buen amor*», RomN, V (1963-64), 88-91; Anthony N. Zahareas, *The Art...*, pp. 26-28, 43-47, 49-59, 70-71.

of the misunderstandings of the signs and that the outcome of the dispute is not of great importance : the nature of the prize (which happens to be learning in this version) is not essential to the tale, nor are the particular interpretations of the various signs, nor indeed are the particular gestures of the contestants. The tale is essentially about the mutual misunderstandings that arise in a disputation conducted by signs, and various outcomes of the dispute are possible, at least in theory. No doubt Juan Ruiz considered it apposite that his version should have learning for the prize and ruffianly interpretation *vs.* learned interpretation for the misunderstandings (we cannot know for certain whether he introduced these details as variations on the unknown source or whether the latter already contained them). The situation in the tale does not appear to fit exactly the situation in the outer framework of the *Libro:* Juan Ruiz does not say «I am the Greek and the foolish reader is the Roman»; what he actually says, in the S version, is «Let it not happen to me with you as it happened to the Greek doctor with the Roman ruffian and (with) his little wisdom» (46*bc*). [11] He is exhorting the reader to think carefully about the meaning of this book, without there being any misunderstanding as there was in the tale of misunderstanding he is about to unfold for the reader's entertainment. The moral lesson emerges from the fact that one interpretation is better than the other; as A. A. Parker has put it :

> Surely the point is that the Roman, who is a tough ruffian, interprets the signs in a ruffianly and aggressive way, while the Greek, who is a wise and learned man, interprets them in terms of the existence and power of God. [12]

This view, which coincides with that of M. R. Lida, is close to the stated moral lesson :

> Por esto dize la pastraña de la vieja ardida :
> «non ha mala palabra si non es a mal tenida»;
> verás que bien es dicha, si bien fuese entendida.   (64*abc*).

[11] *S*: «non me contesca contigo commo al doctor de greçia / con nel rribaldo Romano e con su poca sabiençia». The sense of the *G* version is: «Let it not happen with you as it happened to the Greek doctor with the Roman ruffian and (with) his little wisdom» («non acaesca contigo commo al dotor de greçia / con el rribal de rroma e con su poco sabençia»), but *G's* use of «con» instead of the dative after «acaesçer» suggests that it is the poorer reading (we should have expected «* non te acaesca», not «non acaesca contigo»; cf. *S's* «non me contesca»). In his recent edition (Madrid, 1967), p. 93, Joan Corominas takes *S* as the better reading.

[12] Review of T. R. Hart, *La alegoría en el «Libro de buen amor»*, MLN, LXXVII (1962), p. 558.

It is as though Juan Ruiz were saying «Pro captu lectoris habent sua fata libelli». It is true that the last line of 64 («entiende bien my dicho [G libro] e avrás dueña garrida») appears to confound the moral, but this playfulness is in the general argument, not in the tale. [13] The tale is of erudite origin, as Lecoy has shown, but it has been put to a popular use. It is clearly a burlesque of the disputations that took place in the medieval schools and in addition it may be a parody of the sign-language used in certain religious orders. But its function in the *Libro,* as well as to bring «solaz» to the reader, is to provide an analogue, at this crucial moment in the Introduction, that will demonstrate the dangers of misunderstanding.

II. FIRST LOVE AFFAIR (77-104)

Tale 2: *The Lion's Share* (82-88).

Motif J 811.1 (The Wise and the Foolish: Wisdom of concessions to power) [Juan Ruiz's version would be better classified under *Motif* J 50+ (Wisdom acquired from observation)]; *Type* 51 (Animal Tales); Lecoy, *Recherches...,* pp. 146-148.

This tale occurs soon after the first love affair begins. It is told by the lady in her discussion with the Archpriest's «mensajera». The lady is prudent and has seen too many other women trapped by the go-between's wiles. She takes warning from their fate, just as the vixen took warning from what happened to the wolf's head (81). Juan Ruiz's version of The lion's share is directed towards teaching the lesson of «learning by example». But the tale is capable of pointing at least one other moral: other versions direct attention to the lesson of «wise concession to power», with emphasis on the lion's eminence. Emphasis on this aspect would have been totally out of place in Juan Ruiz's episode; thus he brings to the fore in the narration of the tale the moral point he wants to extract and it is stated firmly by the vixen:

ella dixo: «en la cabeça del lobo tomé yo esta liçión,
en el lobo castigué qué feziese o qué non.»   (88cd).

---

[13] Stephen Reckert's suggested emendation of «dueña garrida» to «buena guarida» (*RFE,* XXXVII (1953), 227-237), although it eases the interpretation of this passage, has not found favour with Gybbon-Monypenny, Zahareas, Chiarini or Corominas.

186

In the next stanza the lady takes up the vixen's moral and applies it to her own situation, even threatening to emulate the lion's striking down of the wolf:

Por ende yo te digo, vieja e non mi amiga,
que jamás a mí non vengas nin me digas tal enemiga,
sy non yo te mostraré commo el león castiga, [G santigua,]
que el cuerdo e la cuerda en mal ageno castiga.   (89).

The function of this tale is to illustrate a point of debate between the lady and the go-between. Juan Ruiz shows great skill in bridging the distance between the tale's more usual moral point and the lesson he requires at this moment in his outer narrative, to which the tale is entirely subordinated.

Tale 3: *Mountain in labour brings forth mouse/mole* (98-102).

Motif U 114 (The Nature of Life: Appearances deceive), cf. K 1800 (Deception by disguise or illusion); no *Type* listed; Lecoy, *Recherches...*, pp. 120-122.

This is the first of the Aesopic tales in the *Libro* and its starting-point is the lady's comment to the go-between in 95*d*: «los novios non dan quanto prometen». In 97 she expands this point, berating the deceitfulness of lovers:

Diz: «quando quier casar omne con dueña mucho onrrada,
promete e manda mucho; desque la ha cobrada,
de quanto le prometió, o le da poco o nada».   (97*abc*).

The moral point to be illustrated is the deceitful breaking of promises, but the more usual moral of this tale is «appearances deceive», which has only a tenuous connection with Juan Ruiz's requirement. Yet, as Lecoy has shown, one medieval version had the «broken promises» moral: the Latin *Romulus* of Marie de France (*LBG*, 90) has «Hoc exemplo monemur promissis non multum credere», but the more usual moral for the tale is that of Walter the Englishman: «Saepe minus faciunt homines qui magna minantur» (see Lecoy, pp. 121-122). Immediately the tale ends, Juan Ruiz has the lady stress the «broken promises» moral:

E bien ansí acaesció a muchos e a tu amo;
prometen mucho trigo e dan poca paja tamo.   (101*ab*).

He thus adjusts the tale to his outer narrative purpose. But in this instance he goes further; in the very next stanza he takes up the other moral point the tale is capable of imparting:

> Omne que mucho fabla, faze menos a vezes,
> pone muy grant espanto, chica cosa es dos nuezes.   (102*ab*),

which leads him to a general philosophical statement that would have been impossible to arrive at from the «broken promises» moral:

> Las cosas mucho caras, alguna ora son rrafezes,
> las viles e las rrefezes son caras a las de vezes.   (102*cd*).

Despite the partial failure of adjustment of this tale, since the concept of deceptive appearances is an essential part of it, it accords generally with the theme of deception by lovers which is central to the episode.

III. REFLECTIONS ON DESTINY (123-165)

Tale 4: *The Astrologers and the son of King Alcaraz* (128-141).

Motif M 341.2.4 + (Prophecy: Five-fold Death); *Type* 934A (Novelle: Tales of Fate); Lecoy, *Recherches...*, pp. 160-163.

This is the only tale in the *Libro* that, despite its Moorish setting, has strong Arthurian connections. In 123, Juan Ruiz begins a discussion on astrology and the influence of the stars on men's destiny. He shows in 125-127 how men's efforts in various fields (academic, religious, military, courtly) will fail if they try to go against the judgement of the stars. He illustrates this argument with the tale of King Alcaraz's son, who dies in five different ways according to the different predictions of five astrologers. He draws the desired moral in 140*a*: «Yo creo los estrólogos verdad natural mente», but immediately modifies it by warning that God can overturn the astrological predestination of any man:

> pero Dios que crió natura e açidente,
> puede los demudar e fazer otra mente.   (140*bc*).

This modification is developed in 141-150, where he compares God's power over fate first to a king's power over the law and then to the

Pope's power over his decretals. In 151-152 Juan Ruiz is modest about his astrological abilities but claims to have daily witnessed the fate of the many men born under the sign of Venus and their vain attempts to woo women. He places himself among their number in 155. Zahareas sees a close connection between this tale and the theme of love:

> The design of Juan Ruiz's presentation is clear: first he changes the traditional story in order to focus better man's helplessness when under a *sentençia*; next he introduces the theme of helplessness: the planet is Venus, the *sentençia* is love, and the helpless «victims» are lovers like himself. The story and the commentary merge in such a way that in the face of love's overwhelming power, man is either unable or reluctant to use his free will and escape his fate, i.e. avoid indulging. (*The Art...*, p. 192).

But this interpretation seems to have come a long way from the text: between 123 and 151 [14] the subject of love never crops up at all; the subject is destiny and the power of the stars. The purpose of the discussion on astrology is to reinforce the Archpriest's assertions about the power of love, while the function of the tale of King Alcaraz's son is to illustrate the discussion on fate. All the changes that Zahareas claims Juan Ruiz introduced (*The Art...*, pp. 191-192) are directed, if they really did originate with him, [15] towards connecting the prophecy with the influence of the stars, as Zahareas admits (*The Art...*, p. 191). There is no explicit connection between Juan Ruiz's version of the tale with the planet Venus or helpless love. These subjects are the outcome of the continuing discussion on destiny, *after* the tale has served its function of giving illustration and authority to Juan Ruiz's initial definition of fate. [16] The tale of King Alcaraz's son is concerned with distinct predictions, all of which are partially correct, and its purpose is to instil a belief that all astrological predictions contain some truth (unless they are altered by God). Although it is clear that Juan Ruiz

[14] P. L. Ullman's theory (*PMLA*, LXXIX (1964), 200-205) that 140-150 were added in the second version as a moralizing corrective would mean, if true, that in the first version the discussion of the sign of Venus followed the Alcaraz tale almost immediately; but nothing in this theory suggests that the subject of love was referred to anywhere in the tale or in the lesson drawn from it.

[15] Zahareas speaks of «the variations which Juan Ruiz introduces» as though there is certain knowledge of what they were; some or all of them may have already existed in the unknown direct source.

[16] For a different view of the function of this tale, see A. D. Deyermond, «The Greeks...».

stresses the inevitability of destiny in order to prepare the ground for making the point that he, as a Venerean, cannot avoid his erotic destiny, it is also clear that the tale's function is to illustrate the general argument, not the particular one. In similar fashion, although the Archpriest explicitly states in the general argument that destiny may be modified by God's intervention (140*bc*), which man can obtain by fasting, almsgiving, prayer and contrition (149*ab*), he only hints at the possibility of altering one's erotic destiny in the particular argument:

> Ca puesto que su signo sea de tal natura
> commo es este mío, dize una escriptura
> que buen esfuerço vençe a la mala ventura [17]
> e a toda pera dura grand tienpo la madura. (160).

IV. THIRD LOVE AFFAIR (166-180)

Tale 5: *The Thief and the Mastiff* (174-178)

Motif K 2062 (Deception through shams: Detection of hypocrisy); no *Type* listed; Lecoy, *Recherches,* p. 122.

Lecoy has shown that this Aesopic tale was capable of providing more than one moral lesson: the usual lesson, based on self-interest, was a warning to gluttons not to lose everything for the sake of one extra meal. This moral survives in Juan Ruiz's version: «por el pan de una noche non perderé quanto gano» says the mastiff in 175*d,* and he emphasizes the point in 176*ab*:

> Por poca vianda que esta noche çenaría,
> non perderé los manjares nin el pan de cada día.

But at least one of the sources of the tale contained a second moral lesson based on self-interest: the bread contained a trap and the hound detected it. The Archpriest interlaces this lesson with the first: the mastiff «diz: 'non quiero mal bocado, non serié para mí sano'» (175*c*) and he repeats the point in the next stanza: «ssy yo tu mal pan comiese con ello me afogaría» (176*c*). Another of the possible sources

---

[17] This maxim occurs in a different context in the *Libro de Alexandre*: «Dizen que buen esfuerço vençe mala ventura, / meten al que bien lidia luego en escriptura» (71*ab*, *P* MS., lacuna in *O*).

(*LBG,* 21) contained the disinterested moral lesson of the mastiff's loyalty to his master, and Juan Ruiz introduces this lesson also: the mastiff tells the thief,

> tu furtarías lo que guardo e yo grand trayçión faría.
> Al señor que me crió non faré tal falsedat...
>
> (176*d*, 177*a*, etc.).

Juan Ruiz exploits these three lessons because they illustrate, but do not exactly match, the lady's motives in rejecting the Archpriest's suit in 171-173. In the first lesson the mastiff recognizes that the thief's bread is a poor exchange for his master's; this is paralleled by the lady's refusal to exchange «grand rriqueza» for «poco» (172*c*) and she comments, «mal mercar non es franqueza» (172*d*). Just as the thief's bread is not what it seems, so the Archpriest's presents are not what the lady expects (171), but the motivation of this second lesson is not developed as fully in the outer narrative as in the tale. The third lesson (of disinterest), which is the mastiff's loyalty to his master in the tale, is paralleled by the lady's loyalty to God in the narrative:

> Non perderé yo a Dios nin al su parayso
> por pecado del mundo que es sonbra de aliso.   (173*ab*).

Juan Ruiz's treatment of this tale demonstrates how he exploits the elements that best illustrate the situation in his outer narrative, but he does not attempt to match the situations exactly; he achieves no more than a broad parallelism.

V. THE ARCHPRIEST'S DEBATE WITH DON AMOR,
Part I (181-216)

Tale 6: *The Young Man who wanted to marry three women* (189-196).

Motif J 21.32 (The Wise and the Foolish: Wisdom acquired from experience); *Type* 910A (Novelle: The Good Precepts); Lecoy, *Recherches...*, pp. 157-158.

This tale is based on the same story as the French *fabliau* called *Le valet aux douze femmes*. The section on the millstone may have existed in the unknown source or it may have been a different tale altogether. [18] The function of the tale is to illustrate the Archpriest's

[18] Jackson has pointed out that multiple tales are sometimes composed out of the débris of earlier tales which have lost some essential point in the

accusation in his debate with Don Amor that love weakens the strongest men :

> non sé ffuerte nin rrecio que se contigo tope,
> que no'l debatas luego, por mucho que se enforce.   (187cd).

Zahareas, in his study of the tale (*The Art...*, pp. 80-83), attributes the differences between Juan Ruiz's version and the extant French versions to a deliberate choice on the Archpriest's part; it is a dangerous procedure, however, to undertake a comparative study when an essential step in the comparison is hypothetical. For all we know, in the unknown source the number of women the young man wanted to marry may have been three, not twelve. Finding the French youth's demand for twelve wives «quite unnatural», Zahareas attributes the Spanish youth's lesser demand to Juan Ruiz's «stricter adherence to reality [*scil.* which] puts him on his guard against unnatural situations» (*The Art...*, p. 81, note). But both situations would have been unnatural had they occurred. The point is that in no version of the tale does any question of further marriage occur after the first. The number chosen to represent the youth's excessive demand is irrelevant from two upwards. [19] The function of the millstone sequence (193-196) is to indicate in a direct way the young man's loss of strength after only one marriage, just as his offer in 192 to share his wife with his brother had indicated it more indirectly.

Tale 7: *The Frogs demand a king* (*King Log*) (199-206).

Motif J 643.1 (The Wise and the Foolish: Wise and Unwise Conduct); *Type* 277 (Animal Tales); Lecoy, *Recherches...*, pp. 122-125.

The relationship of this tale to its Aesopic sources has been studied by Lecoy. Its function is to illustrate a statement of the Archpriest in his Debate with Don Amor:

> Los que te non provaron en buen dya nasçieron,
> folgaron sin cuydado, nunca entristeçieron,
> desque a ti fallaron todo su bien perdieron,
> fueles commo a las rranas, quando el rrey pidieron.   (198).

hands of unskilled tellers; they could temporarily be saved by the skilful patchwork of an expert teller (*The International Popular Tale...*, p. 59) and there can be no doubt that Juan Ruiz was such.

[19] One is reminded of Mme. du Deffand's remark to Cardinal Polignac on the legend that the beheaded St Denis walked two leagues carrying his head in his hands: «La distance n'y fait rien; il n'y a que le premier pas qui coûte.»

The situation of the lover is paralleled by the frogs in their pool who «cantavan e jugavan» (199a) until «creyeron al diablo, que del mal se pagavan» (199c). The moral lesson is first stated by Jupiter to the frogs: «en poco tovistes / ser libres e syn premia; rreñid pues lo que-sistes» (205cd) and then by Juan Ruiz in the following stanza:

> el que non toviere premia non quiera ser apremiado,
> lybertat e ssoltura non es por oro conplado.   (206cd).

Juan Ruiz skilfully adjusts the tale's usual lesson, «Be happy with what you have», to the moral point required in the Debate, «Love ensnares its servants»; but as in many of the other tales there is no exact match of situation: while the stork can be equated with Don Amor and the frogs with lovers, King Log has no match in the outer narrative.

VI. SEVEN DEADLY SINS (217-371)

Tale 8: *Dog drops his meat for the reflection* (226-229).

Motif J 1791.4 (The Wise and the Foolish: Absurd misunderstand-ings: Shadow mistaken for substance); *Type* 34A (Animal Tales); Lecoy, *Recherches...*, pp. 125 and 142; the tale also occurs in the *Calila e Dimna* (ed. John E. Keller and Robert White Linker (Ma-drid, 1967), ch. II, 4, pp. 31 and 33).

This tale illustrates the sin of covetousness and stresses the danger to self-interest: «Por la cobdiçia pierde el omne el bien que tiene» (225a), but Juan Ruiz also emphasizes the element of self-deception in covetousness. Although the tale might be considered a trite illustra-tion of the sin, especially since it follows the examples of Troy (223) and Egypt (224), it is a fine example of Juan Ruiz's narrative skill and economy; the tale is told in one stanza (226) and is then developed mo-ralistically in 227-229. Zahareas considers that the tales in the Debate with Don Amor section «are fables which do not compare in originality and in skill of execution with the other stories of the *Libro*» (*The Art...*, p. 115 and note 108).[20] In speaking of this section, however,

---

[20] Zahareas exempts Tales 6 and 9 from this criticism.

María Rosa Lida took a different and, in my opinion, a more acceptable view :

> Juan Ruiz is an outstanding fabulist, skillful in breathing drama into the characters, and in bringing to life scenery and action with lively concrete touches. Many of his best lines are to be read in his fables and, stranger yet, in the morals appended to them. (*Two Spanish Masterpieces...*, p. 36).

Most of the tales in this section concern animals and M. R. Lida correctly stresses and exemplifies Juan Ruiz's brilliance in describing his animal protagonists, especially «in brief, secondary evocations» (*Two Spanish Masterpieces...*, pp. 27-28, note 13).

Tale 9 : *Ass jealous of war-horse until he sees him defeated* (237-245).

> *Motif* L 452.2 (Reversal of Fortune : Pride brought low); *Type* 214 * (Animal Tales); Lecoy, *Recherches...*, pp. 125-126.

The direct source for all the details in Juan Ruiz's version of this Aesopic tale is uncertain, but Lecoy has indicated some close parallels with Walter the Englishman's version. It constitutes a most skilfully executed illustration of the sin of pride and Juan Ruiz draws a very wide moral from it :

> Aquí tomen ensyenpro e lyçión de cada día
> los que son muy sobervios con su grand orgullya,
> que fuerça e hedat e onrra, salud e valentya
> non pueden durar syenpre, vanse con mançebía.　　　(245).

Zahareas claims that Juan Ruiz is consciously parodying the *ubi sunt* motif in 243-244, when the ass asks the degraded war-horse :

> ¿Dó es tu noble freno e tu dorada silla?
> ¿dó es tu sobervia? ¿dó es la tu rrenzilla?
>
> (244*ab*) (see *The Art...*, pp. 213-214) [21]

He suggests also that Juan Ruiz inserts the motif into this tale rather than into the Lament for Trotaconventos

---

[21] A. D. Deyermond takes a similar view elsewhere in this volume (see p. 68.

...where he knows it normally belongs because its traditional function — to discredit worldly values— conflicts with his immediate artistic purpose — here [*scil.* in the Lament] to emphasize his worldly concerns. (*The Art...*, p. 214).

But Zahareas does not tell us that Lecoy had discovered a possible source for the *ubi sunt* passage of the tale in Walter's version of it: «dic, sodes, ubi sella nitens, ubi nobile frenum? ... cur illa superbia fugit?» (*Recherches...*, p. 126), which seems to invalidate his claims about its re-positioning in the *Libro*. Although the function of the tale is to illustrate the sin of pride, it is worthy of note that at two points the subject of love is brought up:

> Yva lydiar en canpo el cavallo faziente
> por que forçó la dueña el su señor valiente.   (237*ab*).

> Desque salyó del canpo, non valya una çermeña;
> a arar lo pusieron e a traer la leña,
> a vezes a la noria, a vezes a la açenia;
> escota el sobervio el amor de la dueña.   (241).

Tale 10: *Crane pulls bone from wolf's throat; wolf refuses to pay* (252-256).

Motif W 154.3 (Unfavorable traits of character: Ingratitude); *Type* 76 (Animal Tales); Lecoy, *Recherches...*, pp. 126-127; this tale also occurs in the *Libro de los gatos* (ed. John Esten Keller (Madrid, 1958), no. II, pp. 35-36).

At first sight this tale appears to be an unpromising one for illustrating the sin of avarice. As can be seen from Stith Thompson's classification, it is usually employed to exemplify ingratitude. Juan Ruiz goes to great lengths to try and adjust it to his purpose: he probably introduced the situation of the wolf's being in the process of eating a goat for lunch when the bone sticks in his throat (see Lecoy, *Recherches...*, p. 127). He stresses the wolf's refusal to pay the crane (254) and uses him as a point of comparison for the man, once poor but now enriched by God, who frowns when he sees a poor man (251). The moral of avarice is emphasized again in 255, but in the following stanza Juan Ruiz also draws the traditional moral of ingratitude for good measure: «omne desagradesçido bien fecho nunca pecha» (256*b*), but he does not stress the ingratitude of lords and masters, for example, which is the main moral in the *Libro de los gatos* version.

Tale 11: *Uriah Letter* (258-259).

Motif K 978 (Deceptions: Fatal deceits); *Type* 930 (III) (cf. *Type* 910-K (Novelle: Tales of Fate); this tale also occurs in the *Corbacho* (ed. Martín de Riquer (Barcelona, 1949), I, ch. xvii, pp. 72-74).

This tale had many popular variants (see Thompson's *Motif-Index*). It is the only Biblical reference in the *Libro* that Juan Ruiz develops into a short tale. It is clearly based directly on Samuel, II, 11, 6-27, but in a much truncated version. It forms the first of the three tales used to illustrate the sin of lust. Juan Ruiz claims that David's punishment was his inability to finish building the temple (259c), but in the *Corbacho* the Arcipreste de Talavera stresses a different punishment: the rebellion of Absalom his son.

Tale 12: *Virgil in the basket* (261-268).

Motif K 1211 (Deception into humiliating position: Humiliated or baffled lovers); no *Type* listed; Lecoy, *Recherches...*, pp. 168-171; this tale also occurs in the *Corbacho*, I, ch. xvii (ed. Riquer, pp. 70-72).

The medieval legend of Virgil the Enchanter has been much studied[22] and Juan Ruiz's version is one of the earliest extant, as Lecoy has pointed out. The *Corbacho* version is similar, but briefer, and provides a reason, lacking in the *Libro,* for the lady's trick on Virgil: he had boasted that he was so wise that no woman could deceive him. The first part of Juan Ruiz's story, Virgil's humiliation supposedly as a consequence of his lust, is a fair illustration of that sin, but the remaining elements, Virgil's theft of fire (although it is a neat revenge), the Tiber turned into copper, the lady's lethal staircase and Virgil's magical foresight of that trap (which really invalidates his initial entrapment in the basket), all these elements have little to do with the point to be exemplified in the Debate. This is one of the few moments

---

[22] See J. W. Spargo, *Virgil the Necromancer* (Cambridge, Mass., 1934); Juan Ruiz's tale is referred to on pp. 35-36 and 333-334.

when Juan Ruiz's enthusiasm for a tale makes it difficult for him to adjust it to his main narrative. He attempts an adjustment in 266cd, without much success:

> fízole suelo de cobre, rreluze más que goma;
> a dueñas tu loxuria desta guisa las doma.

Since the tale has developed too far from the desired moral lesson, at the end of it he does not try to give a detailed reasoning and ends with a general statement:

> ansy por la luxuria es verdadera mente
> el mundo escarnido e muy triste la gente.   (268cd).

Tale 13: *Eagle killed with arrow made with its own feather* (270-275).

Motif U 161 (The Nature of Life: Misfortune with oneself to blame the hardest); no *Type* listed; Lecoy, *Recherches...*, pp. 127 and 45.

No direct source has been found for this tale, yet it is of Aesopic type (see Claybourne and Finch, «The Fables of Aesop...», 308). It constitutes the third tale used to illustrate the sin of lust, but with it Juan Ruiz is narrowing our attention to one aspect of sexual over-indulgence: physical self-destruction. He begins by saying that no one who indulges in lust survives the experience and then makes the point that lechers in fact kill themselves:

> De muchos ha que matas non sé uno que sanes;
> quantos en tu loxuria son grandes varraganes,
> mátanse a sy mesmos, los locos alvardanes,
> contésçeles commo al águila con los nesçios truhanes.   (269).

The hunter uses the eagle's moulted feather to make an arrow with which he shoots down the eagle. The narrative point is contained in the eagle's dying remark, evoking the ancient voodoo-type superstition: «de mí salyó quien me mató e me tiró la vida» (272d). The Archpriest connects this with the lecher, whose destruction is brought about by a force from within himself:

> El loco, el mesquino, que su alma non cata,
> usando tu locura e tu mala barata,
> destruye a su cuerpo e a su alma mata,
> que de sy mesmo sale quien su vida desata.   (273).

197

Although the tale does not deal with lust, it contains the point of a physical loss or weakness leading to the shortening of life. The incorporation of this seemingly unpromising tale demonstrates Juan Ruiz's skill in connecting his analogues to an exact point in his main argument.

Tale 14: *Jay in peacock's feathers unmasked* (285-290).

> *Motif* J 951.2 (The Wise and the Foolish: Wise and Unwise Conduct: Presumption of the Lowly); *Type* 244 (Animal Tales); Lecoy, *Recherches...*, pp. 127-128.

The function of this Aesopic tale in the *Libro* is to exemplify the sin of envy, although it could equally well illustrate vanity or vainglory. Its starting-point is in 284*ab*:

> Por que tiene tu vezino más trigo que tú paja,
> con tu mucha envidia levantas le baraja.

Lecoy has found only two other versions where the jay (or crow) strips off his own feathers before donning the peacock's. This detail leads to a more trenchant moral: «lo suyo e lo ageno todo se va a perder» (290*c*). In addition, Juan Ruiz stresses the further lesson against vainglory: «quien se tiene por lo que non es loco es; va a perder» (290*d*).

Tale 15: *The Lion and the Horse* (298-303).

> *Motif* K 1121.1 (Deceptions into self-injury); *Type* 47B (Animal Tales); Lecoy, *Recherches...*, pp. 128-129.

The sin to be illustrated here is gluttony but the Aesopic tale chosen by Juan Ruiz more usually warns against deception or pretence (Stith Thompson's title for the tale is «Wolf (lion) as sham doctor for horse's foot, kicked in face»). The Archpriest ties the tale firmly to the idea that gluttony brings sudden death (297) and introduces new elements and alters others, as Lecoy has shown, in order to adjust the tale to his immediate purpose. The lion dies because of his greed (in attempting to kill the horse) and the horse dies as a consequence of his earlier gluttony before the lion's arrival on the scene. The element of deceit still exists in Juan Ruiz's version but it is muted in favour of the moral to be stressed. Immediately the tale ends, Juan Ruiz repeats the moral: «anssy mueren los locos golosos do tú y vaz» (302*d*) and uses Hippocrates as authority for his statements (303*c*).

Tale 16: *Ass insults dying Lion* (311-316).

> *Motif* W 121.2.1 (Unfavorable traits of character: Cowardice); no *Type* listed but it resembles *Type* 50C (Animal Tales); Lecoy, *Recherches...*, p. 129.

This Aesopic tale was capable of providing various moral lessons: the cowardice of the ass, the vainglory of the lion, pride brought low, etc. Juan Ruiz, however, requires an illustration for the sins of vainglory and anger, which he treats together (304 *et seq.*). He mentions the two sins at the beginning of the tale (311*a*), but quickly gives priority to anger (311*c*), failing to bring out the element of vainglory at all. He retains the element of the ass's cowardly behaviour, but in his version it has become a mere indication of the lion's humiliation. The whole emphasis has been shifted on to the lion's position and his final fury and suicide. The two sins are mentioned again at the end: «yra e vana gloria diéronle mal gualardón» (315*d*), but an additional moral is drawn in the next stanza, based on the contrast between the lion's ill-treatment of the other animals in his youth and their revenge in his old age:

> El omne que tiene estado, onrra e grand poder,
> lo que para sy non quiere, non lo deve a otros fazer. (316*ab*).

Tale 17: *Wolf objects to fox stealing cockerel although he himself is a thief* (321-371).

> *Motif* U 21.4+ (Justice and Injustice: Justice depends on the point of view); no *Type* listed; Lecoy, *Recherches...*, pp. 129-130.

The function of this, the longest tale in the *Libro,* is to illustrate the sin of hypocrisy, which Juan Ruiz regards as a concomitant of sloth: «otrosy con açidia traes ypocresía» (319*a*), but the tale is also a burlesque of contemporary law-courts. In his florid and romantic comparison of the passage with the fourteenth-century legal system, Martín Eizaga y Gondra forms a favourable impression of Don Ximio's judgement :

> ...el análisis de los preceptos legales, aplicables a la cuestión debatida, nos autorizan a [*scil.* decir] bien del saber jurídico del alcalde de Bugía. [23]

But he later appears to contradict this view when he speaks of «la ignorancia presuntuosa del narrador» (*Un proceso...*, p. 55), for it is difficult to see how Don Ximio can exhibit juridical knowledge if the author is forensically ignorant. María Rosa Lida sees a strong didactic element in the tale :

> En contraste con «las Disciplinas, Documentos y Castigos» de la literatura didáctica de su época, también encierra enseñanza no cuentística y no ética, sino jurídica... («Nuevas notas...», p. 44).

Zahareas is correct in stating that Juan Ruiz relates this tale «in order to illustrate hypocrisy» (*The Art...*, p. 94) [24] and it is clear that Juan Ruiz wishes to compare the hypocrisy of Don Amor with the hypocrisy of the wolf; he states this both at the beginning and at the end of the tale :

> engañas todo el mundo con palabra fermosa,
> quieres lo que el lobo quiere de la rrapossa.   (320*bc*).
> Tal eres como el lobo, rretraes lo que fazes.   (372*a*).

There is not, however, any justification in the text for assuming that the comparison goes beyond the immediate point to be compared : Don Amor is like the wolf, but the Archpriest is not like the fox. It is difficult to accept Zahareas's view that

> It is now evident that Juan Ruiz uses the fable of the wolf to open this parody [*scil.* on the liturgy] in order to prepare the amusing situation of one hypocrite attacking another hypocrite. The parallel is very sly but evident : as a thief accuses another thief about thievery, so an opportunist lover attacks another about opportunistic love. (*The Art...*, p. 98).

[23] *Un proceso en «El libro de buen amor»* (Bilbao, 1942), p. 52.
[24] Joan Corominas considers that Juan Ruiz had written the tale earlier as «una pieza de apólogo moral contra los hipócritas» and incorporated it later into the *Libro* (*Edición crítica*, p. 54).

But the real bridge between the tale and the Debate is the parallel Don Amor (hypocrite) = wolf (hypocrite), *not* wolf (hypocrite) *vs.* fox (thief) = Don Amor (hypocrite) *vs.* Archpriest (what?). This tale demonstrates clearly that Juan Ruiz cannot have intended that the situation in the tales and the situation in the outer narrative should exactly match each other, else the matching would always be faulty: in addition to the serious lack of a parallel to the fox which I have already indicated, there would be no point of comparison for Don Ximio, let alone for the other animals in the tale.

VII. THE ARCHPRIEST'S DEBATE WITH DON AMOR, Part II (372-575)

Tale 18: *Mole and frog tie paws together to cross river; both eaten by kite* (407-416).

Motif J 681.1 (The Wise and the Foolish: Wise and Unwise Conduct: Forethought in alliances); *Type* 278 (Animal Tales); Lecoy, *Recherches...*, pp. 130-131; this tale also occurs in Clemente Sánchez de Vercial's *Libro de los exenplos por a.b.c.*, no. 358 (ed. J. E. Keller (Madrid, 1961), p. 277) and in *El libro de los gatos*, no. xviii (ed. J. E. Keller, p. 63).

This Aesopic tale is introduced into the Debate when the Archpriest is reproving Don Amor for tricking men and women into his snares. Before the tale he calls Don Amor a devil (405*a*) and compares him to a bird-catcher (406). Those who put their trust in him are to be equated with the mole in the tale (407*ab*), but there is no exact match: the reader is not intended to equate Don Amor with the deceitful frog, nor with the kite, who is merely the instrument of the animal's destruction (416*abc*). The comparison with the devil is recalled in 415:

> A los neçios e neçias que una vez enlaças
> en tal guisa les travas con tus fuertes mordaças
> que non han de Dios miedo nin de sus amenazas,
> el diablo los lyeva presos en tus [*G* sus] tenazas.

The point stressed by Juan Ruiz at the end of the tale is that their ensnarement in love brings disaster to the «neçios» of this world just as the foolish trustfulness of the mole and the deceitfulness of the

frog bring about their destruction. The moral lesson drawn from
the tale by Sánchez de Vercial is somewhat different: the frog receives
his just deserts for deceiving the mouse, the kite apparently being
regarded as a just avenger; no comment is passed on the mouse's fate,
but presumably we are to regard him as a victim of his own credulity:

> ¡Ploguiesse a Dios que ansi peresciesen los ombres deste mun-
> do que engañan a los sinples por palabras engañosas prometien-
> doles ayuda, pensando engaño en sus coraçones!

In the brief version of the tale in the *Libro de los gatos* the frog's intention to deceive the mouse is not mentioned, but it can be seen from
the moral that the behaviour of both is to be regarded in a bad light
since they are to be equated with «algunos clérigos e algunos monjes
que non saben nada de bien» who are given high office but whom the
devil (= the kite) will carry off: «Estonçe viene el diablo, que se entiende por el millano, e lievalos amos a dos». The author of the *Libro
de los gatos* shifts the emphasis on to the kite = devil equation to
best illustrate his anticlerical theme.

Tale 19: *Contest in laziness* (457-467).

Motif W 111.1 (Unfavorable traits of character: Laziness); *Type*
1950 (Jokes and Anecdotes: Tales of Lying); Lecoy, *Recherches...*,
pp. 155-157.

No direct source has been found for this tale, though Lecoy puts forward the reasonable hypothesis that Juan Ruiz took up either a popular story of the time or a *fabliau* that had been used by preachers
as an *exemplum*. The emphasis in the *Libro* is clearly on its comic
elements, but it also has an exemplary function. Don Amor uses the
tale to demonstrate the dangers of laziness in amatory matters (456*cd*).
This tale constitutes the first of three (the others are Tales 20 and 21)
which do not provide a direct moral lesson. This is because they are
used as illustrative points in the Debate by the Archpriest's opponent,
Don Amor, who employs them not to warn against moral defects but
rather against the imperfections of lovers' behaviour. This is not to
say that these three tales are not capable of providing a moral lesson
in the proper sense; but Juan Ruiz has muted the moral lesson in
favour of an amatory lesson because this change is required by his

outer structure to which all the tales are subordinated. This tale could quite well be used, in a comic way, to illustrate laziness as a concomitant of the sin of sloth, but Juan Ruiz adjusts it to the immediate point of argument. In his discussion of the tale (*The Art...*, pp. 83-85), Zahareas rightly emphasizes its strong comic spirit, yet, although the tale and its moral seem to me to end at 467, Zahareas considers it to be connected to the advice given in 468:

> The story is used as an *exemplum,* and the arguments of Don Amor again recall some of the attitudes expressed in the fabliaux: if a man is not lazy with a woman, he helps her to lose her sense of shame. A shameless woman, as in the spirit of the fabliaux, «mas diabluras faze que quantas ome quier» (468*d*). (*The Art...*, p. 83, note 51.)

I cannot see that Don Amor's advice on laziness, or the tale that illustrates it, is connected at all with the new piece of advice («ffaz le una vegada la vergüença perder») in 468. Don Amor has been giving a string of «dichos» since 425 on how to be a successful lover: «Don't be shy» in 454*c* is followed by «Don't be lazy» (together with the tale) and this is succeeded in turn by «Get the woman to lose her sense of shame» (468). This is a consecutive series of pieces of advice without interdependence.

Tale 20: *The Adventure of Don Pitas Payas* (474-487).

Motif J 2301 + (The Wise and the Foolish: Gullible Husbands); *Type* 1419 (Jokes and Anecdotes: The Foolish Man and his wife); Lecoy, *Recherches...*, pp. 156 and 158-160.

The source of this tale is uncertain (it may well have been oral, as L. G. Moffatt has suggested), but it is likely that María Rosa Lida was right to say that it is «of probable French descent» and «a true *fabliau* in its theme, structure, and licentious tone...» (*Two Spanish Masterpieces...*, p. 8). [25] Zahareas has examined the subtleties that he consid-

---

[25] Irma Césped, however, thinks that it may originate in Spain (see *BFC,* IX (1956-57), 35-65). A similar motif is to be found in the tale known as *De Mercatore* (or «The snow child», *Motif* J 1532.1, *Type* 1362). The Latin versions that survive appear to have been written in France in the twelfth century, see Alphonse Dain, «De Mercatore», in Gustave Cohen, *La «Comédie» Latine en France au XIIᵉ siècle* (Paris, 1931), II, pp. 259-278: «Si l'on juge par le nombre des redactions que nous en avons conservé, tant en latin qu'en langue

ers Juan Ruiz has introduced into this tale (*The Art...*, pp. 85-91). He sees a shift of emphasis from the faithlessness and trickery of the wife in the *fabliaux* versions on to the husband's error in absenting himself and attributes this to Juan Ruiz's artistic aim of developing a more subtle irony:

> Juan Ruiz's appreciation of different ironic contrasts is clearly perceptible in the denouement of the story. In the usual fabliau outcome, the husband discovers the infidelity and the unfaithful wife has to answer... Juan Ruiz, however, shifts the interest from the wife's infidelity to the husband's absence and to the ironic implications of their conversation... (*The Art...*, pp. 89-90).

Be that as it may, it is clear that Juan Ruiz has an urgent structural reason for shifting the attention on to the husband's absence, since the tale is used by Don Amor to illustrate the dangers of absence from the beloved. Zahareas sees this as only one of

> ...two separate problems, one having to do with a husband outsmarted by his young wife, the other with the problem of negligence in love which is part of the *ars amatoria*. (*The Art...*, p. 86).

But the tale has only one *function*, which is to exemplify the risks of negligence in love (Zahareas's second problem). The *fabliau* chosen by Juan Ruiz probably exemplified cuckoldry and the infidelity of women (Zahareas's first problem) and the Archpriest is therefore obliged to adjust its emphasis and its moral lesson to conform with its function — an adjustment of the kind that he undertook in a number of the tales.

Tale 21: *The Hermit who became a drunkard, seducer and murderer* (529-543).

> *Motif* V 465.1.1.1 (Religious Orders: Clerical Vices); *Type* 839 + (Religious Tales: One vice carries others with it [The three sins of the hermit]); Lecoy, *Recherches...*, pp. 150-154 and 157; a version of this tale occurs in the *Libro de Apolonio*, 54-55; partial versions occur in Clemente Sánchez de Vercial's *Libro de los exen-*

vulgaire, cette assez grosse plaisanterie semble avoir eu un succès inégalé pendant tout le cours du moyen âge...» (p. 262). Bédier considered the «Snow child» tale to be a *jocus monachorum* (*Les Fabliaux...*, p. 417).

plos por a.b.c., nos. 92, 176 and 404 (ed. J. E. Keller, pp. 88-90, 143-144 and 313). [26]

Lecoy has shown that this tale is probably a combination of two earlier tales but it is not certain whether Juan Ruiz combined them or whether this process had already been carried out before his time, since his direct source is unknown. It forms the last of the three tales used by Don Amor to illustrate his amatory instructions. In 528 he tells the Archpriest always to have «buenas costumbres» and warns him against «mucho vino bever»; he mentions the example of Lot and then embarks on the «ensienpro estraño» of the hermit. The function of the tale is made clear in 544-545: over-indulgence in wine affects the eyesight, shortens life and induces palsy. In particular it causes bad breath: «uele muy mal la boca, non ay cosa quel vala» (545*b*). The moral is then clearly stated: «si amar quieres dueña del vyno byen te guarda» (545*d*). But the usual moral of the tale is that drunkenness will lead to other vices (lust, murder, apostasy, etc.). Juan Ruiz has adjusted the lesson to correspond to Don Amor's argument, but, just as his delight in story-telling in the tale of Virgil the Enchanter leads to an imperfect adjustment, so here his urge to moralize temporarily blinds him to the situation in his main narrative and in 546-547 he extracts the full traditional moral from the tale. This produces a curious but momentary shift in Don Amor's position from that of an instructor in amatory skill to that of the medieval preacher.

VIII. DOÑA ENDRINA (576-891)

Tale 22: *The Swallow and the Hemp Seeds* (745-754).

Motif J. 621.1 + (The Wise and the Foolish: Wise and Unwise Conduct: Forethought in the prevention of other's plans); *Type* 233C (Animal Tales); Lecoy, *Recherches...,* pp. 131-132; the tale also occurs in the *Conde Lucanor,* I, no. 6.

This Aesopic tale is used by Trotaconventos to illustrate one of her arguments in her exhortation of Doña Endrina to accept Don Melón's suit. After pointing out the dangers for a woman of living alone

[26] See also Luis Jenaro Maclennan, «Las fuentes de las estrofas 544-545 del *Libro de buen amor*», *VR,* XXI (1963), 300-314, and Janet Chapman, «A Suggested Interpretation of Stanzas 528 to 549a of the *Libro de buen amor*», *RF,* LXXIII (1961), 29-39.

IAN MICHAEL

without a man to defend her (743), she hints that people are plotting all kinds of traps and law-suits against Doña Endrina (744). It is this point that she illustrates by the tale: Doña Endrina is to be equated with the foolish bustard and she, Trotaconventos, with the swallow, who gives good advice that goes unheeded. She repeats the lesson at the end of the tale:

> Que muchos se ayuntan e son de un conssejo
> por astragar lo vuestro e fazer vos mal trebejo.   (754ab).

Juan Ruiz did not need to carry out much adjustment here, since the lesson he required coincided with the usual moral of the tale.

Tale 23 (part missing): *De Lupo Pedente (Sow kicks wolf into stream when he comes to baptize her young)* (766-779).

> *Motif* K 1121.2 (Deceptions into self-injury); Type 47B (Animal Tales); Lecoy, *Recherches...*, pp. 148-149.

The first part of this Aesopic tale is missing: there is a lacuna of six stanzas between 765 and 766. In 764-765 Doña Endrina has begun her reply to Trotaconventos and the connection between what she says and the incomplete tale that follows is not altogether clear, but she is concerned to rebut what Trotaconventos has said and one of the go-between's arguments has a connection with the moral lesson of the tale. In 761d, after urging Doña Endrina to accept Don Melón in marriage, she says that there is a good omen: «hado bueno que vos tienen vuestras fadas fadado». It is likely that it is Doña Endrina who tells the tale (there would hardly have been space in six stanzas for her to end her speech and for Trotaconventos to begin again and start the tale)[27] and it is also probable that its function is to illustrate the dangers of trusting in omens. The omen, which the wolf experiences at the beginning of the tale and which he takes as a sign of future good fortune, must clearly have been the sneeze that he mentions in 768d: «'a la fe', diz, 'agora se cumple el estornudo'» and in 767c: «dixo: 'diome el diablo el ageno rroydo, / yo ove buen aguero...'». After his disastrous but hilarious attempts to attack in turn sheep, goats and

---

[27] In his recent critical edition, Joan Corominas is strongly of this opinion (pp. 53 and 292) and gives an account of the various discussions on this point (p. 292).

206

pigs (in his recent critical edition, pp. 294 and 296, Joan Corominas attempts to reconstruct the missing details of the wolf's dealing with the sheep on the basis of the version in the *Ysopete historiado,* in which the wolf is asked to act as a judge), the moral is stated: «bueno le fuera al lobo pagarse con torrezno» (779c), «Omne cuerdo non quiera el ofiçio dañoso» (780a), but here and in the following stanza the stress is on «Be satisfied with your present lot» rather than on «Don't trust false omens» which probably opens the way for the tale. But unfortunately we cannot check that this was the actual function of this tale because after 781 there is a further lacuna of thirty-two stanzas.

Tale 24: *The ass without a heart* (892-906).

> *Motif* K 402.3 (Deceptions: Thefts and cheats: Thief escapes detection); *Type* 52 (Animal Tales); Lecoy, *Recherches...,* pp. 140-142; this tale also occurs in the *Calila e Dimna* (ed. J. E. Keller and R. W. Linker, ch. VII, 1, pp. 247-250).

Juan Ruiz has skilfully combined elements from both the Oriental and Western branches of this tale. He has introduced considerable alterations by shifting the traditional emphasis from the wolf's cunning in deceiving the lion to the ass's stupidity. This modification was made necessary by the different lesson he wished to draw. As can be seen from Stith Thompson's classification, the traditional point was that a cunning thief escapes detection. But the function of the tale is quite different in the *Libro:* it is used by Juan Ruiz in his moralistic address to women at the end of the Doña Endrina episode. The point to be illustrated is: «entendet bien las fablas, guardat vos del varón» (892b). The lesson is again made clear at the end of the tale:

> Assy, señoras dueñas, entended el rromançe,
> guardat vos de amor loco, non vos prenda nin alcançe
> abrid vuestras orejas, vuestro coraçón se lançe
> en amor de Dios lynpio, vuestro loco no'l trançe.   (904).

This mention of the ladies' ears and heart relates them directly to the ass in the tale: they must use their ears and heart and not be like the ass, who behaved so foolishly that the other animals could say that he must have been born without heart and ears. The bridge between the tale and the main argument is the conduct of foolish women = the conduct of the ass, but there are no other real points of contact. Juan Ruiz does not often attempt close parables; that the analogue has one point of contact is sufficient for his exploitation of it as a cautionary illustration.

IX. DOÑA GAROÇA (1332-1507)

Tale 25: *The Gardener and the Snake* (1348-54).

> *Motif* J. 1172.3 + (The Wise and the Foolish); *Type* 155 (Animal Tales); Lecoy, *Recherches...*, pp. 132 and 144-145; this tale also occurs in Clemente Sánchez de Vercial's *Libro de los exenplos por a.b.c.*, no. 312 (ed. J. E. Keller, p. 244).

This tale is used by Doña Garoça to illustrate her argument that in helping Trotaconventos when she was poor she was nurturing a viper in her bosom. The moral is clearly stated at the end of the tale: «alégrase el malo en dar por miel venino» (1354a). There is a double parallel: Trotaconventos is like the snake and Doña Garoça is like the gardener. The moral that Juan Ruiz stresses is the ingratitude of evil people. The tale, however, has many versions, both Graeco-Latin and Oriental, but Juan Ruiz shows no signs of having known the latter. After demonstrating its ingratitude, in some versions the snake is thrown out of the house and in others is returned to captivity. In Sánchez de Vercial's version, after the snake has coiled itself around the man's neck to choke him, a passing fox is asked to act as judge. He cunningly tells the snake that he must see a re-enactment of the events; when the snake agrees and returns to his branch the man is freed. The moral in the *Libro de los exenplos* could be rendered as «Bad blood will out», as can be seen from its title, «Natura insita deficile negari potest».

Tale 26: *The Hunter and the Greyhound* (1357-66).

> *Motif* W 154.4 (Unfavorable traits of character: Ingratitude); no *Type* listed but it resembles *Type* 160 (Grateful Animals, Ungrateful Man); Lecoy, *Recherches...*, pp. 132-133.

Trotaconventos uses this Aesopic tale to counter Doña Garoça's tale of the Gardener and the Snake. Its function at first is to illustrate ingratitude (her counter-accusation):

> quando trayo presente só mucho falagada,
> vine manos vazías, finco mal escultada. (1356*bc*).

As well as ingratitude the tale can also illustrate disrespect for old age and it is this aspect that Trotaconventos begins to exploit at the end of the tale: «por ser el omne viejo non pierde por ende prez» (1362*c*). In 1364-65, however, she returns to the moral of ingratitude. As in the previous tale there is a double parallel: Trotaconventos is like the aged greyhound and Doña Garoça is like the ungrateful hunter.

Tale 27: *The Town Mouse and the Country Mouse* (1369-85).

Motif J 211.2 (The Wise and the Foolish: Wise and Unwise Conduct: Choice between evils); *Type* 112 (Animal Tales); Lecoy, *Recherches...*, pp. 133-134; this tale also occurs in the *Libro de los gatos,* no. xi (ed. J. E. Keller, pp. 49-51).

The function of this well-known Aesopic tale is to illustrate Doña Garoça's fear of giving in to Trotaconventos's persuasions:

> Mas témome e rreçelo que mal engañada sea,
> non querría que me fuese commo al mur del aldea. (1369*ab*).

There is an unusual feature here in that the long moral lesson at the end of the tale (1379-83) is stated by the country mouse, but Doña Garoça sums it up:

> Más vale en convento las sardinas saladas
> e fazer a Dios serviçio con las dueñas onrradas,
> que perder la mi alma con perdizes assadas
> e fyncar escarnida con otras deserradas. (1385).

The moral of the version in the *Libro de los gatos* is the same: «Ciertamente, non queria que todo el mundo fuese mio si siempre oviese de bevir en tal peligro», but the moral is then applied, predictably, to the «muchos benefiçiados · en este mundo de yglesia, que son usureros»

and the cat of the tale is there interpreted as the devil, on the watcn
for souls. Since Juan Ruiz's requirements here matched the tale's
traditional lesson, no adjustment was necessary.

Tale 28: *The Cockerel and the Sapphire* (1387-91).

Motif J 1061.1 (The Wise and the Foolish: Wise and Unwise Conduct: Value depends upon real use); no *Type* listed; Lecoy, *Recherches...*, p. 134.

This Aesopic tale is capable of providing at least two moral lessons: 1) that the value of a thing depends upon its usefulness; 2) that
the fool will not perceive a great treasure (cf. pearls before swine). It
is the second of these possibilities that Juan Ruiz exploits. The starting-point is Trotaconventos's statement to Doña Garoça: «dexar plazer e viçio, e lazería queredes» (1386*b*). At the end of the tale the
moral is stated by means of a new image:

> Muchos leen el libro, toviendo lo en poder,
> que non saben qué leen nin lo pueden entender.   (1390*ab*).

Juan Ruiz completely suppresses the other possible lesson, for its
presence would not be appropriate to Trotaconventos's argument.

Tale 29: *Ass tries to caress his mistress* (1401-08).

Motif J 2413.1 (The Wise and the Foolish: Foolish imitation); *Type*
214 (Animal Tales); Lecoy, *Recherches...*, pp. 134-135.

The usual lesson of this Aesopic tale is a warning against foolish
imitation, or going against the limits set on one by God and nature.
The point is made at the end of the tale:

> lo que Dios e natura han vedado e negado
> de lo fazer el cuerdo non deve ser osado.   (1407*cd*).

But Juan Ruiz has to adjust it to the situation at this moment in the
Doña Garoça episode; its lesson is therefore modified to illustrate the
folly of useless persistence. Before she begins the tale Trotaconventos
says that she does not wish to emulate the ass (1400*b*). At the end of
it she states the usual moral in 1407 and then in the next stanza applies

it to her situation: she will not foolishly go over again the arguments of the previous day, for «callar a las de vegadas faze mucho provecho» (1408d). This is a good example of the strain Juan Ruiz sometimes imposes on a tale in order to adjust it to its function in his outer narrative.

Tale 30: *Vulpes* (*or The Fox who played dead*) (1412-21).

Motif J 351+ (The Wise and the Foolish: Choices: small inconvenience, large gain) [cf. K 522 (Deceptions: Escape by shamming death)]; *Types* 1 and 33 (Animal Tales); Lecoy, *Recherches...,* pp. 138-140; this tale also occurs in the *Conde Lucanor,* I, no. 29.

The function of this tale is to illustrate Doña Garoça's refusal to enter a dangerous situation («tan mal juego», 1410d) from which she can see no possible escape. Don Juan Manuel's version has greater logic and verisimilitude than Juan Ruiz's, but the latter has a strong comic element which is lacking in the *Conde Lucanor* version. A further difference is that Don Juan Manuel draws the moral of «Put up with small inconveniences but resist a serious threat», while Juan Ruiz concentrates on the warning about the difficulties of escaping from a trap. Although the fox in the *Libro* version (1420abc) begins by drawing the same moral as we find in the *Conde Lucanor,* there is then a clever adjustment to make the lesson correspond to Doña Garoça's situation:

«lo que enmendar non se puede non presta arrepentyr».

(1420d).

Deve catar el omne con seso e con medida
lo que fazer quisiere, que aya d'él salyda,
ante que façer cosa quel' sea rretrayda;
quando teme ser preso, ante busque guarida.   (1421).

The lesson is thus directly related to Doña Garoça's possible ruin if she goes further into the affair.

Tale 31: *The Lion and the Mouse* (1425-34).

Motif B 371.1 (Animals grateful for release); *Type* 75 (Animal Tales); Lecoy, *Recherches...,* pp. 135-136.

This Aesopic tale is used by the wheedling Trotaconventos in her attempt to be restored to Doña Garoça's favour: despite her unimportance and poverty, she says, she still might be able to be of great service to Doña Garoça. The function of the tale is to exploit the idea of the small helping the great:

> Puede pequeña cossa e de poca valya
> fazer mucho provecho e dar grand mejoría. (1434*ab*).

With great skill Juan Ruiz then expands the concept to include the go-between's prime assets: «manera e seso, arte e sabidoría» (1434*d*).

Tale 32: *The Fox and the Crow* (1437-43).

Motif K 334.1 (Deceptions: Thefts and Cheats: Means of hood-winking the guardian or owner); *Type* 57 (Animal Tales); Lecoy, *Recherches...*, p. 136; this tale also occurs in the *Conde Lucanor,* I, no. 5, and in the *Libro de los exenplos por a.b.c.,* no. 11 (ed. J. E. Keller, pp. 34-35).

The *Libro* version of this famous Aesopic tale has been studied by Don Ramón Menéndez Pidal (*Poesía árabe...,* pp. 118-123). Juan Ruiz's narrative skill and concision reach a high point in this tale. Its function is straightforward: Doña Garoça has doubts about Trotaconventos's «dulçes falagos» (1436*a*) and she does not wish to be like the crow. There is a simple double parallel here of Garoça = the crow and Trotaconventos = the fox. Sánchez de Vercial's version is similar to Juan Ruiz's in that the fox tells the crow that he is as white as a swan; Lecoy has shown that this comparison was already in Walter the Englishman's version. Don Juan Manuel's courtly and sophisticated crow would not have been deceived by such an absurd comparison.

Tale 33: *Hares think the sound of waves is a great danger to them* (1445-50).

Motif J 1812.2 (The Wise and the Foolish: Fools: One thing mistaken for another); no *Type* listed but it resembles *Type* 1321 (Jokes and Anecdotes: Numskill Stories: Fools frightened); Lecoy, *Recherches...,* pp. 136-137.

This is the last of the Aesopic tales in the *Libro.* Trotaconventos uses it to calm Doña Garoça's alarm, which she claims is unjustified and typical of nuns in amatory matters (1444); here she is drawing the moral that fools become alarmed unnecessarily (cf. 1451: one nun, like one hare, starts all the others off). In 1449*cd* Trotaconventos somewhat alters the lesson:

> en tal manera tema el que bien quiere bevir,
> que non pierda el esfuerço por miedo de morir;

here she is really making a new point: the fool who fears losing his life is more likely to die because of his loss of courage. This new point is repeated in 1450*cd,* but now in a military image:

> los covardes fuyendo mueren deziendo: «¡foyd!»
> biven los esforçados diziendo: «¡daldes, ferid!»

Tale 34: *Devil at gallows repudiates his bargain with robber* (1454-79).

Motif M 212.2 (Ordaining the Future: Bargains with the Devil); no exact *Type* listed but it resembles *Types* 810 and 821 (Religious Tales: The Man Promised to the Devil); Lecoy, *Recherches...,* pp. 154-155; this tale also occurs in the *Conde Lucanor,* I, no. 45.

Lecoy has indicated the main differences between Juan Ruiz's version of this preacher's tale and Don Juan Manuel's; in addition he discusses the numerous French and Latin versions. In this case the moral is firmly entrenched in the substance of the tale: those who sell their souls to the Devil will come to a bad end (though in Berceo's *Milagro de Teófilo,* which has a similar Faustian theme, there is, of course, a miraculous intervention by the Virgin). Perhaps because of the trenchancy of the moral, Juan Ruiz made this the last tale in the Doña Garoça episode; Trotaconventos's reaction to it is almost one of despair and she does not attempt to counter it with another tale: «'Señora', diz la vieja, 'muchas fablas sabedes'» (1480*a*).

X. Tale 35: *Song of the Clerics of Talavera* (1690-1709).

Motif V 465.1 + (Clerical Vices: Incontinence of the Clergy); no exact *Type* listed but it resembles *Types* 1725-1849 (Jokes and Anecdotes: Jokes about Parsons and Religious Orders); Lecoy, *Recherches...,* pp. 229-236.

Menéndez Pidal has shown that this song is not a unique account of contemporary events but had firm antecedents in the Goliardic tradition, particularly in the *Consultatio Sacerdotum*[28]. Although Juan Ruiz reshapes the story and introduces topical references, Don Ramón indicates that he must have known more than one earlier version of the tale. It can therefore be considered in the same light as the other popular tales in the *Libro,* for it must have been enjoyed by the laity as much as by the clergy. It only differs from the other tales in that its source was Goliardic rather than Aesopic, Oriental or in the *fabliaux.* Its function, however, is difficult to assess. Lecoy does not see it as a structural part of the *Libro*:

> Le manuscrit *S* ... se termine par un choix de pièces de notre auteur, étrangères certainement au *Libro de buen amor* proprement dit... (*Recherches...*, p. 229).

L. G. Moffatt also considers it to be totally unconnected with the *Libro* since it comes after the formal *explicit.*[29] Without committing herself on the structural problem, María Rosa Lida opined that the «propósito moral» of the *Libro* was as firmly expressed in this *Cantica* as elsewhere in the work («Nuevas notas...», p. 44). Zahareas, on the other hand, suggests a structural role for the *Cantica*:

> ...the story serves a humorous purpose, but may also have a structural utility: it is a means of varying Juan Ruiz's angle of vision... He chooses a story which reflects the structure of the *Libro*... (*The Art...*, pp. 112-113, note 103).

Zahareas's suggestion is attractive, but difficult to maintain because of the odd position of the *Cantica.* Juan Ruiz himself makes no attempt to define the function of the tale. The narrative technique is the same as in the other tales, except that here it is direct narration by the author in the third person;[30] there is, however, no stated moral lesson either

[28] *Poesía juglaresca y orígenes de las literaturas románicas* (Madrid, 1957), pp. 205-207.
[29] «The Imprisonment of the Archpriest», *Hispania* (Stanford), XXXIII (1950), 321-327, at p. 324.
[30] The first person is used twice: «bien creo que lo fizo más con midos que de grado» (1691*b*); «Pero non alonguemos atanto las rrazones» (1709*a*). Zahareas's assertion that 1708 is spoken by the narrator (*The Art...*, p. 112) seems doubtful. The passage is anyway obscure since we are not told who «Don Gonçalo canonigo» is, but it is more likely that the stanza is still part of the speech made by «el chantre Sancho Muñoz» (it is regarded thus in the edition of the *Libro* by Criado de Val and Naylor (Madrid, 1965), p. 574). Corominas (*ed. crit.*, p. 628) takes the first hemistich of 1708*a*, «don Gonçalo canonigo», as the end of the speech of Sancho Muñoz, and the rest of 1708 as «aclaración que el arcipreste hace a la alusión de don Sancho», but this seems to be a somewhat violent reading.

at the beginning or at the end of the tale. If the tale has no clear function and no explicit lesson, has it an implied moral? M. R. Lida recognized its «juego irónico» but she made the excellent point that Juan Ruiz's irony presupposed firm moral values:

> Varias formas de humorismo predilectas de Juan Ruiz, como la ironía, la paradoja y la parodia, presuponen muy firmes valoraciones, y no reciprocidad de valores. («Nuevas notas...», p. 35).

The irony [and the moral] of the *Cantica* lies in the fact that «el elogio de las medidas disciplinarias del Papa emana de las palabras hostiles de los clérigos amancebados» («Nuevas notas...», p. 35). Zahareas goes much further and sees irony also in Juan Ruiz's moral judgements throughout the poem (*The Art*..., p. 113, end of note 103). It is difficult to accept his view of the *Cantica* that

> ... while giving the impression that he deals with the problem of priestly behavior, Juan Ruiz avoids getting involved in a controversy such as the immorality of the clerics, of which he himself as the hero of the *Libro* is a prime example. (*The Art*..., p. 112).

On the contrary, Juan Ruiz is involved in the controversy by his very mention of the subject; moreover, as author he is distinct from the Archpriest as protagonist. As M. R. Lida has pointed out, the implied moral lesson of the *Cantica* is revealed through, not despite, its irony.

CONCLUSIONS

This examination of the tales in their contexts permits certain conclusions:

1) In every case except the last the function of the tales is to illustrate a point of argument. It is clear that they perform the function of the illustrative analogue, not that of the allegorical parable. There is always one bridge between the tale and the outer narrative, in a few cases there are two or more, but it is rare for the events or situation in the tale to match exactly those in the outer narrative. This may be

because, as Corominas claims, the tales, as well as many of the moral, satirical and didactic pieces, had been written earlier (*Edición crítica*, pp. 52-53) and were not perfectly adjusted into the *Libro*:

> ... en cuanto a las Fábulas, los Cuentos ejemplares y algún trozo semejante, se tomó muy en serio la tarea de integrarlos dentro de su gran obra. Y, sin embargo, se advierten bien claras las suturas que las unen a esos conjuntos mayores... (*Ed. crít.*, p. 53).

But it is also possible that many of the faulty adjustments noted by Corominas were not considered as such by Juan Ruiz: he may not have been aiming at a fuller integration and thus, after making one connection between a tale and the outer framework, he felt free on occasion to exploit the tale for its own sake (cf. Tales 12, 17, 21, 23 and 24).

2) The tales occur in particular groups in the *Libro* because they occur only at moments of argument or debate: the author's address to the reader, the Archpriest's Debate with Don Amor, Trotaconventos's arguments with Doña Endrina and with Doña Garoça. Thus their function to some extent resembles that of the *exempla* of the medieval preachers.

3) There is a preponderance of animal tales, which demand the reader's acceptance of a convention and a typification that are usual in the *contes d'animaux*, as Bédier noted:

> ...ils supposent ... cette convention, acceptable à tout homme, que les animaux parlent, et un symbolisme très peu caractérisé, qui fait de chacun d'eux le type de certaines passions humaines. [31].

4) Stith Thompson's classification of the tales by theme reveals that fourteen of them come under category J (The Wise and the Foolish) and seven under category K (Deception); six more tales have claims

[31] *Les Fabliaux...*, p. 223. This predominance of animal tales is not peculiar to Juan Ruiz; R. S. Boggs has noted the great popularity of these tales in Spain (see *A Comparative Survey of the Folktales of Ten Peoples* (Helsinki, FF Communications no. 93, 1930), p. 10). Not only is it acceptable for animals to talk, but, without surprising us, Juan Ruiz has the sapphire talking to the cockerel in Tale 28.

to a cross-reference with J and five others with K. Even allowing for Juan Ruiz's shifts of emphasis in the usual themes of some of the tales in order to adjust them to his main narrative, it is noticeable that many of the tales he chose correspond to his main thesis in their display of the themes of wisdom and folly, and the various types of deceit: self-deception, deception of others, deception by others.

5) The study of the tales in their contexts also sheds some light on their dual function of entertainment and moralization. Although Bédier rightly pointed out that the moral lesson is not usually an organic part of a popular tale but an optional adjunct, the fact remains that in most cases the sources of Juan Ruiz's tales appear to have stressed a moral point. In many of the tales the Archpriest continues to stress the same moral as the source, but only when that moral happens to coincide with the tale's function in his narrative. In a number of cases, as I have tried to show, he mutes or suppresses the moral of the source and brings to the fore a different lesson, which may not be moral in the religious sense. Whereas the usual lesson of The Adventure of Don Pitas Payas (Tale 20) was to beware of the wiles of women, Juan Ruiz makes it provide an amoral lesson: «Absence is dangerous in amatory matters». [32] This is not because Juan Ruiz is giving amoral advice but because it forms part of Don Amor's *ars amatoria*. There are, however, occasional signs that Juan Ruiz's strong didactic sense overcomes his artistic sense of function: in the tale of the Hermit (Tale 21), the amoral lesson of Don Amor is «Don't drink heavily because the lady will be offended by bad breath», but Juan Ruiz is unable to refrain from adding all the moral and medical lessons of the tale and temporarily makes nonsense of the *ars amatoria*. For this reason alone it is difficult to accept Zahareas's view that

> Juan Ruiz uses the traditional pattern of the allegorical manner chiefly as a framework to develop a variety of ambiguous intentions and humorous stories which in turn he exploits at length for comic entertainment and ironic complexities. (*The Art...*, p. 60).

---

[32] The usual moral lesson is, of course, still vaguely implicit in the tale, but in this broad sense, in Bédier's words, «Il n'y a pas, en effet, de bourde ni de *trufe* si indifférente qu'on n'en puisse tirer quelque leçon» (*Les Fabliaux...*, p. 271), or, in the words of the Duchess in *Alice in Wonderland*, «Everything has a moral, if only you could find it».

Juan Ruiz does have a sense of artistry and a strong sense of fun, but even when he playfully misleads the reader it is obviously a game, not seriously meant. The fact that he had to make adjustments to the moral lessons of some of the tales for functional reasons does not provide sufficient grounds for thinking that he deliberately wished to subvert the firm moral values of his time.

University of Manchester

R. B. TATE

Adventures in the 'sierra'

> La parte en cuaderna vía refiere con colores realistas y caricaturescos el encuentro de la serrana, y a continuación se repite el mismo encuentro en forma de canción, de tonos idealistas, en fuerte oposición con el relato precedente. (R. Menéndez Pidal, *Poesía juglaresca y orígenes de la literatura románica,* 6th edn. (Madrid, 1957), p. 212.)

> No veo... contraste entre el tono caricaturesco de la versión en cuaderna vía y el supuesto tono idealista de la versión zejelesca. (María Rosa Lida de Malkiel, «Nuevas notas para la interpretación del *Libro de buen amor*», NRFH, XIII (1959), p. 45.)

The above quotations from two scholars who have contributed so much to the understanding of the *Libro de buen amor* show how even a passage which contains no serious textual difficulties can give rise to apparently irreconcilable differences of opinion. The present article intends to examine the aforesaid passage to see whether any accommodation at all is possible between such points of view.

We may take the episode of the adventures in the sierra as having fixed limits, stanzas 950-1042. Within these limits there are no references to other parts of the *Libro* which can explicitly locate it in a larger sequence, except perhaps that of 950*a*, a somewhat distant echo of 76*c*, and the fact that we may associate the time of year, March (951*a*), with the opening of the mountain-passes in the Guadarrama. The place-names given in the poems are unquestionably linked with this area, the poet having followed the same traditional practice as he did in accommodating well-known topics within his localised version of the *Pamphilus,* and as Juan Manuel did with his *ejemplos.* The rural upland setting and early spring may thus be taken as two of the unifying factors.

The experiences are presented in the form of four *zéjeles,* each of

219

which is preceded by a narrative «prologue» of variable length in *cuaderna vía*. The whole episode can therefore be distinguished clearly from the rest of the *Libro* inasmuch as the balance between lyric and narrative is explicitly contrived both as regards volume and content. It must be remembered that there have been no extant lyrics since 115, although there are references to poems not included at 171*d*, 915*a*, 918*b*, 947*b*. At none of these points, however, can it be stated incontrovertibly that the lyrics formed part of some original version.

The internal sequence, for purposes of reference, may be classified in the following fashion: Narrative I, 950-958; Lyric I, 959-971; Narrative II, 972-986; Lyric II, 987-992; Narrative III, 993-996; Lyric III, 997-1005; Narrative IV, 1006-1021; Lyric IV, 1022-1042. In order to appreciate the relationship between lyric and narrative, it will help to consider the lyrics one by one in isolation. This is a different procedure from that employed by Lecoy, Le Gentil, or María Rosa Lida, in that they have treated the section as a pure sequence, with the result that the lyric acquires some of the tone and quality of the preceding *cuaderna vía*. Even though the purpose of Le Gentil is to study the lyrics in themselves, his interpretations are inevitably coloured. For instance, in the case of Lyric III, Le Gentil declares: «Le poète conclut, alors, et, *d'un ton ironique* [my italics], annonce qu'il part pour s'occuper des derniers préparatifs. Cette fois, c'est à son tour de rire, car il a bel et bien mystifié la *serrana,* qui l'a sottement pris pour un gardien de troupeau (cf. 993 et 994).» Lida approaches the same lyric in much the same frame of mind. The *serrana,* she says, is: «a slow-witted lass very much disposed to marrying the poet, who cleverly dodges her under the pretext of going to buy her wedding gifts».[1] It is our intention, initially, to work outwards from the lyric to its context, in order to see whether such commonly accepted assumptions are totally justified.

Firstly, it is important to note that the lyrics in themselves have no link with any part of the *Libro* outside this episode, nor with each

---

[1] Pierre Le Gentil, *La poésie lyrique espagnole et portugaise à la fin du moyen âge. Première partie: les thèmes et les genres* (Rennes, 1949), p. 545. A more detailed treatment, modifying the earlier views in some respects, is to be found in «Les Canticas de Serrana de l'Archiprêtre de Hita», *Wort und Text: Festschrift für Fritz Schalk* (Frankfurt, 1963), pp. 133-141. However, he does not change the underlying approach to the *Canticas* as indivisible wholes. See, for example, p. 136, with reference to Lyric III and the theme of the marriage offer and presents. María Rosa Lida de Malkiel, *Two Spanish Masterpieces: the Book of Good Love and the Celestina* (Urbana, 1961), p. 42. Manuel Criado de Val, *Teoría de Castilla la Nueva* (Madrid, 1960), p. 240, begins his analysis in a similar way to mine, but his concern is distinct.

other in terms of concrete particulars. In respect of genre and structure, they are broadly of one family, even though distinctions are important. They all concern a casual encounter with a peasant girl or
woman in the spring on mountain path or in the valley pastures, precisely located and presented in the first person in dialogue. The protagonist, a stranger, makes a request for directions, food and shelter or
companionship, and this is met with counter-demands couched in a
variety of terms. These are either concerned with sex or marriage,
and the response determines the outcome of the poem, for all the lyrics
move towards a climax of some sort. It would be misleading to seek
common elements beyond those mentioned above without distorting
the content, meaning or tone of each separate lyric. However, these
variations would not in any way lead to severe modification of the
affiliations proposed at various times by Menéndez Pidal, Lecoy or Le
Gentil.

In Lyric I, complete in itself, the encounter is clearly between
serrana and *escudero* (961*b*), between the cold, hungry, frightened and
empty-handed traveller and the brutal, coarse and demanding peasant.
The burlesque of the pastoral meeting is not exceptional, with its animal view of sexuality, but the specific point of the lyric is that, despite
inconvenience and forced submission, the protagonist gains at least
as much as he loses in self-respect. One cannot attach without some
distortion any moral meaning to the lyric itself.

Lyric II, also complete in itself, shares with the above many elements, particularly the traditional contrast of court and country, but
in a more hyperbolic fashion. This is more characteristic of the burlesque pastoral in that it is the protagonist who opens with flattering
remarks (note the use of the second person plural, 988*f*-989*g*) which
are brushed aside by the *serrana*. She implies that he should have used
brute force (in 987*b, valyente* should be interpreted as 'husky'). The
same peasant meal is followed by rather more violent demands, and the
poem ends not *post coitum,* but at the moment before. The specific
intention seems to lie in the contrast of the erotic experience expected,
however inappropriately, and that which is suggested in the closing
remarks. There are reasonable grounds, therefore, for considering Lyrics I, II as being closely related in form, content and comic purpose.

Lyric III, however, must first be seen independently of the narrative.
The encounter is neither in rain or snow, the protagonist is neither im-
portunate nor importuned. Both parties are clearly of the same social
background and speak the same rustic language; the tone is innocent

and optimistic with no undertones of sexual urge. The lyric is in two equal parts; in the first the young unmarried shepherd in search of a bride outlines his qualifications as a breadwinner, in the second the young girl makes clear what she demands in presents from a bride-groom. There are little grounds for reading coarse materialism into her lines, which conclude in a *noviazgo* and plighting of troth. This is, in effect, a traditional rural courting song, of which examples can be seen in Pero González de Mendoza and Juan del Encina. [2] If the «rustic tasks and paraphernalia doubtless provoked the laughter of a city audience» as María Rosa Lida de Malkiel has remarked, then we will have to revise our views on a number of similar songs in Lope de Vega's *comedias* where the emphasis lies squarely on the charming ingenuousness of the participants. [3]

Lyric IV, the longest by far, must also be held apart in preliminary consideration from the well-known narrative prelude. The conditions of encounter are similar to Lyric II, but very much less caricaturesque, with an offer of service to a *serrana* whose name suggests a courtly rather than a country background, and who is described, as well as addressed, as «fermosa, loçana / e byen colorada» (1024*d,e*) and «moça» (1027*a*). [4] María Rosa Lida claims that these words «no res-

[2]
¡Si supiesses como corro
bien luchar, mejor ssaltar!
las moçuelas en el corro
pagan sse del mi ssotar...

Cancionero de Baena (Madrid, 1851), p. 258.

Con dos mil cosas que se
yo, mia fe, la servire
con tañer, cantar, baylar,
con saltar, correr, luchar
y mil donas le dare.

Darele buenos anillos,
cercillos, sartas de prata,
buen çueco y buena çapata,
cintas, bolsas y texillos:
y manguitos amarillos,
gorgueras y capillejos,
dos mil adoques bermejos,
verdes, azules, pardillos...

Egloga representada en requesta de vnos amores... in Juan del Encina, *Cancionero, ed. facs.* (Madrid, 1928), f. cxii verso.
[3] Lida de Malkiel, *Two Spanish Masterpieces...*, p. 43. The criticism that she levels against Kellermann in «Nuevas notas...», p. 41, note 35, could well be turned against herself. Corominas does modify lightly her view of the passage: see his edition of the *Libro de buen amor* (Madrid, 1967), p. 390, note to 997-1005.
[4] The name Alda (ms, *G*) fits the prosody more accurately than the Aldara

ponden a intención embellecedora» («Nuevas notas...», p. 45 n. 39). One can hardly call for a plain reading in other parts of the poem and deny it here, especially as a few lines further on she adds, «no sólo no describe su fealdad, sino que pondera su hermosura». Marriage or some equivalent sort of liaison is what the girl wants, even if the man is married. The traveller himself claims to want shelter only and after a, to him, indifferent meal, encourages the girl to list her demands which he has little intention of satisfying. Clearly the girl does not yield against promises and the traveller is disgruntled, which explains his exclamation of 'heda' (1040a). However materialist she may be, she is neither coarse nor violent, nor any more morally loose than her urban counterparts elsewhere in the *Libro*. In fact, the erotic note is only present by inference, and the element of parody difficult to discern, a view which Corominas seems ready to accept on p. 398 of his edition (note to 1022*ss*), but curiously enough rejects on p. 400 (note to 1024*de*).

One cannot draw easy conclusions from the common elements in the lyrics. Suffice it to say that I and II are at a remove from III and IV and that the protagonist cannot be clearly identified as the same figure in each song. In I and II we have the characteristic lost figure, given the accustomed epithet of *escudero* in the latter (961*c*); in III it is a peasant figure seeking marriage, in IV a *fidalgo* (1031*b*) and married, or so he claims (1028*b*). Nor can we refer to the relationships between man and woman as being even remotely similar in all four. The traditional *serrana* certainly appears in I and II, where the protagonist plays a sad second fiddle and violence and bawdy brutality is the substance. In III and IV the tone is neither ironic nor *outré*. In III the girl is an *ingénue* of rustic charm, reminiscent of Christine de Pisan's figurines; in IV the character is less explicit, but there is neither crudity nor caricature.

Consider briefly the linkage of the lyrics to their primarily narrative prologues. Narrative I in its opening lines suggests an association with the protagonist of the rest of the *Libro* in pursuit of a *loca demanda*, clutching at something he can never hold on to (951*d*: cf. 225*a*, 229*d*). The *serrana* in narrative and lyric is linked by name, ap-

of ms. *S*, although, as Corominas notes, the latter cannot be peremptorily rejected (p. 398). Whether the name Alda is a reminiscence of Roland's *fiancée* or the young girl of the twelfth-century Latin comedy of the same name (see in particular her description in lines 125-136 of the ed. of G. Cohen in *La Comédie latine en France au XIIᵉ siècle* (Paris, 1931), vol. I, p. 135), her appearance and behaviour are anything but rustic.

pearance and employment; the setting and conditions, the mode of dialogue are similar, as is the initial sequence of events, i.e. in the brusque demand for toll and promise of payment. Curiously enough, the resemblance ceases there, for on receipt of the promises the protagonist is carried on the back of the peasant over hill and stream. The peasant meal, the central erotic element, and indeed the substance of the final lines of the lyric are omitted. The narrative and lyric are therefore not co-terminous. The former is more succinct where it covers the same ground, but adds a conclusion as *point de départ* for the next stage. The latter is stronger in tone, the initial confrontation more abrupt (cf. 955*a*, 962*d*), perhaps to add more bite to the finale. It has been suggested that there might be missing verses at the end of the narrative (958), but the construction of the final verse could provide a counter-argument.

Narrative II is explicitly set in sequence to Narrative I (cf. 972*ab*, 974*b*) and also follows the pattern of events set in the corresponding lyric. The response to exaggerated flattery is, firstly, suspicion and, as the traveller makes more obvious advances, physical opposition. This, explicably, changes to compliance to the original demands and it is the protagonist's turn to prevaricate. If one were to set aside the two stanzas 983-984, present in ms. *S*, the line of argument in the narrative derives clearly from the lyric, preceded and followed by additional material. The additional two stanzas, however, deliberately emphasize the erotic element, which is only faintly implicit in the lyric.

Narrative III, in contrast to I and II, is the briefest of introductions to the lyric and solely connected to it by the interest of the *serrana* in marriage. In complete contrast, the *serrana* is described as slow-witted enough to mistake the traveller for a rustic like herself, while the traveller is cynical and condescending. There is no attack, no eroticism, no recrimination; the mode is purely narrative and the two parts have no overlap. Here is a clear opposition in practically every plane, out of which one cannot, without distortion, create a composite plot.

Narrative IV is the most openly grotesque of all four; like III it lacks any dramatic dialogue and in the same way stands as a preliminary to the lyric. Basically a descriptive *enumeratio* of the caricaturesque wild woman of the sierra, it is contrived as a photographic negative of the ideal woman described at 431-435, 443-445, 448 of Don Amor's address. [5] Outside the facts that the traveller is near Tablada,

---

[5] The version of ms. *S* is more elaborate than that of ms. *G;* cf. G. B. Gybbon-Monypenny, «The Two Versions of the *Libro de buen amor:* the

is cold, needs shelter and finds he can only get it on payment, the narrative bears little other relationship to the lyric. As in Narrative I, there has been the suggestion that verses may be missing; in this case only one song out of three is recorded.

The most obvious over-all conclusion is that there are more resemblances between the four narratives than between the four lyrics. In all cases the weather is foul, the *serrana* wilful, dominating, ugly or stupid, the sexual experience either frightening or comic and hardly rewarding for the traveller. On the other hand the narrative can vary widely in its relationship with the lyric. Only in the case of II can they both be said to conform to one another. Narrative I could be added to this only if one accepts the argument of missing verses: in III and IV the narrative is a pure preliminary and totally distinct in tone and mode. Can one in the light of the above talk of a progression, a sequence of steps to a climax? There could be a simple geographic sequence. In the lyrics, Malangosto, Sotos Alvos, Riofrío, Cornejo, la Tablada lie more or less on the North flank of the Guadarrama. The narrative adds Loçoya, Fuentefría, Segovia, Ferreros and could be said to link the scattered points into the pattern of a journey from South to the North side of the sierra and back again (974*a*). It is true that the first two pairs are about sensual experience of the most basic kind, and the last two revolve around marriage in the rustic sense of matching offer with offer. One may also sense an attempt to learn from experience between I and II, with no positive results, but this does not carry over into III and IV in any clear line. What could be said with more conviction is that the impression of love in the sierra as nasty and brutish in contrast to the town or court, is something which derives more clearly from the narratives than from the lyrics. The moralising tone, the elaboration by *sententia* or refrain (950*d*, 951*d*, 954*d*, 955*c*, 957*b*, 973*d*, 977*b*, 978*c*, 983*b*, 995, 1007*bc*) is also exclusive to the narrative and can be extended both before and after (946*b*, 1043*c*).

This leads on to the conclusion, often expressed, that the lyrics in their variety pre-exist the narrative, itself contrived as a simple support. In tone and attitude the narrative coheres more or less closely to the rest of the *Libro;* the character of the protagonist is also more clearly at one with the work as a whole than in the lyrics, where he is at

Extent and Nature of the Author's Revision», *BHS*, XXXIX (1962), p. 218. See also, on the rhetoric of the passage, A. N. Zahareas, *The Art of Juan Ruiz, Archpriest of Hita* (Madrid, 1965), pp. 147-152.

once the *escudero,* or the *serrano,* married or single, cynical or innocent, successful or unsuccessful. The interplay between narrative and lyric is not solely in terms of correspondence or contrast, so that both Menéndez Pidal and María Rosa Lida are equally right and wrong. Menéndez Pidal would be accurate if he took Narrative and Lyric III (and possibly IV) as his norm and María Rosa Lida could equally well state her case with Narrative and Lyric I and II. Both critics have oversimplified in response to assumptions about unity of treatment throughout the poem. The important point is that the poet has imposed no *a priori* selection upon these songs, which belong to the same *genus* but not the same *species.* They are, by tradition, in autobiographical form, and the songs are so framed that they could continue to exist in perfect independence from the frame, just as the lyrics of many a writer of *comedias* derive their reputation initially from free circulation and then by their incorporation into a play, or as the songs in a musical comedy are written under the sign of a known tradition, designed to function equally bound or unattached. In this particular case we cannot wholly deny to Juan Ruiz some degree of poetic sophistication when he follows a pair of closely identified passages of narrative and lyric with two where the contrary is evident, even if we discard arguments about sequence and symbolism as insufficiently pertinent. [6]

Finally, in consideration of the vexed question of how to situate the whole passage in the *Libro,* Lecoy's liturgical cycle or Kellerman's juxtapositions raise as many questions as they answer. María Rosa Lida has never hazarded a precise structural guess, and Gybbon-Monypenny is openly tentative about the latter half of the *Libro.* [7] Roger Walker, in assuming a poematic process in which the sense of sin and impending death weigh heavier and heavier on the Archpriest, runs into self-confessed difficulties with quite a few episodes, including the *serranas,* which seriously weaken his case. [8] Its links with the rest of the *Libro* are tenuous enough; the only clear reference to it from outside is in the subsequent short bridge passage prior to the two Passion songs, where Juan Ruiz alludes to his escape from the past «uproar» (1043c), again more appropriate to the previous narrative. It might be added that the initial lines of both *cuaderna vía* passages could be

[6] Cf. T. R. Hart, *La alegoría en el «Libro de buen amor»* (Madrid, 1959) and the review of *La alegoría...* by María Rosa Lida de Malkiel in *RPh,* XIV (1960-61), p. 342; Gybbon-Monypenny, «Two Versions...», pp. 217-218.

[7] Gybbon-Monypenny, «Two Versions...», p. 216.

[8] R. M. Walker, «Towards an Interpretation of the *Libro de buen amor*», *BHS,* XLIII (1966), p. 7.

taken as parallel (950a, 1043ab). But if we turn back to the geographical pattern suggested, it is difficult to extend this logically to the following bridge-section. For if Santa María del Vado is correctly located at the foot of Pico Ocejón in one of the Somosierra passes, it is an appropriate resting place after crossing the sierra, but it is at the opposite end of the trajectory covered, which ends at La Tablada. Had the traveller obeyed the advice of the first *serrana* (962f) he would more than likely have ended up in the right place by the shortest route. On the other hand, the return home, alluded to in 974a, could well run through Santa María del Vado in the direction of Hita (1067b). Such an approach might well suggest the gradual enlargement of this section to the detriment of elementary geographical accuracy, but it is a hazardous line of argument. [9]

Returning to the part of the *Libro* preceding the *serrana* section, stanzas 910-949 are of course missing from MS *G*, making the Endrina episode precede directly. Ulrich Leo would like to see a link between the two adventures of MS *S* here interposed, but merely as aspects of the «Trotaconventos Epos». [10] Yet the second of these episodes is also dated March (954a), the first of a sequence of chronological references which led Lecoy to his theories of liturgical cycles. But such ligatures as have been mentioned have more in common with rough stitching fore and aft than careful organisation, similar to the way that the Don Furón episode, also dated in March, is tacked casually on by a probable reference to Trotaconventos's death (1619a).

In sum, one may easily accept that Juan Ruiz, across an indeterminate number of originally independent lyrics of varying tone, constructed an elementary set of bridge passages, relatively uniform with the rest of the *Libro*. The purpose of each individual lyric is fairly clear, as is that of the sum total of the narratives, but juxtaposed they create no recognisably clear pattern other than that of exuberant variety. [11] If Menéndez Pidal and María Rosa Lida's vision of the macrocosm has led them to distort and simplify their vision of the micro-

---

[9] Criado de Val, *Teoría...*, pp. 244-245.
[10] Ulrich Leo, *Zur dichterischen Originalität des Arcipreste de Hita* (Frankfurt, *Analecta Romanica*, vi, 1958), Section VII, pp. 42-47.
[11] Le Gentil, in doubting the «didactisme jovial» of Mrs Malkiel, has proposed the alternative term of «*pré-quichottisme*, qui suppose un mélange très particulier de bienveillance et de sarcasme, de sérieux et de fantaisie» («Les *Canticas...*», p. 139). This leads him to suggest that parody of the Cervantine type, with all its deliberate ambiguities, may well provide a more satisfactory explanation of the poet's intention: «elle a l'avantage de faire une large place au jeu littéraire» (p. 140). It is to be hoped that Le Gentil will elaborate this point at some future date.

cosm, it would be rash to assert the inverse; but it is equally clear that, in virtue of this variety, it would be even more injudicious to set the whole section on the road to some undetermined climax.

Much more tentative conclusions may be derived from a comparison of the author's manner of insertion of three other extensive episodes or «set pieces» in the *Libro*, that of Doña Endrina, the allegorical *Batalla* and the tent of Don Amor. These are similar in that we have clear evidence for the existence of materials prior to the poem. In all cases the digestion of this material into the «bloodstream» is only partial. By this I mean that in the case of the first episode the identity of Juan Ruiz as protagonist is carelessly renounced half way through, while the interpolated observations of Juan Ruiz the commentarist, are, as with the *serrana* episode, more in tune with the nominally didactic narrative of the framework, as can be seen from the final summing up (904-909). The association of the autobiographical narrative line with the substance of the *Batalla* does not derive from any but the most tenuous internal logic (viz. 1069c; 1077c) and the author as protagonist disappears completely for just short of 180 verses (1080-1257), to appear sporadically (1258; 1260a; 1263c, etc.) in the ambiguous role of either protagonist or commentator, it does not matter which. And within the confines of the *Batalla* episode, box within box, as it were, one can see again, *in parvo,* how a bridge is manufactured (1128-1130; 1161-1162) to contain a series of topics at the centre of which is Christian penance.

However sympathetic one may be to the efforts of critics like Zahareas who properly hold reservations about the selective vision of María Rosa Lida, one must, I think, be prepared also to admit that any global artistic vision of the *Libro* will have to confront apparently insoluble incongruities. Whether or not one may turn aside the author's remarks in verse 1629, one must accept it as an explicit invitation. This would suggest that the author is a protean figure who assumes in turn the many roles that his imagination creates freely or adapts from other sources, without renouncing his position as master of ceremonies, and that the «meaning» of the work is the «meaning» at any one point in its unfolding. Or put another way it is only with difficulty that one can assert a total meaning any more than a one-man series of dramatic sketches, characterised chiefly by their entertaining variety, can be said to have accumulative effect on the audience at the conclusion. What we do admire in the end is the actor and his abilities to conjure up a variety of scenes and emotions at all levels. It will of course be advanced, and properly, that there are plenty of data to suggest that the author has attemped to impose a unity on his work, but it would be unwise to move this to the centre of any argument about internal aesthetic structure, since one can equally invoke much of the data to suggest that many elements are super-imposed rather than organic. One is tempted to think of the work as something initially like an artistic «transcript» of a juglaresque «performance» which, on the written page, in a fixed form or sequence, has invited the author to treat it like an organised and composed unit demanding an introit and epilogue. Our difficulties, then, in reading the work, will primarily derive from our uncertain but inevitable assumptions about the relations between the speaker, his various roles, and ourselves as audience or as readers.

University of Nottingham

ROGER M. WALKER

'Con miedo de la muerte la miel non es sabrosa': Love, Sin and Death in the 'Libro de buen amor'

The most puzzling feature of the *Libro de buen amor* is its apparent dualism of attitude. The author seems to be recommending and savouring the pleasures of life, particularly the pleasures of sexual love, and at the same time stressing the need to live according to the commandments of the church and the moral law of God in order to save one's soul. Because the Archpriest expresses himself with equal vigour on the subject of the joys of love and on the dangers of sin, many different and conflicting interpretations of his book have been advanced. Unfortunately many of these interpretations have been arrived at by virtually ignoring one side or the other. Consequently some early critics maintained that Juan Ruiz was quite simply an immoral man, a disgrace to the priesthood, and that all his preaching and moralizing was merely a hypocritical front to protect him from the censure of his ecclesiastical superiors. But there were others who tried to present the Archpriest as a shining example of Christian virtue who felt forced to use highly coloured and sometimes scurrilous stories to make the point of his moral lesson more vividly and hold the attention of his audience.[1] However, as Félix Lecoy rightly pointed out, «toute interprétation qui voudrait sacrifier l'un de ces deux aspects à l'autre est incomplète».[2] Not only is such an interpretation incomplete, it is unnecessary. Those who would have us see Juan Ruiz as either a licentious hypocrite or a holier-than-thou moralist do so because they feel that the two attitudes shown in the *Libro* are mutually exclusive. And so they would be, of course, in a work of abstract didacticism,

[1] Although more recent critics have tended to avoid such extreme judgments, they are still divided more or less clearly into those who regard the *Libro* as primarily a didactic work and those who see it as essentially a merry work.

[2] *Recherches sur le Libro de buen amor* (Paris, 1938), p. 349.

231

whether it be a manual of seduction or a guide to the Christian life: the preacher must adopt and maintain a single standpoint if he wishes to make his point clearly. The *Libro de buen amor,* however, is cast not in the form of a sermon but in the form of an autobiography (whether true or imagined is not important here). In this work we are concerned not with humanity in the abstract, but with one man's struggles and temptations, one man's character and its many and contradictory facets. It is surely possible to accept on both the human and aesthetic plane that a man, especially in the guilt-ridden atmosphere of the Middle Ages, can be both 'homme moyen sensuel' and a convinced Christian. I believe that Juan Ruiz is such a man and that in the *Libro* he is dramatizing the very real conflict between his sensuality and his religious beliefs.

To my mind, what gives this conflict its particular poignancy and brings it clearly into focus is the theme of death. For Juan Ruiz death has a twofold significance: it is the end of earthly life and its pleasures, and it is also the point at which the fate of his immortal soul will be decided. My purpose in this article is to examine the conflict between the love of women and the love of God in the *Libro de buen amor,* particularly in the light of what the Archpriest has to say about death.

Pedro Salinas, in his *Jorge Manrique, o tradición y originalidad* (3rd edition, Buenos Aires, 1962), quotes Gómez de la Serna's superb definition of death as «un estado en que no se pueden fumar puros» (p. 49). In purely human terms death means simply the end of life and the irrevocable loss of all that makes life most enjoyable. For Juan Ruiz life's supreme joy is love and the pursuit of women. It has been suggested in previous studies[3] that the first part of the *Libro de buen amor* (up to and including the successful seduction of Doña Endrina) stresses this positive side of love and sets out the various stages of what Lecoy calls «un apprentissage amoureux» (*Recherches...*, p. 357). In the first half of his book the Archpriest not only describes his early amorous escapades, his instruction at the hands of Don Amor and Doña Venus, and the ultimate triumph over the virtue and better judgment of Doña Endrina, but he also tries at some length to justify his conduct. He says that sex, apart from affording man the greatest

---

[3] See F. Lecoy, *Recherches...*, pp. 357 ff.; G. B. Gybbon-Monypenny, «The Two Versions of the *Libro de buen amor:* the Extent and Nature of the Author's Revision», *BHS,* XXXIX (1962), 205-221 (especially pp. 215-216); Roger M. Walker, «Towards an Interpretation of the *Libro de buen amor*», *BHS,* XLIII (1966), 1-10 (especially pp. 1-3).

possible pleasure — «Ca en muger loçana, fermosa e cortés / todo bien del mundo e todo plazer es» (108cd) — is also in the natural order of things, and he cites the considerable authority of Aristotle in support of his contention:

> Omnes, aves, animalias, toda bestia de cueva
> quieren segund natura compañía sienpre nueva,
> e quanto más el omne que a toda cosa se mueva.   (73bcd).

The Archpriest also has recourse to the 'scientific' arguments of the astrologers to explain and justify his desire for women (151 ff.): as he was born under the sign of Venus he was inevitably endowed with a lecherous temperament. He even goes so far as to imply that God cannot disapprove too much of sex since he made woman such an attractive creature and created her specifically to be man's companion:

> Ssy Dios, quando formó el omne, entendiera
> que era mala cosa la muger, non la diera
> al omne por conpañera nin d'él nin la feziera;
> ssy para bien non fuera, tan noble non saliera.   (109).

Jorge Guzmán has recently made the point that «este yo, a lo largo del *Libro,* no tiene más carácter distintivo que su deseo de mujeres; el yo de las aventuras amorosas es ciertamente un incansable amador y nada más».[4] For Juan Ruiz, then, love is virtually synonymous with life, life that is characterised above all by light, movement, noise and company, forming the sharpest possible contrast to the darkness, stillness, silence and loneliness of death. His attempts at seduction involve constant comings and goings, intrigues and disputes. Whenever he loses or is rejected by one woman, he immediately looks for another to avoid the horror of loneliness: «E yo como estava solo syn conpañía, / codiciava tener lo que otro para sy tenía» (112ab).

In his long lecture to the Archpriest, Don Amor constantly stresses the need for unflagging enthusiasm and unremitting effort in the pursuit of women if the prospective lover is to have any hope of success: «Que el grand trabajo todas las cosas vençe» (452d). Laziness and apathy in the wooer are unforgivable:

> Son en la grand pereza miedo e cobardía,
> torpedat e vileza, ssuziedat e astrossya;
> por la pereza pyerden muchos la mi conpañía,
> por pereza se pierde muger de grand valya.   (456).

---

[4] *Una constante didáctico-moral del Libro de buen amor* (México, 1963), p. 58.

Don Amor hammers this point home with the story of the two sluggards who fell in love with and wanted to marry the same woman. As a direct result of their lethargy one has been crippled and the other has lost an eye.

Man, then, throws himself into frenzied activity dedicated to love, pleasure and the gratification of his senses, but designed above all to give him a sense of life and to prevent him brooding upon his inevitable death. Yet in the end it is all fruitless; man has to admit to death that «non puede foyr omne de ty nin se asconder» (1523*a*). The first part of the *planto* for the *tercera* Trotaconventos stresses the essentially life-destroying aspect of death.[5] Death is «enemiga del mundo» (1520*c*) and «con todo el mundo tyenes continua enamistat» (1522*b*). The frantic activity stops —«Trotaconventos ya non anda nin trota» (1518*d*); conversation and communication are no more— «enmudeçes la fabla» (1546*c*); the senses through which man appreciates the pleasures of life are destroyed —«El oyr e el olor, el tañer, el gustar, / todos los çinco sesos tú los vienes tomar» (1547*ab*). A dead man is finally and irrevocably alone, a wretched thing so alien to life that he is abhorred even by those who loved him most:

> Eres en tal manera del mundo aborrida,
> que por bien que lo amen al omne en la vida,
> en punto que tú vienes con tu mala venida,
> todos fuyen del luego como de rres podrida.

> Los quel' aman e quieren e quien ha avido su conpaña,
> aborresçen lo muerto como a cosa estraña;
> parientes e amigos todos le tyenen saña,
> todos fuyen d'él luego como si fuese araña.

> De padres e de madres los fijos tan queridos,
> amigos e amigas deseados e servidos,
> de mugeres leales los sus buenos maridos
> desque tú vienes, muerte, luego son aborridos.   (1525-27).

---

[5]   After I had completed this present paper there appeared an article by Rafael Lapesa, «El tema de la muerte en el *Libro de buen amor*», *Estudios dedicados a James Homer Herriott* (Wisconsin, 1966), pp. 127-144. Lapesa also stresses this aspect of the *planto*: death for the Archpriest is «ante todo, y en el fondo casi exclusivamente, implacable y pavorosa destrucción» (p. 135). Later in his study, however, Lapesa comes to conclusions about the theme of death in the *Libro* that are very different from my own. These have been noted in the appropriate places.

Death makes everything a man regards as good or beautiful or worth-
while in life seem ugly and sordid:

> Tyras toda verguença, desfeas fermosura,
> desadonas la graçia, denuestas la mesura,
> enflaquesçes la fuerça, enloquesçes cordura,
> lo dulçe fazes fiel con tu mucha amargura.
>
> Despreçias loçanía, el oro escureçes,
> desfazes la fechura, alegría entristezes,
> mansyllas la lynpiesa, cortesía envileçes:
> Muerte, matas la vida, al mundo aborresçes.   (1548-49). [6]

This last line is a simple statement of the true significance of death
to the hedonist. It is not surprising that the Archpriest cries out in
exasperation:

> ca beviendo omne sienpre en mundo terrenal,
> non avrién de ti miedo nin de tu mal hostal,
> nin temerié tu venida la carne umagnal.   (1553*bcd*).

If only man could live for ever and not have the shadow of death
hanging over him he could be perfectly happy with the world and its
pleasures. But as death is so obviously part of the natural order of
things —indeed, the one certain thing in the whole of life— we are
obliged to see all earthly things in the light of it and come to the
inevitable conclusion that they are finite and transitory. This conclusion lies at the basis of most great religions: man does not like
to accept that his existence has no more meaning than that of the
animals and plants, but if he is doomed to die just as they are, then
the significance of human existence must reside in a life after death.
Once this is accepted, it is an easy step to regard this world and all
its attractions as a delusion and a distraction from the serious business
of preparing oneself for the next.
    It is Juan Ruiz's religious convictions and fear of death that force
him into virulent attacks on the pleasures he obviously appreciates so
much. He goes to great lengths to try and convince us —and, one
suspects, himself— of the futility of earthly love. Of the thirteen

---

[6] A. H. Schutz, «La tradición cortesana en dos coplas de Juan Ruiz»,
NRFH, VIII (1954), 63-71, makes the interesting point that the qualities listed
in 1548-49 are precisely those which were regarded as essential for the courtly
lover. They are also the qualities that Don Amor recommends his disciples
to cultivate.

encounters with women in the book only two end in real success and
another leads to a frustrating platonic relationship.[7] Of the other
women, five refuse to have anything to do with the Archpriest, one
leaps into bed with his messenger, and three of the four *serranas* subject him to degradation and humiliation. His lifelong pursuit of
women, therefore, brings him little else but pain, frustration and humiliation. Can this be seriously taken as an illustration of the joys of
love?

This singular lack of success is surely emphasised so as to make
us ready to accept the more serious charges he brings against love,
which can be classified under three heads: (*a*) Love is deceitful;
(*b*) Love is sinful; (*c*) Love is destructive. I propose to examine each
of these charges in turn.

Very early in the *Libro de buen amor* the Archpriest utters a warning about the deceitfulness of love:

> Una tacha le fallo al amor poderoso,
> la qual a vos, dueñas, yo descobrir non oso;
> mas, por que non me tengades por dezidor medroso,
> es esta: que el amor sienpre fabla mentiroso. (161)

He returns to this point in his tirade against Don Amor:

> eres mentiroso, falso en muchos enartar. (182*c*)

> Toda maldad del mundo e toda pestilençia;
> sobre la falsa lengua mintirosa aparesçencia. (417*ab*)

Not only is Don Amor himself a liar and deceiver, he also inspires his
followers to imitate his evil ways and forget the true purpose of their
lives:

> El que tu obra trae es mintroso puro,
> por conplyr tus deseos fazes lo erege duro,
> más cree tus lysonjas el neçio fadeduro
> que non la fe de Dios; vete, yo te conjuro. (389)

Don Amor and Venus freely admit the importance of deceit in successful wooing and urge the lover to choose a go-between skilled in

---

[7] Joan Corominas, in his edition of the *Libro* (Madrid, 1967), maintains
that the protagonist's affair with Doña Garoça is in fact fully consummated
and not platonic (*Commentary*, 1503). This view was first put forward by
Ulrich Leo in his book *Zur dichterischen Originalität des Arcipreste de Hita*
(Frankfurt, 1958), pp. 67 ff., but is still far from receiving general acceptance.

the craft of lying («sepa mentir fermoso» — 437c) and deceiving («que saben bien çegar» — 442d). The lover too must learn the arts of deception and misrepresentation in his turn, as Venus emphasises more than once: «Non olvides los sospiros, en esto sey engañoso» (627c); «Las mentyras a las devezes a muchos aprovechan, / la verdat a las devezes muchos en daño echan» (637ab); «Sey sotil e acuçioso e avrás tu amiga» (648b).

Such is the power of love to mislead that it makes men lose their sense of proportion and see value in things and persons that have none:

> El que es enamorado, por muy feo que sea,
> otrosí su amiga, maguer que sea muy fea,
> el uno e el otro non ha cosa que vea
> que tan bien le paresca nin que tanto desea.

> El bavieca, el torpe, el neçio, el pobre
> a su amiga bueno paresçe e rrico onbre.   (158-159ab)

Janet Chapman has pointed out that Juan Ruiz attributes the same transformational ability to money in his biting satire on the power of wealth (490 ff.).[8] Two of the things that men value most —love and money— are thus characterised by their power to deceive and alter appearances. But death also has this power to transform (see 1548-49, quoted on p. 235 above). There is, however, a significant difference here: love and money make us see nobility, beauty and worth where none really exists, whereas death shows us corruption and decay where we thought there was something of value and substance. The pursuit of love, therefore, is not only fruitless, but also deceives a man into thinking he has found something permanent and good, worthy of the energy that he should be expending on the salvation of his soul.

But love not only deceives man and makes him careless of his duty to God, it also leads him directly into mortal sin and so puts his soul in even greater danger of damnation by causing him to add sins of commission to sins of omission. The sinfulness of sexual love is, of course, a medieval commonplace, and throughout the *Libro* there is ample evidence that the Archpriest sees no reason to question its truth, from the clear statement in the prose prologue that «desecha e aborresçe el alma el pecado del amor loco deste mundo», to the almost casual parenthesis of «E yo como ssoy omne como otro pecador, / ove

---

[a] «A Suggested Interpretation of Stanzas 528 to 549a of the *Libro de buen amor*», *RF*, LXXIII (1961), 29-39.

de las mugeres a las vezes grand amor» (76*ab*). Several of the women he pursues also recognise that what he is asking of them is contrary to the moral law and a danger to their souls. His third potential bed mate, for example, sends him away with this blunt refusal: «Non perderé yo a Dios nin al su parayso / por pecado del mundo que es sonbra de aliso» (173*ab*). As one might expect, the nun Doña Garoça is the most insistent of all on this point during her long disputation with Trotaconventos (see, for instance, 1355*d*, 1385, 1443*cd*).

However, Juan Ruiz's clearest indictment of the sinfulness of *loco amor* is the long passage on the Seven Deadly Sins (217-371). This *topos* was one of the favourite themes of medieval preachers, but the Archpriest in his tirade against Don Amor gives it a new dimension by specifically accusing love of being the cause of all the sins:

> Contigo syenpre trahes los mortales pecados;
> con mucha cobdiçia los omnes enganados,
> ffazes les cobdiçiar e mucho ser denodados,
> passar los mandamientos que de Dios fueron dados. (217)

Each sin is dealt with in turn, and the clear connection between love and the various affronts to God is emphasised by the constant use of the second-person address form and by making *Cobdiçia* the root sin instead of the more usual Pride. There can be no doubt here at least of the Archpriest's message: the pursuit of wordly love brings in its wake every kind of sin and must consequently be regarded as the greatest single danger to the salvation of a man's soul.

The Archpriest makes it quite plain, then, that whatever its superficial attractions might be, sexual love is not only futile, but also deceitful and sinful. Furthermore it is destructive; and this is one of the most interesting features of the theme of love in the *Libro de buen amor*. Not only does love confuse man's sense of values and endanger his soul, it also weakens him physically and so hastens his death. This point is first made in the attack on Don Amor:

> Traes enloquecidos a muchos con tu saber,
> fazes los perder el sueño, el comer e el bever;
> ffazes a muchos omnes tanto se atrever
> en ti fasta que el cuerpo e el alma van perder. (184)

> Eres padre del fuego, pariente de la llama;
> más arde e más se quema qualquier que te más ama;
> Amor, quien te más sygue, quemas le cuerpo e alma;
> destruyes lo del todo, como el fuego a la rrama. (197)

The story of the young man who wanted to marry three women, which the Archpriest uses to illustrate this point in his accusation of Don Amor, emphasises graphically (albeit comically) the harmful physical effects of love. After only a month of marriage to his first wife the man tries to stop the millstone with his foot (as he had been able to do so easily in the past), but sex has weakened him so much that this time the stone «levantó le las piernas, echó lo por mal cabo» (195*b*).

Love has the same destructive power as the other activities that spring from the sensual side of man's nature. The story of the hermit, for example, illustrates the terrible consequences to oneself and to others of excessive drinking. In drink the hermit commits the sins of covetousness, lust and pride, and finally the crime of murder (540), for which he is executed. Not only has he taken another person's life, he has occasioned the loss of his own: «Perdió cuerpo e alma el cuytado maltrecho» (543*c*). After this story the Archpriest describes in more general terms the harmful physical effects of overdrinking:

> Faze perder la vysta e acortar la vyda,
> tyra la fuerça toda, sys' toma syn medida,
> faze tenbrar los mienbros, todo seso olvida;
> adó es el mucho vyno toda cosa es perdida. (544)

> Los omnes enbriagos ayna envejecen. (546*a*)

The destructive nature of man's animal sensuality is, I think, clearly brought out in the allegorical battle between Carnal and Cuaresma. Doña Cuaresma graphically describes the destruction wrought by Don Carnal, who represents in the allegory the sensual side of man: «Astragando mi tierra, faziendo mucho dapño, / vertyendo mucha sangre, de lo que más me asaño» (1070*cd*). After his escape from captivity Carnal issues a summons to all his supporters which begins: «De nos, don Carnal, fuerte matador de toda cosa» (1190*b*). When Cuaresma admits defeat and leaves the field, Carnal celebrates his victory with a great slaughter of everything he can find:

> Traya en la su mano un assegur muy fuerte,
> a toda quatropea con ella da la muerte,
> cuchillo muy agudo a las rreses acomete,
> con aquel las degüella e a desollar se mete. (1217)

Man's sensuality, then, brings death and destruction in its wake, as well as leading him into sin and the danger of damnation. This close connection between death and damnation is one of the most constant themes of the *Libro de buen amor* and one which demands closer examination. On several occasions the Archpriest specifically links the disastrous effects love has on the body with the dangers it holds for the soul. In his *pelea* with Don Amor, for instance, he accuses love no fewer than five times of causing this double destruction: «Ffazes a muchos omnes tanto se atrever / en ti fasta que el cuerpo e el alma van perder» (184*cd*); «Amor, quien te más sygue, quemas le cuerpo e alma» (197*c*); «Tú, después, nunca piensas synon por astragallos, / en cuerpos e en almas asy todos tragallos» (207*cd*); «Das muerte perdurable a las almas que fieres, / das muchos enemigos al cuerpo que rrequieres» (399*ab*); «Almas, cuerpos e algos como huerco las tragas» (400*b*). Doña Garoça expresses similar sentiments in answer to Trotaconventos' attempts to convince her of the joys of love: «E pues tú a mí dizes razón de perdimiento / del alma e del cuerpo e muerte e enfamamiento» (1423*ab*). [9]

Nowhere, however, is Juan Ruiz's emphasis on the common origin of death and damnation more evident than in the sermon on the Seven Deadly Sins. Each of the sins is accused in turn not only of bringing about the loss of the soul (which one would of course expect), but also of causing the death and destruction of the body:

I. COBDICIA: Por que sus almas e los cuerpos lazraron
(221*d*)

Murieron por los furtos de muerte sopitaña
(222*a*)

---

[9] A similar formula is used (*a*) in the prose prologue: «Entiendo quantos bienes fazen perder el alma e al cuerpo» (p. 5); (*b*) to describe the end of the drunken hermit: «Perdió cuerpo e alma el cuytado maltrecho» (543*c*); (*c*) in the denunciation of seducers by Endrina: «Pyerde el cuerpo e el alma» (885*c*). Other examples of the clear use of *cuerpo* when linked with *alma* to mean 'man's life in this world' are provided in C. C. Smith and J. Morris, «On 'Physical' Phrases in Old Spanish Epic and Other Texts», *PLPLS*, XII (1967), Part V, 129-190 (especially pp. 167-168). My colleague Mr A. D. Deyermond has informed me that this type of formulaic threat combining temporal and eternal punishment is common in legal documents of the Middle Ages; it is reflected, for example, in the *Poema de Mio Cid*, 27-28 and again in 1022. However R. Menéndez Pidal, in a note on 27-28 in his edition of the *Poema* (Madrid, 1911), points out that «Alfonso VI usó realmente de esta cláusula en sus diplomas, pero su nieto Alfonso VII la abandonó, y, por lo tanto, iba ya haciéndose arcaica cuando se escribió el Cantar». G. G. Coulton, *Five Centuries of Religion*, III (Cambridge, 1936), also shows quite clearly how as time went on documents placed more and more emphasis on the threat of legal and secular punishments and largely abandoned the threats of excommunication and damnation (pp. 34-40). Smith and Morris also provide evidence to show that the most common legal formula was the threat of the loss of *cuerpo* and *aver* (*art. cit.*, p. 168). I think, therefore, we are safe in assuming that in the *Libro* the phrase *perder cuerpo e alma* would have a clear religious significance for its hearers.

Por tu mala cobdiçia los de Egipto morieron,
Los cuerpos enfamaron, las ánimas perdieron;
(224*ab*)

2. SOBERBIA: Mueren de malas muertes, non los puedes tú
[quitar,
Lyeva los el diablo por el tu gran abeytar,
(232*bc*)

El omne muy sobervio e muy denodado...
ante muere que otro más fraco e más lazrado;
(236*a, c*)

3. LUXURIA: De muchos ha que matas, non sé uno que
[sanes;
quantos en tu loxuria son grandes varraganes,
matan se a sy mesmos los locos alvardanes;
(269*abc*)

Destruye a su cuerpo e a su alma mata,
(273*c*)

Entristeze en punto, luego flaqueza siente,
acórtase la vida...
(274*cd*)

¡Quién podrie dezir quantos tu loxuria mata!
(275*a*)

4. ENVIDIA: Estorva te tu pecado, façe te ally moryr.
(280*d*)

Por la envidia Cayn a su hermano Abel
matólo, por que yaze dentro en Mongibel.
(281*ab*)

Ffue por la enbydia mala traydo Jhesuxris-
[to,...
por enbydia fue preso, e muerto e conquiśto;
(282*a, c*)

5. GULA: Mató la golosyna muchos en el desierto,
(295*a*)

Muerte muy rrebatada trae la golossyna
al cuerpo muy goloso e al alma mesquina;
(297*ab*)

6. VANAGLORIA/
IRA: [Samson] A sy mesmo con yra e a otros mu-
[chos mató.
(308*d*)

[Saul] El mesmo se mató con su espada...

(309c)

7. ACIDIA: Con tus malas maestrías almas e cuerpos ma-

[tas.

(318d). [10]

Jorge Guzmán notes the number of references to death in the Garoça episode, but comes to the conclusion that the *muerte* meant here «ya no es la muerte física, sino más bien el pecado, la perdición» (*Una constante...*, p. 79). He bases this assumption on a number of biblical texts in which he believes «la Biblia iguala muerte y condenación». But in view of the considerable number of very clear references to the loss of both *cuerpo* and *alma* as a result of sin, I think we must understand *muerte* here and elsewhere to mean physical death as well as damnation.

I believe that the Archpriest's inspiration for this theme of the double danger of sin is the church's doctrine of the Fall of Man; damnation *and* death were first introduced into the world as a direct result of the sin of Adam. Catholic teaching on the doctrine of Original Sin is summarised as follows: (*a*) God gave Adam Sanctifying Grace and immunity from death; (*b*) By his sin Adam forfeited these gifts, became an enemy of God and a slave of the devil, and was changed for the worse in body and soul; (*c*) He transmitted to all his posterity his guilt and its evil consequences. [11]

The biblical text on which this doctrine is based is *Genesis,* II, 17, in which God says to Adam: «De ligno autem scientiae boni et mali ne comedas; in quocumque enim die comederis ex eo, *morte morieris*» (Vulgate version; my italics). God's warning is later repeated by Eve to the serpent: «De fructu vero ligni quod est in medio paradisi, praecepit nobis Deus ne comederemus, et ne tangeremus illud, ne forte moriamur» (III, 3). According to the interpretation placed on them by the church, these references to death mean that when Adam disobeyed he would suffer immediate spiritual death (by being cut off from God), and would also be put under sentence of physical death. These

---

[10] When the Archpriest refers back to the Seven Deadly Sins before beginning his sermon on the arms of the Christian, he stresses once again their danger to both body and soul: «Los mortales pecados ya los avedes oydos, / aquestos de cada día nos trahen muy conbatidos, / las almas quieren matar pues los cuerpos han feridos, / por aquesto devemos estar de armas byen guarnidos» (1583).

[11] This summary and the discussion of Original Sin which follows are based on M. Sheehan, *Apologetics and Catholic Doctrine* (Part II: *Catholic Doctrine*), 2nd. edn. (Dublin, 1957), pp. 60-67.

two separate consequences of disobedience are confirmed later in the same chapter of *Genesis*. After the fruit has been eaten God condemns Adam to what is quite clearly physical destruction: «Donec revertaris in terram de qua sumptus es: quia pulvis es et in pulverem reverteris» (III, 19). Man's sentence to spiritual separation from God, on the other hand, comes at the end of the chapter: «Et emisit eum Dominus Deus de paradiso voluptatis, ut operaretur terram de qua sumptus est. Ejecitque Adam, et collocavit ante paradisum voluptatis cherubim, et flameum gladium, atque versatilem, ad custodiendam viam ligni vitae» (III, 23-24).

By his disobedience Adam lost for himself and all his descendants the four gifts bestowed upon him at his creation: the supernatural gift of Sanctifying Grace, and the preternatural gifts of Integrity, Immortality and Enlightenment. The Fall, then, brought to the world damnation, through the loss of Sanctifying Grace which enabled man to participate in God's divine nature and eternal happiness; sin, through the loss of Integrity which gave him control over his passions and his lower nature; death, through the loss of Immortality which also would have preserved him from suffering and physical decay; and confusion, through the loss of Enlightenment which gave him wisdom and understanding of God and the world around him.

The seriousness of the Archpriest's attack on *loco amor* is brought home to us forcibly when we realise that he is in fact attributing the same terrible consequences to sexual love as the theologians do to Original Sin. Love alienates a man from God and causes his damnation; it leads him into further sin, since it is the root of the Seven Deadly Sins from which all other wickedness derives; it causes him to lose his health and hastens his death; and it blinds him to his duty to God by giving him a false set of values based on *engaño*. Bearing all this in mind, would it be too fanciful to suggest that Juan Ruiz may have believed that the sin of Adam was in fact the sin of *loco amor?* The church teaches that the nature of Original Sin is a mystery; but the fact remains that the biblical account of the Fall is full of erotic overtones, and indeed Adam's very first recorded act after his expulsion is to 'know' his wife (*Genesis,* IV, 1). This strongly implied connection between sex and the Fall accounts for the church's very high regard for virginity and chastity and its insistence on a celibate priesthood —features that distinguish Western Christianity from most other religions. At all events, the disastrous effects clearly ascribed to *loco*

243

17

amor in the *Libro* bear a striking resemblance to those normally ascribed to Original Sin. [12]

Juan Ruiz, then, despite his gay façade and his much praised *alegría*, in fact presents on closer examination a very sombre picture of the human predicament. Through his inheritance of the sin of Adam, man is alienated from God, attracted to evil, and doomed to death and damnation. However, for a Christian this is not the end of the story: a second Adam was sent by God to redeem the transgression of the first; but to do this he had to suffer the same fate as Adam and all his descendants: he too had to suffer physical death, not as a punishment but as a sacrifice to appease God's anger. As Christ was without sin he was able to conquer death, a clear indication of the theological connection between sin and death; he rose again, not only spiritually but physically. He was the first man since Adam to overcome the alienation of man from God, the desire to sin, the death of the body, and Satan's power over the souls of the dead.

This doctrine of redemption is the central point of the Archpriest's *planto* for Trotaconventos. (It is only by omitting any reference to the climactic account of the death and resurrection of Christ that A. N. Zahareas is able to come to the extraordinary conclusion that the *planto* is basically comic). [13] The first part of the lament, which has already been examined (pp. 234-235 above), presents a horrific picture of the power of death to destroy and corrupt human life and worldly values. The tirade goes on to describe how death even managed to pene-

[12] In a future paper I hope to be able to shed further light on this point after a detailed study of the ideas on Original Sin propounded by contemporary preachers and theologians. Lapesa («El tema de la muerte...», p. 37) notes correctly that «Juan Ruiz identifica y engloba en un solo mal radical el pecado, la muerte corpórea y la condenación, muerte segunda y eterna»; but he then goes on to claim that «en vez de situar en el pecado la causa de ambas muertes, según la doctrina bíblica y cristiana, [Juan Ruiz] invierte los términos y hace que la muerte sea promotora del pecado». He bases this, to my mind, quite wrong conclusion on the fact that the Archpriest accuses death of being the basis of all evil in 1546d («en ti es todo mal») and 1552b («tú eres mal primero»), and of creating hell to cater for its victims. I think I have assembled enough evidence in the course of this paper to show that Juan Ruiz was completely orthodox in his beliefs about sin and death. The main weakness of Lapesa's argument is that it is based entirely on the invective against death in the *planto* for Trotaconventos.

[13] *The Art of Juan Ruiz, Archpriest of Hita* (Madrid, 1965), pp. 209-217. Lapesa, on the other hand, does not evade the problem and he presents a convincing explanation for the juxtaposition of the parodic and serious parts of the *planto,* suggesting that the invective against death was written before the lament for Trotaconventos herself as a quite separate piece and was only later incorporated into it. He believes that the phrase «Mataste a mi vieja» was inserted into the opening stanza of the invective (1520) in order to make the connection («El tema de la muerte...», p. 139).

trate heaven to bring about the fall from grace of Lucifer and the rebel angels (1555). [14] Not content with this victory, death even dared to make Christ afraid and finally perpetrated its greatest enormity of all and claimed the son of God as its victim:

> El Señor que te fizo, tú a este mataste,
> Ihesuxristo Dios e omne tú aqueste penaste,
> al que tiene el çielo e la tierra, a este
> tú le posiste miedo e tú lo demudeste.
>
> El infierno lo teme e tú non lo temiste,
> temió te la su carne, grand miedo le posiste,
> la su humanidat por tu miedo fue triste,
> la deydat non te temió, entonçe non la viste.   (1556-57).

Death claimed the human Christ, but the final victory belonged to the divine Christ, and the power of death was broken:

> Al infierno, a los suyos e a ty mal quebrantó,
> túl' mataste una ora, él por sienpre te mató.
>
> Quando te quebrantó, entonçe lo conoçiste,
> sy ante lo espantaste, mill tanto pena oviste,
> dio nos vida moriendo al que tú muerte diste,
> sacó nos de cabptivo la cruz en quel' posiste. (1558cd-1559).

So Christ's sacrifice made it possible for a man to obtain grace and save his soul; no longer would death inevitably mean damnation. But although this grace is a gift from God, man does not receive it automatically: he has to make great efforts to overcome his desire to sin and his taste for worldly pleasure. [15] He must prove to God the goodness of his intentions by trying to live according to the moral law and the commandments of the church (i.e. by good works), and above all by showing his sorrow for sin by prayer and penance. This is an essential part of the Archpriest's message. The *Libro* not only has its

---

[14] This is a further interesting example of the close connection between sin and death in the *Libro*: Lucifer's fall is normally attributed to the sin of pride, not to death.
[15] Lapesa refers to this section of the *planto* which describes the victory of Christ as «la lucha suprema entre la vida y la muerte», ending in «el triunfo definitivo de la Vida» («El tema de la muerte...», p. 138). But this statement is misleading in the context of his article, since he fails to distinguish clearly at this stage (although he remedies this failure later) between earthly life and the eternal life of heaven, which is granted only to those who reject earthly pleasures. I maintain that there is a quite different significance given to *vida* in «Muerte, matas la vida, al mundo aborresçes» (1549d) and in «Dio nos vida moriendo al que tú muerte diste» (1559c).

negative side, depicting the futility, deceitfulness, sinfulness and destructiveness of love, but also its positive side, showing how man can overcome his baser instincts and gain salvation. Very early in the work Juan Ruiz refutes his own arguments about the ineluctable influence of the stars on one's character by citing the superior power of what the catechism calls the «three eminent Good Works» (prayer, fasting and almsgiving):

> Anssy que por ayuno e lymosna e oraçión
> e por servir a Dios con mucha contriçión,
> non ha poder mal signo nin su costellaçión.   (149*abc*).

This basic formula for salvation is developed throughout the book. There are, for example, no fewer than thirteen prayers in the *Libro,* in most of which the Archpriest stresses his own unworthiness, the redeeming power of Christ, the mercy of God towards sinners, and the value of Mary's intercession. [16]

But prayer alone is not enough; faith in God's mercy must be accompanied by determined efforts on man's part to live according to the moral law. We must, in Juan Ruiz's own words, «fazer buenas obras». In the lament for Trotaconventos he stresses the great importance of good works in man's search for salvation, repeating his exhortation to «fazer bien» four times in as many stanzas: «El que byen fazer podiese, oy le valdría más / que non atender a ty [i.e. Muerte] nin a tu amigo cras, cras» (1530*cd*); «El byen que fazer podierdes, fazed lo oy luego, / tened que cras morredes ca la vida es juego» (1531*cd*); «El byen que farás cras, palabra es desnuda, / vestid la con la obra ante que muerte acuda» (1532*cd*); «Amigos aperçebid vos e fazed buena obra, / que desque viene la muerte a toda cosa sonbra» (1533*cd*). The point could not be made with greater simplicity or clarity. [17]

---

[16] The thirteen prayers are the opening *Oraçion* (1-10); the four *Gozos de Santa María* (20-32, 33-43, 1635-41, 1642-49); the four *Canticas de Loores de Santa María* (1668-72, 1673-77, 1678-83, 1684-89); the two other Marian poems, the *Ditado* (1046-48) and the *Ave María* (1661-67); and the two poems on the Passion of Christ (1049-58, 1059-66). In addition to these, one could also consider as prayers the two *Cantares de çiegos* (1710-19, 1720-28).

[17] Lapesa («El tema de la muerte...», p. 134) plays down this aspect of the *planto,* saying that Juan Ruiz «repite formulariamente la lección recibida». He is more concerned to emphasise the Archpriest's cynical description of how, almost before the dead man is decently buried, his relatives pounce on his possessions and his widow starts looking for a new husband. But this bitter satire of human behaviour in no way invalidates the «lección recibida»: it is a further indication of the worthlessness of worldly goods and attachments.

The long section on the arms the Christian needs to fight the infernal trinity (1579-1605) is a catalogue of the various means established by the church to help a man to gain salvation. The three theological virtues, the four cardinal virtues, the seven sacraments and the seven works of mercy are all systematically set out and their particular efficacy explained.

But a man cannot do good works or behave virtuously unless he first brings his sinful nature into submission. And this he can only do by acts of penance which discipline his body and prepare his spirit to receive God's grace. This is the most difficult part of the Christian life — the long and bitter struggle against the flesh. It is fitting that the main episode in the *Libro de buen amor* which deals with penance should take the form of a battle, an allegorical *pelea* between Carnal and Cuaresma who represent the two sides of man's dual nature: his destructive sensuality and his desire to tame it. These two aspects of his character alternately gain the upper hand. At the beginning of the *pelea* it is Carnal's turn to be defeated, and the friar sent to confess him insists on a separate penance for each of the seven days of the week, so that Carnal may atone for each of the Seven Deadly Sins he has committed. It is significant that later on Juan Ruiz links the two well-worn medieval allegorical themes of the battle of Carnal and Cuaresma and the triumphal procession of Love. It is Amor, as we have seen, which is the root of all evil, holding out so many temptations to sin, and it is Carnal, man's own sensual nature, which makes him follow Amor and commit the sins. [18]

The fact that Carnal soon escapes from Cuaresma's prison has more significance than simply to show how the rejoicing of Easter follows the austerities of Lent; indeed, the church's conception of these rejoicings is far removed from the orgy of sex and gluttony depicted in the joint triumph of Carnal and Amor. The escape of Carnal is meant to convey above all that man's urge to sin is strong and that unless constant vigilance is maintained it will emerge more virulent than ever after a period of enforced restraint. The Archpriest stresses this point almost at the end of the work when we see that, even after the long homily on the arms the Christian needs to fight the infernal trinity, even after recognising the warnings for himself in the deaths of three people who were very dear to him, the sensual urges are still not conquered: even now there is one last despairing effort «por aver juntamiento

---

[18] See the article in this volume by K. M. Laurence for a more detailed treatment of the *pelea*.

con fenbra plazentera». The attempt is a disastrous failure, but it serves to emphasise that repentance is not once and for all, that the battle against the flesh continues to the end. The three lines that introduce this last adventure stress the theme of the constant recurrence of sinful desires:

> Ssalida de febrero, entrada de março,
> el pecado que sienpre de todo mal es maço,
> traya [de] abbades lleno el su rregaço. (1618*abc*).

Eternal vigilance, then, is necessary, as the Archpriest himself comments after the defeat of Cuaresma by Carnal:

> Quien a su enemigo popa a las sus manos muere;
> el que a su enemigo non mata, si podiere,
> su enemigo matará a él, si cuerdo fuere. (1200*bcd*).

Here again we find Juan Ruiz expressing his spiritual struggle in terms of killing and death: if we underrate the strength of our baser instincts they will kill us, both physically and spiritually; to prevent this we must ourselves kill the old Adam within us and keep the flesh in subjection.

Despite all the irony and ambiguity, all the parody and burlesque, all the comedy and *alegría* in the *Libro de buen amor*, I think there can be no doubt about Juan Ruiz's basic orthodoxy. He stays faithful to his stated intentions in writing the book which he sets out in the prose prologue (a 1343 addition, and therefore in effect an epilogue): «fue por rreduçir a toda persona a memoria buena de bien obrar e dar ensienpro de buenas constunbres e castigos de salvaçión. E por que sean todos aperçebidos e se puedan mejor guardar de tantas maestrías como algunos usan por el loco amor» (p. 7). Not only does he state his main aim in these unequivocal terms, he also brings into the prologue the principal points of the attack he mounts against *loco amor* in the body of the work. He attributes man's tendency to sin to «la fraqueza de la natura humana que es en el omne, que se non puede escapar de pecado» (p. 4). He stresses the shortness of life and the inevitability of death for the «cuerpo umano que dura poco tiempo» (p. 5), and gives added weight to his solemn warning by quoting Job's «Breves dies hominis sunt» (*ibid.*) and David's «Anni nostri sicut aranea meditabuntur» (*ibid.*). We are warned of love's deceitfulness, of the «sotilezas engañosas del loco amor del mundo» (*ibid.*); of love's sinfulness «que faze perder las almas e caer en saña de Dios» (p. 6); and of love's destructiveness, «apocando la vida e dando... muchos daños a los cuerpos» (*ibid.*). On the other hand, the great spiritual qualities of *entendimiento, voluntad* and *memoria* «traen al alma conssolación e aluengan la vida al cuerpo» (p. 3). If these are cultivated man will arrive at «el buen amor de Dios e sus mandamientos» (*ibid.*), and strive to «fazer buenas obras, por las quales se salva el ome» (p. 4) so as to die in a state of grace, since «Beati mortui qui in Domino moriuntur» (*ibid.*).

According to the prologue, man has a clear choice between «el buen amor de Dios» and «el loco amor del mundo», and he must make the choice; there is no compromise. So that we may choose freely Juan Ruiz claims that this book will provide both sides of the argument, and it is this which has laid him open to charges of hypocrisy. However, although he slyly suggests that anyone who decides after all to choose the way of *loco amor* will find «algunas maneras para ello» (p. 6) in the book, he not only immediately denies that this is his true intention («lo que non los conssejo»), but goes on, as we have seen, to present us with a very powerful series of arguments against sexual love, and also to show the frustration and humiliation that was the lot of at least one man who spent his life chasing women. Only twice (or possibly three times; see note 7 above) does the protagonist-lover succeed in his intention, and in the light of what I regard as the prevailing tone of the work, it is worth looking a little more closely at these 'successes'.

The episode of Doña Endrina is an undeniable triumph for the methods outlined by Don Amor and Venus; but it is also intended to serve as an illustration of the wickedness and deceitfulness of lovers and their *terceras* and thus provide a salutary warning to women who might be tempted to follow in Endrina's footsteps. [19] We see how Trotaconventos finally succeeds in winning over the young widow by playing on her vanity and her fear of loneliness, as well as on her basic sensuality: the *tercera*'s simple remark that «sola enveječedes» (725*b*) sums up her whole argument. It is not an edifying spectacle. At first Endrina behaves with prudence and shows that she has no illusions about Don Melón's motives: «Bien así engañan muchos a otras muchas Endrinas; / el omne tan engañoso engaña a sus vezi-

---

[19] J. Guzmán makes out a good case for seeing this whole episode as a warning to women about the dangers of love (*Una constante...*, pp. 39-58). See also the article in this volume by G. B. Gybbon-Monypenny.

nas» (665*ab*).   But we see her gradually worn down until she is willing to accept Trotaconventos's cynical assertion that «Es maldat e
falsía las mugeres engañar» (848*a*).   Eventually she succumbs, but after
the seduction she bitterly regrets her folly and compares herself and
other women who have been similarly deceived to birds which get
caught in a snare and «Mueren por el poco çevo, non se pueden defen-
der» (883*d*).   Once again we have the idea of love leading to death
(here, of course, a metaphor for dishonour).

This reference to death is particularly interesting when we recall
that this is far from the first time that love and death have been closely connected in the course of this episode: the idea of dying of love
appears at different times on the lips of all three principal actors in
the drama —the lover (whether the Archpriest or Don Melón), Endrina and Trotaconventos.   Here are some examples:

> Coytado sy escaparé, grand miedo he de ser muerto;
> oteo a todas partes e non puedo fallar puerto;
> toda la mi esperança e todo el mi confuerto
> está en aquella sola que me trahe penado e muerto.   (651; lover).

> Vuestro amor e deseo que me afinca e me aquexa,
> nos' me tira, nos' me parte, non me suelta, non me dexa,
> tanto me da la muerte quanto más se me abaxa.   (662*bcd;* lover).

> Pues que la mi señora con otro fuer casada,
> la vida deste mundo yo non la preçio nada;
> mi vida e mi muerte, esta es señalada:
> pues que aver non la puedo, mi muerte es llegada.   (791; lover).

> Desque con él fablaste, más muerto lo trahedes;
> pero que aun vos callades, tan bien como el ardedes;
> descobrid vuestra llaga, sy non ansy morredes;
> el fuego encobyerto vos mata e penaredes.
> (837; Trotaconventos).

> El grand amor me mata; el su fuego parejo,
> pero quanto me fuerça, apremia me sobejo.   (839*ab*; Endrina).

> Con el ençendymiento morides e penades.
> (843*c*; Trotaconventos).

> Más quiero moryr su muerte, que bevir vida penada.
> (855*d*; Endrina).

> Fija, la vuestra porfía a vos mata e derrama,
> los plazeres de la vyda perdedes si non se amata.
> (857*cd*; Trotaconventos).

Dar vos ha muerte a entranbos la tardança e la desira.

(859*c*; Trotaconventos).

The theme of the lover dying of love is one of the commonest hyperboles of the courtly love tradition (see Corominas, *Commentary*, 791*c*); but in the *Libro de buen amor* in which, as I have shown, love and death are so intimately and frequently linked, this erotic commonplace can acquire a startlingly simple new significance, which is underlined in Trotaconventos's words to Endrina: «Que sinon la muerte sola non parte las voluntades» (860*d*). [20]

The episode immediately following the seduction of Endrina is again successful from the lover's point of view. This adventure was added by the Archpriest to his revised version of the *Libro* in 1343, probably to clarify any misunderstandings his readers might have about the real point of the Endrina story (see Guzmán, *Una constante...*, pp. 59-68). This time the lady does die and it is stressed that her death is a direct result of her sinful behaviour: «Ovo por mal pecado la dueña a ffallyr» (943*b*). [21]

If we are to accept the view of Leo and Corominas that Doña Garoça is in fact seduced (see note 7 above), then of course her sudden death, after knowing the Archpriest for only two months, can be seen as a consequence of her sinful love, particularly in the light of the number of references to death contained in the episode (see, for example, 1379-81, 1420, 1422-23). Guzmán examines the Garoça story in some detail (*Una constante...*, pp. 76-90) and suggests that the medieval reader would consider that the nun, as a bride of Christ, was placing herself in very great spiritual danger by agreeing to meet the Archpriest at all.

It is my contention that at no point in the *Libro de buen amor* can the Archpriest be accused of seriously recommending worldly love as a course worth following. Although he announces that «todo bien del mundo e todo plazer» (108*d*) may be found in women, he has just been telling us that «las cosas del mundo todas son vanidat» (105*b*). Small

[20]   This loading of a single term with a multiplicity of meanings and overtones is typical of the Archpriest. His use of the word *muerte* seems to be, on examination, almost as complex and full of ironic subtleties as his use of *buen amor,* for a discussion of which see G. B. Gybbon-Monypenny, «Lo que buen amor dize con rrazon te lo pruevo», *BHS*, XXXVIII (1961), 13-24; Brian Dutton, «'Con Dios en buen amor': a Semantic Analysis of the Title of the *Libro de buen amor*», *BHS*, XLIII (1966), 161-176; and the same author's contribution to this present volume.
[21]   Corominas interprets «por mal pecado» as an exclamation, with the sense of «qué lástima», but gives no reason for doing so (*Commentary*, 943*b*).

women may well afford us «plazer del mundo» (1611*d*) and even «te-
rrenal parayso» (1616*b*), but this eulogy of «dueñas chicas» is carefully
placed so that the echoes of the sermon on the infernal trinity, of which
this very same *mundo* is a member, are still ringing in our ears. At
times the Archpriest may seem to be contradicting himself, but in
fact he is never in any doubt about which side he must eventually
come down on. Nowhere does he deny that love is sinful; nowhere
does he doubt the need for penance; nowhere does he question the
reality of death and damnation. But he does not underestimate the
strength of his sex urge and the attractions of love. The ironic shifts
and twists serve to emphasise the violence of the conflict within him.
As I said at the beginning, the *Libro de buen amor* is not an abstract
treatise, but a highly personal reaction to the human problems of love,
sin and death. The *yo* is real, even if the details of the episodes are
fictitious. The man who prostrates himself sorrowfully before the
Virgin is the same man who later offers a lodging to Don Amor and
Don Carnal. The temptations of the flesh and the fear of death are
real and personal problems to him, and the conflict becomes more and
more acute as his own time of death approaches and both sides intensify their efforts in the battle for his soul. [22]

Birkbeck College,
University of London

[22] For a fuller discussion of the progressive intensification of the Archpriest's sense of death and desire to atone for his sins as the work proceeds,
see my article «Towards an Interpretation of the *Libro de buen amor*», BHS,
XLIII (1966), 1-10.

INDEX *

Ad Herennium, 32, 43-44.
Aesop, 187, 190, 192, 194, 197-199, 201, 205-207, 209-212, 214.
Aguado, J. M., 25.
alborada, 62.
Alda, 222n.
Alison, 69, 75n.
Alfonso X, King of Castile and León, 103, 105.
   see also *Primera Crónica General*.
alliteration, 8.
ambiguity, 33n, 34, 57, 95-96, 120.
amplificatio, 28, 131, 139.
Andreas Capellanus, 64, 116.
annominatio, 7-8, 43-45.
Aquinas, St. Thomas, 57, 150.
Arabic, 98-99, 116.
Arabic influence, 77, 93, 96, 164-165.
Archpoet, the, 61.
Aristotle, 83, 93, 233.
Artes Poeticae, 32, 82, 91.
Artes Praedicandi, 29-32, 35.
Arthurian romance, 74-75, 188.
Ash Wednesday and Shrove Tuesday, 167, 171n.
assonance, 3, 5-6.
astrology, 81, 83-89, 92-93, 188-190, 233.
auctoritates, see *sententiae*.
Audigier, 65.
Augustine, St., 48-50, 57, 109.
autobiographical form, 47, 79-80, 123, 127, 155, 228, 252.
Auto de los Reyes Magos, 60.

Bataille de Caresme et de Charnage, 159-160, 162-164, 173, 175.
Belenoi, Aimeric de, 104.
Berceo, Gonzalo de, 2-10, 15, 23-24, 26, 60, 98-101, 103, 109, 117, 119, 213.
Bible, 29-51 *passim*, 67, 91, 108, 109, 152-153, 196, 205, 242-243, 248; see also exegesis.

Bolseiro, Juião, 64.
Brasdefer, Jehan de, 124n, 127.
Bromyard, John, 161.
Breughel, Pieter, 171n.
buen amor and *loco amor*, 33, 45, 95-121, 231-252.
burlesque, see parody.

Calanso, Guiraut de, 105, 107.
Calila e Dimna, 193, 207.
Cancionero de Baena, 116n.
Cancionero de Palacio, 102-103.
Cantar de Mio Cid, 65, 74, 240n.
cantiga de amigo, 140n.
Canzone d'un Fiorentino al Carnevale, 172.
caritas and *cupiditas*, 124.
Castigos y ejemplos de Catón, 120n.
Castilianisation of source material, 127.
Cato, see *Disticha Catonis, Castigos y ejemplos de Catón*.
Cavalcanti, Guido, 64.
Cavallero Zifar, 66n, 121n.
Celestina, La, 125 n.
Cervantes, Miguel de, 227n.
Chanoinesses et des Bernardines, Des, 170.
Chanson de Roland, 223n.
Chaucer, Geoffrey, 29, 48, 75n, 82, 87, 125n.
Clement V, Pope, 42.
clergy, regular and secular, 59, 151, 154-157.
Cluny, 58.
conduplicatio, 43-44.
confession, 149-157, 165-170, 247.
Consultatio Sacerdotum, 74, 214.
contentio, 43, 45.
Contrasto di Carnevale e de la Quaresima, 163-164, 169, 173.
Corominas, Joan, 142-143n.
corteza and *meollo*, 58-60; see also meaning of *Libro de buen amor*, hidden.

* This index lists the occurrences of (i) topics discussed, e. g., ambiguity, Arabic influence, (ii) references to classical or medieval authors or works and, generally, to later literary works, (iii) references to modern critics of the *Libro de buen amor* where there is substantial discussion of their views.

253

COLECCION TAMESIS

SERIE A - MONOGRAFIAS

EDWARD M. WILSON and JACK SAGE: *Poesías líricas en las obras dramáticas de Calderón*, pp. xix + 165.

PHILIP SILVER: *'Et in Arcadia ego': A Study of the Poetry of Luis Cernuda*, pp. xv + 211.

KEITH WHINNOM: *A Glossary of Spanish Bird-Names*, pp. 157.

BRIAN DUTTON: *La 'Vida de San Millán de la Cogolla' de Gonzalo de Berceo. Estudio y edición crítica*. El tomo I.° de las *Obras completas* de Gonzalo de Berceo, pp. xiv + 248.

A. D. DEYERMOND: *Epic Poetry and the Clergy: Studies on the 'Mocedades de Rodrigo'*, pp. xix + 312, with two maps.

ABDÓN M. SALAZAR: *El escudo de armas de Juan Luis Vives*, pp. viii + 136.

P. GALLAGHER: *The Life and Works of Garci Sánchez de Badajoz*, pp. x + 296.

CARLOS P. OTERO: *Letras, I*, pp. xviii + 202.

EMMA SUSANA SPERATTI-PIÑERO: *De 'Sonata de otoño' al esperpento (Aspectos del arte de Valle-Inclán)*, pp. viii + 341.

'Libro de buen amor' Studies. Edited by G. B. Gybbon-Monypenny, pp. xiii + 256.

SERIE B - TEXTOS

LOPE DE VEGA: *Triunfo de la fee en los reynos del Japón*. Edited by J. S. Cummins, pp. xlix + 116, with seven illustrations and one map.

FERNÁN PÉREZ DE GUZMÁN: *Generaciones y semblanzas*. Edición crítica con prólogo, apéndices y notas de R. B. Tate, pp. xxvii + 112.

El sufrimiento premiado. Comedia famosa, atribuida en esta edición, por primera vez, a Lope de Vega Carpio. Introducción y notas de V. F. Dixon, pp. xxvii + 177.

José de Cadalso: *Cartas marruecas.* Prólogo, edición y notas de Lucien Dupuis y Nigel Glendinning, pp. lxiii + 211.

Virgilio Malvezzi: *Historia de los primeros años del reinado de Felipe IV.* Edición y estudio preliminar por D. L. Shaw, pp. liv + 206, with 3 illustrations and 3 maps.

La comedia Thebaida. Edited by G. D. Trotter and Keith Whinnom, pp. lxi + 270.

SERIE D - REPRODUCCIONES EN FACSIMIL

Cayetano Alberto de la Barrera y Leirado: *Catálogo bibliográfico y biográfico del teatro antiguo español, desde sus orígenes hasta mediados del siglo XVIII (Madrid, 1860),* pp. xi + 727.